FEEL

FEEL

My Story

FREDDIE SPENCER

with Rick Broadbent

1 3 5 7 9 10 8 6 4 2

Virgin Books, an imprint of Ebury Publishing,
20 Vauxhall Bridge Road,
London SW1V 2SA

Virgin Books is part of the Penguin Random House group of companies
whose addresses can be found at global.penguinrandomhouse.com

Penguin
Random House
UK

First published by Virgin Books in 2017

www.penguin.co.uk

A CIP catalogue record for this book is available from the British Library

ISBN 9780753545614

Designed and typeset by K.DESIGN, Winscombe, Somerset
Printed and bound in Great Britain by Clays Ltd, St Ives PLC

Penguin Random House is committed to a sustainable future for our
business, our readers and our planet. This book is made from Forest
Stewardship Council® certified paper.

MIX
Paper from
responsible sources
FSC® C018179

Dedicated to Jordyn and Connor and all the people who made this story possible

To Linda and my mom who worked so many hours. Their unselfishness allowed my dad and me the chance to go to many events and that gave me the opportunity to hone my craft. Without their sacrifices we couldn't have done it.

In memory of my dear friend Mr Williams

Jere Ivy Williams, 9 February 1934 – 24 June 2014

Mrs Williams asked me one day after Mr Williams had passed whether knowing Jere had made my life better.

I said 'The privilege of having Mr Williams in my life not only made it better but it helped me to know my purpose and he was always there when it mattered most.'
She smiled and said: 'He did okay then!'

Contents

Part 3 – EXIT (2008 to now)

Prologue: **At the Nations Grand Prix, Mugello, 1985**

SITTING IN my motorhome on Sunday afternoon, there are two silver trophies on the table. This is the moment I have worked towards ever since I was a young kid riding in my yard with a protective sock covering up my burnt hand and scarred memories. I am the first man for 12 years to win both the 500cc and 250cc Grand Prix races at the same event. I have a chance to become the first to win both titles. The trophies for the two wins are proof. They glint in the Tuscan sun.

I feel an overwhelming relief. After all the struggles I sit down on the bed and look down the length of the motorhome to the table. I reflect on the races. I think briefly of Spain and how I heard the sound of the helicopter and won there despite the broken hand, swollen ankle and hole in my elbow. I connect the dots from my past to this glorious present. This is everything I have ever wanted or could have imagined. This is the greatest day.

On the 500cc podium, the last notes of my national anthem softening to silence, I had looked ahead to the 250cc race. I ran to the pre-grid. Eddie Lawson, my great rival for the 500 crown, looked at me and shrugged: 'Better you than me.' It was hard but it would be worth it.

I stand up and touch the trophies. And a strong feeling washes over me. Now I know that it was a foreshadowing of what was to come, but then it is as if a small window opens and, fleetingly, today, at the pinnacle of what I do, I wonder if this was all I am supposed to know.

Is this all there is?

Part 1
ENTRY
(1961–85)

Chapter 1: **FIRE (1961–73)**

LEVY C was already an old man when he pulled me out of the fire. At least he seemed old to me. He was in his fifties, a short man, probably no more than five feet four inches tall, and like many black people at that time he had faced more than his fair share of suffering. I just saw a kindness in him. He was a family man, not necessarily his own flesh and blood, and seemed to enjoy that sense of belonging. Previously, he had worked on the property of Big Momma, my great-grandmother on my mother's side, in Blanchard, Louisiana, helping out in as many ways as he could, and now he was part of our family too.

Mom would go and bring him over so he could do jobs around the place. She would say, 'Levy C, come in the house,' but he would say, 'No, ma'am, I'm all right, Miss June, I will stay out here.' My parents never talked about race: about Rosa Parks and the bus boycott of December 1955, when a schoolgirl had caused a storm by breaking the segregation that was deemed normal; of how you might hear the 'N' word used so easily by both adults and children; or that prejudice was ingrained and passed on to a new generation like a hereditary defect. They were just more open-minded than most. Levy C would sit at his little TV tray table outside on the patio and would not want to bother anyone. From the age of around five, I would join him out the back on our little covered porch, him eating his pimento cheese sandwich and me my peanut butter–jelly version, surrounded by vast pine trees stretching into the backyard, a vision of beauty as the colours changed in the fall.

I was almost three years old in late October 1964. These were shifting times in the USA. Bob Dylan had not long since released 'Blowin' in the Wind' and John F. Kennedy had been assassinated the year before. The country was in a state of flux and chaos, but tremors from the fault lines of the wider world did not reach a young boy in Shreveport, Louisiana. We didn't subscribe to the local paper except the Sunday edition and we had only three TV channels. We didn't have cable until 1974 and when we became one of the first areas in Shreveport to get HBO it opened up a whole new world.

My memory of what happened that year, 1964, would only be filled in years later by my sister, Linda. My mother would never talk about the episode because it was so traumatic for her and Linda. The only story she told was about the old wooden rocking chair that sat in the corner of the bedroom. She got it from Grandma and would sit in it and rock me all night long when I couldn't sleep in the months after what happened.

During the fall, leaves would cover the ground and people would rake them into huge piles, up to ten feet wide, and then burn them to break them up. Because we were out in the country, outside the city limits, this was legal. Put them in bags and you'd have had hundreds, so this was a way of saving money and effort. You just had to make sure you didn't make the piles too big or they would catch a tree and cause a fire. These were mighty leaf mountains to a little boy.

That fateful day Mom and Linda were out there. The leaves had been burning for a day and Mom started walking towards the pile of leaves closest to the red garage in the back of the property. Unbeknown to her, I was following. Levy C was tending another pile close by and out of the corner of his eye he saw me. He dropped his rake. My sister heard the sound of it hitting the ground and looked up. She saw Levy C catch up to me as I tripped on one of the roots surrounding the garage and then fell forwards into the pile of leaves. These leaves had been lit the previous day and so had been quietly crackling and smouldering for 12 hours, one of the giant silhouetted pyramids dotted around the yard. I plunged into the sizzling cinders with my arm stretched out in front of me. I was only in briefly as Levy C caught me by the back of my shirt before my entire body would have been engulfed by the blazing black remains.

The damage was grave. The skin on my left hand was completely burnt and it began to melt like wax.

I was too young to have the memory of my sister's scream as she held me in the passenger seat of the car on the way to the hospital. That scream would echo around her head for ever.

When we arrived at the emergency room Mom and Linda were told to go across the street to Dr Birdwell's office, our family doctor, because they didn't know what to do. It was 1964 and barely imaginable today. There was no burn unit at the hospital and the doctors did not sugarcoat the prognosis. My parents were told that I would very likely lose my hand if the skin grafts didn't take. For years I had to wear a protective sock on it when I went outside in the sunlight and I became acutely self-conscious. I ended up having seven skin grafts from my upper back and I quickly became inured to anodyne hospital wards and adults talking in hushed tones.

I did not know the details of this for many years. Nobody spoke about the fire and I was left with only my vague memory. That was another thing that drew me closer to Levy C, another connection. He was the one who saved me, and years afterwards, when I was around five, sitting on the porch, he turned to me and said: 'Listen, little Freddie, everything happens for a reason.'

As I got older I still did not see a man who raked leaves and worked in our yard, but something else and I never understood why he wasn't accepted by all. Moreover, I felt *a reason*. That's why his words echoed around my thoughts; it's also why it matters what you say in front of children.

When I truly started reflecting on these things, I would imagine the racism he had experienced and balance that against the care and respect he had for our family. I recognised his insight even if I didn't fully understand what it meant. That leaf fire made me realise that where I saw an extremely kind soul, other people's perception was different because of the colour of his skin and his job. He was an easy target to be dismissed.

I remember being in the car with Mom and Levy C would say, 'Miss June, I need to go to the bathroom.' We would stop in many different places and he would be refused all the time. He always ended up in the back of some building, the only place he could go, but he never said a word and never got angry. I remember thinking in my little-boy mind how something as natural as going to the bathroom could be refused to a human being just because of the colour of his skin.

I was born in 1961, the time when Martin Luther King and the Ku Klux Klan were at their zenith. Perhaps it was apposite that this was also a time of growing awareness in the USA. My own story is one of awareness lost and found, and that time in American history saw many people begin to turn away from the wrongs of past generations.

It was a truly seismic time of social evolution. The Civil Rights Act was passed in 1964, but cultures change at a slower pace than paper bills. My parents had a few stores over the years, always in the black area of town. They were good businesses. They had a store in Shreveport called Washington Park when I was eight or nine, and I would get on my bicycle and go on deliveries with a young black kid called Donnie. The segregated restaurants had started to change, but I could sense the discomfort on the faces of people in cars who passed us. They'd look at us and silently say, 'What's he doing with *him*?'

Whether on the bike or off it, I have often taken different lines. What Levy C had known was probably only neglect and pain, but there was a true power in his kindness. He had a choice – to be angry and hurtful and walk on by or to save me. I didn't understand it then, but I knew that his choice meant something beyond flesh and bone.

My family

Mom's parents divorced when she was young. My grandfather drank a lot which is why my grandmother left him and took the kids – Mom, Janet, Joyce and Uncle Jack. Mom had a hard childhood and, during my early years, she stuttered pretty badly when she was stressed or nervous. We'd go to TG&Y, a five and dime store in a strip mall up the street from our house, where you could supposedly get 'turtles, girdles and yoyos'. It was a place where you went for everything before the advent of the big shopping malls. Mom would go to pay and sometimes when she had to speak to the cashier, she would grow hesitant and begin to struggle with her words, and that would make her feel even more nervous and self-conscious. Sometimes grown-ups would laugh or get impatient and their children would chime in. I never understood that response and it bothered me, especially from the adults. It wasn't embarrassment that I felt; it was an awareness of the insensitivity that other people had. I knew it was their discomfort and I know that some people just don't like to get involved, but none of them truly understood what she had gone through and it made my heart ache for my mom.

When Mom was young her dad would get up at dawn to go to work and come home after dark. It was a routine existence until Friday night ushered in the weekend and he had no place to go. Gone was the comfort of bath-time and a story before bed. Grandpa Attaway would always get home late on Fridays and, when they heard the car pull up, the four children would tense up in fear at what might come next. First, the front door would open and they would hear him yelling. What then? Would Mom have to defend herself again like so many other Friday nights? Would the four of them have to come together and escape the yelling and uncertainty by sneaking out the back of their little house and hiding in the yard? On those occasions they would huddle together for strength and comfort, hoping it would not be a night like before, but it usually was. Grandma could not stop him from going over the edge. The combination of his own disappointment and alcohol was too much and he would take his shotgun and open the back door. 'Where are you?' he would yell, and then fire over their heads. It was an unimaginable scenario but it happened and I can only wonder what it would be like for those children, crouched low in the dirt of their yard in the pitch black, deafened by bullets and terrified of the people they depended on.

He stopped drinking when Grandma left him and he died before my second birthday. Mom didn't tell me this story but I overheard it being discussed. And when I heard the sniggering in TG&Y I was thinking of Mom being shot at once more.

Mom's side of the family made Christmas special. Two weeks beforehand Aunt Joyce would get all the family together, including distant relatives from Blanchard where Mom was born. There were so many of us that we would have to wear name tags. One time I asked my mom if she thought they would remember this year. She said everyone had to wear a name tag and that was that.

'Well, everybody must be pretty forgetful then,' I said.

'Can you remember everyone's name?' she said.

'No.'

'Okay then.'

She had made her point.

The upside was there were so many presents and everyone would have to pick a number and then get in line. Once I remember being so happy when I got number three. There was so much to choose from that I couldn't decide. It was a kid's dream.

On the way home from the store one evening there was a street we would cross called Hollywood Boulevard. Mom turned on to it because she had to pick up something at the airport. We passed a big building that was lit up with different coloured lights and the words 'Hollywood Palace'. I thought maybe this was the Hollywood I had seen on TV. I was five and this place was my whole life.

Chapter 1: FIRE (1961–73)

The South at that time was extremely conservative. In many ways it still is. We were not a religious family but there was a King James Bible on the book shelf above the TV in the living room, second book from the left, and a Baptist church out the back, where I would watch the people go in and out. We never went to church or prayed in the house. Later, articles would appear and there was paddock gossip about how I was deeply religious and even that I was a Mormon or part of some religious cult. People thought they couldn't cuss around me and that I would never drink wine. None of it was true. I was not religious but I always had faith.

We lived in the country and the tolerance of our neighbours, the Hammocks, the Pughs and others, amazes me even more as I now look back. Every day, from the age of four to fourteen, I spent three or four hours riding after school until the sun went down and I couldn't see any more. When we weren't racing on a weekend I would ride then too.

Then, at night, lying in my bed, I would see myself riding, going faster, and I would imagine what I wanted to do the next day. I couldn't wait. In my imagination and in my yard my hand didn't hurt.

Riding in my yard, honing my skills, feeling the bike sliding and learning to control the movement was my therapy. I close my eyes now and I can see vivid pictures, sense the air going over my skin and feel the handlebar grips in my hands because I didn't wear gloves as a kid. I wanted to feel the pressure in my fingertips and that increased my sensitivity. The more relaxed I was, the longer I could ride, and the more I could feel the bike through my hands and body. I learned the different movements of the bike and I learned how to recognise and anticipate them. When I got a little older, my hand stopped hurting and I didn't have to wear a protective sock any more.

My dad, Frederick Senior, raced locally. He once raced in the national go-kart championships at the Rupp factory in Mansfield,

Ohio in the 1950s. I'd listen to the adults talking and hear them say he had the record for the most laps completed in an hour on a two-engine Mac 40 go-kart at Green Valley Raceway in Dallas – he did 44 laps. My sister Linda raced too, but by 1960 they had stopped racing karts. Then it became Dad and my brother, Danny. Dad got out of go-karts and started racing very basic 250cc Yamaha street bikes. There was no road racing and so it was just local TT scrambles, enduros and turkey runs with the local White Eagle Motorcycle Club. He was a relentless tinkerer and Mom and I joked that had there been lawn-mower racing he would have been into that too, but what he really liked to do was drag race at the local strip south of town.

I wanted to feel what the acceleration was like at the drag strip. Dad had a Pontiac GTO and was racing one Sunday. I convinced him to let me ride in the back.

'Why do you want to do that?'

'I just want to.'

I was relentless, bugging him constantly, so finally he shrugged. 'Ah well, okay.'

He hid me on the floorboard behind the driver's seat because you were not allowed to have passengers. I liked the sensation of acceleration and I loved the vibration from the floor of that Pontiac and the connection with the car. There was something really powerful in that relationship.

Dad had been in World War II in the western conflict against Japan. He was drafted right after his high-school graduation. There were some guns from the war locked in the closet by the front door, and although he never spoke much about what he had seen or done, it clearly affected him. He contracted typhoid fever in the Philippines and, worse, what we would now call post-traumatic stress syndrome. The problems he had later in life could be traced back to the death and horror his generation saw.

He was in hospital not long after I was born. Later I'd wonder whether it was really a fever or actually some sort of breakdown.

One of the only things he told me about his time in the forces was how he sometimes felt claustrophobic and would climb into the lifeboats on ships at night to get away from the packed sleeping areas.

He was a hard worker. He was born in Pratt, Kansas, and as a young man worked on the railroads with Union Pacific, a job he got through his uncle Lewis, and then he moved to Shreveport from Wyoming and became a Foremost milkman in the early 1950s with the shirt, tie and hat. It was exactly what you would imagine a milkman to look like at that time. By the seventies he was working at various jobs and on Saturdays during the winter he would deliver Morton's potato chips, before going to work nights unloading freight; anything to make extra money for the racing.

He had the store at the same time, so his routine was open up in the morning, work on bikes in the afternoon, unload freight at night. By the time I came along he was already 35, so it was by no means the beginning of his adult life. Linda was 14 and my brother, Danny, was 11.

The first time I felt fear for my dad was around 1969. He came home one night from the Washington Park store and I could tell something was wrong. He had been at the store with Murphy, the butcher, and they had been robbed. I could see the fear in his eyes as he described being tied up and having something put over his eyes. The robbers were two teenage boys and my dad tilted his head when he heard one of the voices. The kid realised that maybe my dad recognised him. 'Do you know me?' he whispered. They held a gun to his head. Dad really didn't think he was going to survive it.

Dad was also a member of the Shriners, an organisation like the Masons that was big in the USA. I didn't understand it and he never brought it up, but I imagine it was something he felt was important to the community. My main memory is he had a Harley painted in the Shriners' green and orange, which he rode in parades.

He set up a company called Spencer and Sons Trucking to provide dump trucks to move and haul dirt. With his dad, who we called Pop, and his brother Gerald, he even helped build part of the I-20 interstate that dissects Shreveport and joins the east and west parts of the southern United States, one of the big post-war projects.

The population in Shreveport was split about 50–50 between black and white, and we lived in a middle-class area at 2620 Amelia Street just outside the city limits. My parents paid $9000 for two acres of land and $9000 to build the house on it. Before I came along they were in a little house in Sunset Acres, a subdivision, next door to Grandma and Pop. One day, ten years after my brother was born, Mom went to the doctor thinking she had a stomach virus. Dr Birdwell had told her she couldn't have more children. This time she was told she was pregnant. It was a surprise for her and shock to the system of my brother.

Danny didn't want me around. He had been the baby for 11 years and then here I was. He used to hide me behind the recliner in the living room as if trying to pretend I wasn't there. I was the runt of the litter in his eyes. The interaction between him and my dad was very confrontational. There was a lot of arguing when Danny was in his late teens. It was a battle of wills that I could never understand because Danny had no chance of winning.

For the most part, it was a simple, semi-country life. We had no city water – only a well – and days were lifted by my riding in the yard, stifled by not being allowed to ride until after high noon on Sunday because of the noise and respect for the Southern Baptist church next to our house. It was the quiet time of the week.

I was a relentless rider. When I was only three, on board my banana-seat pushbike, I nearly took out everyone's legs at Pop and Grandma's fiftieth wedding anniversary. By the time I was four I got my first little Briggs & Stratton mini-bike. That was all that was available to kids until I turned five and they introduced the mini-trail 50cc Honda. That was amazing. At seven I stepped up to the Yamaha Mini-Enduro 60.

There was no racing for kids when I first started riding – it was not even a thought yet – so I just tagged along when Dad and Danny went racing. While there, a small group of us would ride out in the paddock and kick up dirt. One night the grown-ups got so sick of it that they thought the best way to appease us, and stop us possibly running over someone in the paddock, was to stick us out there in the intermission and let us have our own race. We were overjoyed. One hot Friday night at Lake Lavon, Texas, there was a big crowd in the stands. I can still picture the track – all the corners, the jump, the little right and then left, back on to the straightaway, even the reflection of the lights on the track surface. It was an assault on the senses with the noise, colour and whiff of petrol.

I was on my little lawn-mower engine Briggs & Stratton bike that I rode in my yard, no Honda or Yamaha yet. Another boy called Terry Poovey, whose brother Teddy raced against Danny, would go on to have a successful career and have 11 AMA Grand National wins. We became friends and rivals. That's how it started.

That first race didn't go well for me. On these little bikes the sprocket was almost as big as the rear tire so when I would lean the bike over too far to the left it would kick the chain off when it touched the ground. On every lap the chain would come off. I came in dead last.

Extremely shy, self-conscious and embarrassed, I was not happy. Dad and Danny were laughing because they thought it was cute. I didn't.

'It's not funny,' I said and stomped off.

When I was four and a half they put in a little oval track for us at Lake Lavon. Before long, I started beating the local Texas boys on my mini-trail Honda 50 and that did not go down well. We were the outsiders. Shreveport was only 180 miles from Dallas, but we were from across the state line and we might as well have been from another planet. The local boys would protest if I won. Tempers would sometimes boil over. The locals would say that we were cheating. Sometimes it almost came to blows between the Louisiana folks and the Texans. It was just hard-core, grass-roots racing. The equivalent would be Friday night football in Texas. It was a bruising, hard baptism.

I observed the passion and anger and it left an indelible impression. Terry and I became good friends and would go to the movies together, but the arguments would often be about our bikes, leaving us perplexed. We'd look at each other and shrug. Our attitude was, 'What's the problem with the grown-ups?' As the years passed we all became friends and, today, looking back, that time was priceless.

The picture on the wall

Getting to Pop's house was an adventure. I would go to the end of the driveway and make sure there were no cops. They would often chase me with their siren blazing and lights blinking blue warnings. I was only going 40mph on my mini-trail 50cc Honda, but my goal was to get to the end of the street where there was a gap after the ditch leading to a little opening in the fence. If I could get there then I was in the clear. For me this was dramatic. I can still feel the fear and tension, and I wouldn't look back until the ditch when I knew I was clear. Of course, the cops thought this chase was hilarious.

'We will catch you next time,' one would shout out of the car window. I had my head down going as fast as I could to outrun their car and words.

Now I was through the ditch and the opening and the fence and into the tank farms. That part of Louisiana was big in oil and gas and I had to negotiate a path through these cavernous cylinders full of petroleum before I came to a quarter mile of woods. In the winter months, with the sun setting and trees forming scary silhouettes, getting through this bit was the hardest due to the monsters I imagined lying in wait, but I'd emerge and push the bike across the road. Through my kid's eyes, it was an exhilarating adventure, the coolest trip. Finally, after crossing the field behind Sunset Acres, I'd get to Pop and Grandma's house. Pop had built a 4x8 plywood ramp up and over the fence for me. Once inside I was safe and I'd have a peanut butter and jelly sandwich.

'You need to eat the crusts,' Grandma would say. And Pop would wink when Grandma wasn't looking and whisper: 'I'll cut the crusts off too.'

It was more than worth that journey because I needed Pop's presence. The main feeling I got from him was kindness, and that was so comforting to me. When I looked at others, I used him as a barometer of goodness, whether they were for themselves or whether they were like Pop and thought of others. It was something I gravitated towards and aspired to be. I felt that conflict in my brother and I felt it in my dad, who was quietly kind with me but could be controlling and jealous with others.

Another thing that made a lasting impression on me was the first time a kid told me he was going to beat me up if I won. It happened at Longview in Texas when I was six and the other kids were all older. The track was a little oval within the TT course and anybody could race, but I had developed a habit of winning. I was never a cocky individual, and my dad frowned upon arrogance, but once I turned around in a race and beckoned the other kids to come on. Looking back, I knew it was not the nicest thing to do and I regretted it, but it was a consequence of those kids threatening me. That happened a lot. I never told my parents about it, but they might have guessed something was wrong because I'd win the race and ride back to the van as quick as I could.

'Hey, let's get the trophy,' Dad said.

'No, let's get going. They can have it.' I always raced against older people and I gave a lot of my trophies to them because I didn't want them to feel bad.

I was scared enough, smart enough and certainly shy enough to want to avoid getting into a fight. But after a while it began to inspire me because it was just wrong. It's that thing about how people are treated. I know how it made me feel.

I was brave enough to take on bullies in my own way, but I was so scared of the dark that I couldn't sleep. Lying in my bed I would distract my fear by listening to the drone of the attic fan and the only thing that would make me feel better was the thought of how I had ridden in the yard that day and how I could improve on it. I could feel the thoughts when they came. That fear of the dark, the pain and the trauma, both of the fire and the physical and emotional pain would paralyse me and I would get the courage to go into my parents' room at night but I would never tell them why. I would lie on their floor or climb in bed with them and decide not to go back. I felt ashamed but I could not tell them because I didn't want to hurt them.

I have wondered my entire life when I should talk about what I experienced when I was five and six years old. What happened was the most painful of things, the most intimate violation. I knew I would talk about it someday. I just didn't know when or to whom. I had always seen it in my thoughts and felt it in its rawest form, almost constantly, if not every day then every week for most of my life.

It happened in the bathroom, and it was a neighbour who lived across the street. The teenage boy and his girlfriend were trusted by Mom and Dad to babysit me while they were off doing their things with the White Eagles or the Shriners. I still see it today in my mind because I never blocked it out. I never told my parents because there was part of me that wanted to protect them. It wasn't their fault. They had no idea. It is an experience many people have had, and it affects their self-esteem and trust in others. I was fortunate because I had my motorcycle and, as I did with the pain in my arm, I worked through it. The trauma of that violation did not define me, but it left an impact. It can strip away your spirit. I had my riding to help me.

Ross Downs was the track where I really began to perfect my craft and learn to race. We'd stay at the Ramada Inn in Euless, Texas. The Friday night races finished late, about midnight, and I would often get such bad stomach cramps that Mom would walk me around the hotel until about two in the morning. The cramps were crippling and got so bad that they took me to the hospital thinking I might have ulcers or worse, but it was just a reaction to being so keyed up. Then, after the race, when I would relax, the pain would come.

One time Mom fixed me with a look of kindness and concern. I was probably seven. 'Why do you want to do this to yourself?'

Mom would often tell the story. She'd say: 'Freddie shrugged his shoulders and said, "Because I have to ride. It's what I do."'

They never pushed me. My dad never wanted any reflected glory or limelight and would eventually shrink to the shadows in an act of heroic self-sacrifice.

My drive was not born of competition with others. I was purpose-driven, always striving to improve and understand and go faster, always pushing myself. I was striving for that. I needed to understand the bike more. I was completely self-motivated in that way. I had a single-minded purpose derived from a sense that I was on a deeper, more intimate path; I just didn't know to where. But it felt right.

My brother was different. I felt he really didn't want to race. He was doing it for Dad or other reasons. Many people talk about wanting to do it but when you are out there it is for real. My dad built Danny a 250cc flat-track bike to race at the Houston

Astrodome, a state-of-the-art arena opened in 1965. My dad told him to be at Marshall Speedway, right off the freeway, at 11am one cold January day to practice. In 1970, it was a typical low-grade grass-roots place where they raced old Fords with oversized engines, one level up from a demolition derby. I brought over my bike too and I spent the next two hours doing lap after lap.

Finally, I came in and there was still no sign of Danny.

'Hey, Dad, why don't you let me ride his bike?'

'No way.'

'Come on. Please. You can hold me up.'

'I said no, Freddie.'

'Why?'

I bugged him and then I begged him for the next hour until, with rain clouds looming and the knowledge that he had spent $100 on a potentially wasted trip, he relented.

'Okay, you go out there and put in some laps.'

'Yes, I'll break it in.' That meant only running the engine up to half throttle. I had never ridden a bike that big and powerful before. I couldn't wait.

The bike was so big for me that I could not even put my foot down. As I began to get comfortable I got faster and faster, forgetting I was only supposed to use half throttle. I was accelerating harder and harder off every corner and I was starting to get this thing going sideways. Dad could see I was going too fast and signalled one more lap when, out of the corner of my eye, I saw Danny's car pull up. At that exact moment the engine seized up and I fell down.

Crashes happen in a flash. I was fine apart from the sight of Danny charging towards me and he was clearly extremely pissed at what he had seen.

'What the hell are you doing?' he shouted, all those times he'd hidden me behind chairs now fully justified.

I just stood there wide-eyed and pointed: 'Dad let me ride it.'

Dad muttered: 'Well, you didn't show up.'

From the ground, I tried to be positive. I called my brother Bubba and smiled. 'Bubba, it's really fast. Well, until it seized. Sorry, Bubba.'

Danny was steaming and shook his head. He got into his car and shot off, throwing up dirt that merged with the steam coming off him.

'You should have showed up,' Dad yelled in his wake and he started to smile at me.

Danny was soft-hearted but hard-headed and would never listen to Dad. He was also hesitant and would back off when racing. It made me nervous though I never really knew why. 'I can't watch him any more,' I told Dad one night.

About a month after that, we went to a place rejoicing in the name of Devil's Bowl Speedway just outside Dallas. I went to sit in the passenger seat in the van when Danny was racing in his heat. Not long after I saw Dad running on to the track. My brother had got run over by a couple of other riders in turn three on the first lap. We rode in the back of the car and he was in excruciating pain with a broken pelvis and back injuries.

We got a hospital bed and put it in the front room of the house. That was him done with racing and he was never really the same after that. But the empathy I had for my brother back then was a powerful thing. All that stuff about hiding me and not wanting me didn't matter; I remembered him playing his organ in the garage with his band. The song most vivid in my memories was 'Light My Fire' by the Doors. What I always understood about my brother was the conflict. I think he raced because Dad did. I never did that. I rode because I wanted to and knew it was what I was supposed to do.

Danny had a lot of issues due to the accident: drugs and alcohol and, eventually, health. He stole some of my memorabilia to feed his habits. So we had to be cruel to be kind and, after a particularly bad episode, he went to jail. It's what saved his life.

It always bothered me, not about whether I could have stopped the crash, but the nagging, overwhelming feeling I had about his hesitancy.

The last time I saw my brother was at the nursing home in Monroe, Louisiana in March 2007. Even though there was a home just a few miles away from our sister's house he wanted to be close to his daughter who had moved from Shreveport with her mom when they divorced. My last memory is standing outside and him staring at the street in front of us with a focus that I had never seen in him. Never in racing, never in anything else. After a little while I realised that he was waiting for Sharon's car to appear in the distance because he knew he was dying and it was close to the end. He didn't have much, he never did, and although we all tried to help him he was his own worst enemy. But he loved Sharon unconditionally and he couldn't wait for her to visit him every Saturday. I watched him looking. If I had the chance I'd give him a hug and say: 'It's okay, Bubba.'

I missed my chance. He passed away later that summer. That feeling I had when I was eight endures.

I waited for Dad vigilantly on Friday afternoons. In sixth period I would look out the window of my classroom in the south-west corner of Westwood Elementary. I'd purposely sit on the desk that enabled me to see out the window and I watched the clock. It would seem to take for ever to move from 12 to 3. Eventually, Dad would turn up in our van and we'd leave for Dallas right from school. The only thing that would make me late is if I talked too much in class. Then my teacher would make me stay behind after class and write 'I must not talk back to the teacher' on the chalkboard. I would do that until the board was full and I would try to slant my words so I would run out of space sooner. If I had the discipline on the bike, it didn't translate to other areas like keeping my opinions to myself at school.

I was actually a good student, though. My parents were only adamant about two things. One, was I had to have good grades if I was to ride my motorcycle. The other, was I could not ride without a helmet. Even that got me in trouble when I was around 12 and I decided to show my friend Jeff Flanagan how I could jump a big roll of bailing wire while doing a wheelie; not the brightest idea. I wasn't wearing a helmet that day and Mom pulled in the driveway just as I was trying it. As I rode over it the wire hooked the pegs and I went flying over the bars and smashed my chin on the hard dust. I never tried that again. What a stupid idea.

I also began to notice girls around that time – I was in the sixth grade. One day, after two weeks and around 100 hours of thinking, I got up the nerve to ask Mom if she would buy me a bracelet with my name on it when we went to TG&Y. She said we would get it on Saturday if I mowed the lawn that week. I was happy to do that. The reason I wanted that bracelet was to impress Paula Henderson, the cutest, coolest girl in my class who I had only ever spoken to once when I offered to give her my soft roll at lunch.

So after I got the gold-plated bracelet I went to school on Monday morning to put it on her desk in the classroom with a note: 'Would you wear my bracelet?'

As the class went on I was too nervous to look her way, but finally, right before the bell rang to switch class, I looked over and she had the bracelet on her left wrist. That was a great moment of relief. She glanced my way and smiled.

That was before 10am. By 3pm she had already given the bracelet back. She lived one street away and I would ride my bicycle in front of her house doing wheelies. I thought it might impress her. It didn't work.

Even then, as a shy kid making his way through the normal pains of adolescence, I had a purpose. I had first sensed it when I was six in JW Gorman's Power Cycle Honda dealership on Texas Avenue in Shreveport. Dad and I went into Mr Gorman's office. I looked around and noticed the things that were at my eye level. One was a photograph, old and grainy, black and white. I recognised Mr Gorman but I did not concentrate on him. I looked at the other figure, the man with the overalls and the white hat with the stripe. This figure seemed so different, an exotic man framed in the picture, shaking hands with JW Gorman. The man was Mr Honda himself.

Breeze, Louisiana, 2010

When I woke up in my hotel room this morning I knew today was the day. I had left my sister's on 23 July. I had been there three months and she asked where I would go. I told her it would be fine. All the striving and uncertainty had prepared me for whatever was next. I had no idea what it would be, but I knew it would be out there. I had to trust in what I felt completely this time, because I'd had chances before and I knew what it felt like when I listened and when I didn't. It wasn't an emotionally driven decision for me; I had a lifetime of experiences and wisdom to guide me.

I got out of bed and, as I had done the last three mornings, I walked over to the window and opened the shades to see what the weather was like. It was hot.

My room on the third floor of the Hilton Garden faced east. I put my hand on the window and could feel the heat from the rising sun. As I took my hand off the window, my thoughts turned to what I should do today. I would call my old friend, Mr Williams, to see if he could come by to pick me up around 11. Where would I go next? I didn't know.

I packed my small suitcase. I had three days' worth of clothes. I put my laptop in my backpack and went downstairs to check out.

Mr Williams pulled up to the front of the hotel at exactly 11. I put my bags in the back seat and got in.

'You got everything?' Mr Williams asked.

'You bet.'

He started out of the parking lot and paused at the exit.

Mr Williams said: 'Which way?'

We could only go left or right down Financial Plaza. I knew there were other hotels down to the right. I told him I wanted to go right but sensed to go left.

'Then we should go left,' Mr Williams said.

After we went left out of the parking lot, Mr Williams said: 'Where to next?'

I smiled and, a little embarrassed, said: 'Closer than you might think, Mr Williams.' And I pointed to the neighbouring Courtyard Marriott. So he turned into the parking lot and pulled up to the front, a drive of about 300 yards.

I had been here before with my wife and kids in 2007, but this time was different. The person at the front desk – Teresa, according to the name badge – said: 'Welcome. Can I help you?'

'I'd like a room.'

'Certainly. For how many nights?'

I paused. 'Probably about a week. I don't know yet.'

I said I needed to check out another couple of places to make sure. It felt right and I knew it was, but how could it be *this* simple?

'No problem,' said Teresa. She smiled. 'You'll be back.'

I walked out to the car and Mr Williams took me to two more places. I walked into the lobbies and out again. Then I went back to the Courtyard Marriott. I thanked Mr Williams, apologising for making him come and get me so we could drive one block up the street.

'Freddie, it's no problem. You know that.'

'I know.' I smiled. 'You know how much I appreciate it.'

I walk back inside. It has stopped raining and the sun is shining. I have a calm feeling. I don't know why but I feel Teresa is part of the reason why I know this is where I am supposed to be. And tonight, 2 August 2010, will be the beginning of the most important four months of my life.

This part of my journey began in earnest in September 2007, when Chelee' and I were talking in the master bathroom of our house in

Summerlin on the west side of Las Vegas and she said: 'I want a divorce.'

A month earlier I asked her: 'If all of this goes away, will it be okay?'

She said: 'What are you talking about? You mean if we divorce I won't have anything left?'

I understand why she asked me that but it is not what the question had meant, although at that time I didn't fully understand that myself.

I didn't have a clue what would happen the next day, week, month or year. I just knew she was right. It was over. 'I know,' I said, but I was sad for the sake of the kids, and for Chelee' and me, sad that it was coming to an end after being together for 16 years, sad for all the changes that it would mean for our family.

It wasn't just my marriage that was over either. I had spent my whole life since I was four years old working towards a goal, always trying to move forwards. But I always felt there was something more. The best moments were never me just winning a race or standing on top of a podium or being the fastest guy in the world on a motorcycle. The moments with others – when it wasn't just about me – were the ones that mattered most. It was about them; it was about *us*.

In December 2009 my divorce from Chelee' was finalised. In January 2010 I began to feel it was time to leave Las Vegas. I told the kids I would be going soon. They understood as much as they could at eight and eleven, but it was important to talk to them about it so they would know without question that it wasn't their fault and that I loved them. It was the start of this incredible journey.

So by that day in August 2010 I had been through a difficult three years. I was divorced and I had lost my home and all my businesses. Between the ages of 18 and 47, I had been used to travelling first class. I was used to beautiful cars. I had wanted for nothing in terms of material goods. I had a life of comfort. Now it was time to let go of all that.

I understood when people closest to me wondered what I was doing. I was a motorcycle racer. Maybe they thought it was a midlife crisis?

Chapter 1: FIRE (1961–73)

That first night, as I was lying in my bed in Room 137 at the Courtyard Marriott, I had the strongest feeling that this is where I was supposed to be. This feeling came from years of honing my attention, but why was it so clear to me? Why was I so certain? Was this how it worked when you begin to understand? But understand *what*?

I went to Walmart the next day and bought a Sony MP3 player. I went back to the Marriott and realised that to connect with iTunes you need an Apple iPod. I thought, 'Where have I been?'

I had only $200 in my pocket. The room rate was $103 for those nights, so I would need to sell some memorabilia I had in storage to keep staying there because my next event was not until September in Holland. I know people will ask why I didn't go back to stay at my sister's for nothing, but I felt this was what I had to do. My past experiences – those moments of clarity in 1984 and 1985 – were how I knew: that was my wisdom. It was now or never.

I worked out a deal and got my rate down to $62. I called Rick, who was a salesman at my Honda dealership in the 1980s, to see if he could sell some things for me. He had done it before. Trust me, it was hard. I wanted my kids to have some of those things. I didn't get top dollar. Rick put boots and gloves and posters on eBay. I was aware how it would look to others, but I couldn't worry about that. It was what I had to do.

I began writing in the first week of my stay, at 7.19am on 8 August to be exact. I started with what I knew so I created a business plan for building custom sports bikes, but it morphed into an idea about the 'Realities of Life', and then, finally, into *Breeze*, my account of the four months that changed my life. I saw that the story was more than just how I started racing and went on to become world champion. It was what I learned and honed through my riding that counted, what I could

see,
sense
and feel

It's why as a racer I could look around a crowd as far as the eye could see, over 120,000 different people, right before the most important Grand Prix of the year, just before the flag was thrown, and feel this was not all that I was supposed to do. Then I would shake those feelings from my mind and immediately refocus.

I woke up early on Wednesday, 18 August and decided I would walk to the Forest Park West Cemetery to visit Mom and Dad's graves. I didn't think I was on a spiritual quest or anything. I had become way too practical for that over the years. Before I began this journey in 2007 I had let practical thoughts restrict my intuition. But when you get one of those glimpses you have to pay attention and I realised it was changing.

Teresa was in reception. She introduced me to another member of staff, Mrs Ada, who had been at the hotel almost as long as Teresa, some ten years.

I said I'd walk to the cemetery and Mrs Ada piped up, 'You don't have to walk. Have Pee Wee "Isaiah" take you in the shuttle van. He's not doing anything right now.' I couldn't help but smile. I knew right away that I would like Mrs Ada. 'That's okay. I want to walk.'

It only took about 25 minutes. It was already hot and humid. The last time I had been there I was with Chelee' and the kids in March 2007. I'd stayed in the Marriott then and Teresa, Mrs Ada and Pee Wee were all working there at that time. I hadn't even noticed them.

As I sat by Mom and Dad's graves I closed my eyes and thought about how much I had missed them and how I would give anything to hug them right now. I realised it *was* about more. They had both done so much to give me every chance of a good life. This time I was really there, not more interested in getting everyone back into the car and deciding what we were going to eat. Before it had all been about getting to Cracker Barrel and their chicken pot pie.

Sitting there, I told Mom and Dad that I was sorry. I thought of how Dad asked the pastor to have 'Amazing Grace' played at his service and of Mom telling me she wanted to watch the Faith Hill concert on

TV the last night we spent together at my home in Vegas in January 2001. I thought of their songs, of the power of grace and faith, of time lost, moments wasted.

As I got back to the hotel I reached into my back pocket and pulled out the kids' last school pictures. The sadness hit front and centre. I thought about how much I loved and missed them and wondered if this was worth it.

'How was your visit?' Teresa asked.

I said: 'Today was like the first time I'd really been there since the services.'

Teresa nodded. 'Sometimes we just go through the motions.'

Mrs Ada came out from the laundry at that point. 'Amen to that.' She was direct and to the point, but you could tell she was sincere too. I agreed.

Today I have the curtains open because the power is out. I walk down to the front desk where a gentleman is complaining to Teresa about being unable to see while shaving. He wants to know what Teresa is going to do about it. She was upset because she truly cares about every customer.

I can see he is beginning to upset her as he carries on and on. Normally, I would not say anything but I cannot believe what I am hearing. 'Sir, do you realise the power is out because of violent storms?'

'Yes, so?' he said.

'Teresa's not the person you should be complaining to. It's above her pay grade. Please show some respect to Teresa because we're all in the dark together.'

He just looks at me angrily and walks away. Teresa wipes away her tears and says: 'Thank you.'

When the power comes back on I start writing again and I decide to write about the first traumatic moment of my life. So I write about the day I tripped into a smouldering pile of black leaves and how Levy C chose to start running after the small, shy boy heading for a fall.

Chapter 2: **ROAD TRIP (1973–78)**

WE COVERED a lot of ground in Dad's Dodge Maxivan during the year of 1977, just the two of us, travelling to meetings in increasingly far-flung places, him drinking Coke and eating salted peanuts – it became easier to just pour the bag of nuts into the Coke – passing neon signs, the little television set with metal rabbit ears in the back plugged into the cigarette lighter, crackling into life whenever we got near a town. I would watch the screen intently before we would lose the signal again. Sometimes we'd get ten minutes of reception, sometimes more.

Dad would endlessly play his tape of Abba's *Arrival* album on the little eight-track player in the van. Hours and hours of the same songs over and over again. When we stopped he would complain about his ankles hurting. It was gout exacerbated by eating too many peanuts. Yet it was a precious period. I was fuelled not only by ambition or a need to win, but I craved racing and the sensations that it brought to me. I loved the precision of it. Dad and I would look in the ads in the back of *Cycle News* for races in new places. There would be little information. A name, location, a time for sign-up, practice and the race, little dollar signs if there was prize money. It was real grass-roots racing. Sometimes there were so many entries that there would be scores of heat races. I was always amazed by the deep fields of competition. I always expected to make the main event, but for most the journey to a faraway track would yield only disappointment. But they would go anyway and, while I respected all competitors, it was those racers I respected the most because of their desire to keep trying no matter what.

I was a dirt-tracker at heart, having learned my craft in my dirty yard, but I had a voracious appetite for all bikes. I'd already started to get a few write-ups in the *Shreveport Times* and one day I was leafing through *Cycle News* looking at the results. In the back there was a story about the latest World Championship road race. I flipped over the page and was taken by another photograph. I just loved the look of that frozen bike. It belonged to a rider named Kent Andersson who was a talented Swede who would win the 125cc road-racing World Championship in 1973. Something about that picture resonated with me. Even though it was just a black-and-white photograph of him and his Yamaha, it was so vivid. It was another glimpse, one that would shape my future.

More than a decade later, I was the 500cc world champion and I was at the 1984 German Grand Prix at the new Nürburgring. I was with Niki Lauda, the Formula One racer, who I got on with. He took me around the old track and showed me where he had the terrible crash that had left him burnt, scarred and in a coma. That Friday evening at a welcome party for all champions, a man approached me and stuck out a hand.

'Freddie, you don't know who I am,' he began but I interrupted him.

'Of course I do, Mr Andersson. You're the reason I knew I wanted to road-race.' When I had finished he had tears in his eyes. I knew he'd like to hear that connection through the ages.

Road racing was a different world though. I knew I wanted to race in the World Championship, just like Kent Andersson, but it seemed impossible. There was not a single American in Grand Prix racing at that time.

A few weeks after seeing that photo of Kent we were at Ross Downs for a dirt-track meeting where I was racing in the 100cc class.

Jack Rhodes was the soundtrack to many a summer in the world of dirt-track and motocross racing. He was the announcer and he called every event, his words buzzing along the public-address system and out over the hum of engines and voices. Wherever you went it was always Jack Rhodes' voice greeting you like an old friend, telling you to buy hotdogs from the concession stand and T-shirts from the vendors. The words would blur into the background, but that night they sprung out in perfect clarity during an intermission break before the main events.

'Don't forget there is a road race this weekend down at Green Valley Raceway,' he said. 'It only costs five bucks so go and support the road-race guys.'

I knew I wanted to go. I just needed a bike and the opportunity. I had to convince the adults to let me ride.

In the summer of 1973 I was an 11-year-old dirt-tracker who did not know too much about road racing except what I'd seen at Daytona Motorcycle Speed Week and in the Steve McQueen movie *On Any Sunday*.

I knew it was important, though, because it was part of the Grand National Championship, which encompassed all forms of racing from dirt to road. I was certain I wanted to be there. I told my dad.

'But we don't have a road-race bike, Freddie,' he said.

'Well, let's ask Mr Carter. He'll help us.'

TC Carter, the owner of Carter's Yamaha, was with us at that dirt-track event. It was almost midnight but Dad and I went to find him during that intermission. He listened to my wish and we all agreed to meet at 5am the next morning because we needed to get to the track before practice started at 8am.

We walked into the store at dawn that next morning and the only bike that was small enough for me to ride was a little Yamaha RD100 street bike, blue with a white stripe. In those days, most everybody in the production classes just rode their bikes to races and taped up the lights. I was so excited.

We loaded the bike into the van and went to Green Valley. There was a small shed where people were signing up. I walked in behind my dad.

'Sign right there,' the man behind the desk said to Dad.

'Not me, my son.'

The guy peered around Dad at me. He raised his eyebrows and failed to hide his scepticism. 'What's *he* going to ride?' he said.

Dad was non-plussed by this attitude. 'We have a Yamaha RD100,' he said. The man shrugged. They'd never had a kid who wanted to road-race so there were no rules that said I couldn't, as long as an adult signed off. 'Sign right there,' the man repeated.

I was 11 and the next youngest rider was a man named J Gleeson who was 21. They all laughed a bit. I was a novelty, a boy in a man's world. It was raining and I wondered if we might not get our chance, but they said they could run in those conditions on road bikes and so we went out. I could barely reach the handlebars and foot pegs, so Dad had to hold me upright on the back of the grid and then catch me when I came off the track. I loved it.

It was not the speed that inspired me, but the ebb and flow, the angles and the precision that would be required to be good at it. It was what would motivate me to do it again. Green Valley went up a drag strip and then you came down the return road, through a parking lot where they'd put some cones out, making an arc, and then back to the straightaway. There was only one right-hand corner, but that was awkward for me after all my years going left on ovals. I finished last but I was grinning from ear to ear. My dad smiled too, as he always would whenever he would tell the story over the years. 'You know, I've never seen Freddie so happy to finish last.'

I was 11 when I saw my first death. One Wednesday night at Dallas International, a quarter-mile flat-track oval with plywood fencing all around it, a kid just hit the fence at the wrong place and careered into a stationary pole. It was horrible, of course, and devastating. There is an emotional part to racing, but it was underpinned by the practical and methodical, and I wasn't that boy with stomach cramps any more. The race restarted and I refocused. That's what you need to do, but you never forget. The empathy is for the family left behind.

Mom was incredibly understanding of what I was doing. She saw the danger and knew what could happen. She had even had a crash herself on a scooter; it was not too serious but it still hurt. I knew the emotional and material sacrifices my family had made to give me the chance to succeed. I was aware that I was the reason why Mom had that same black-leather living-room furniture that she disliked for all those years. She and Dad were putting all their money into my racing.

The family ran a convenience store, called Hotchkiss Street Grocery, named after the original dirt road long since developed and now called Milam Street, where the old wooden floor was so uneven that we'd joke you could get seasick just walking up and down. It was just a local neighbourhood existence. Mom never complained about not having things and it was only 15 years later that I could replace that furniture for her.

In 1972, the year before I began road racing, was the first time I saw Kenny Roberts ride at the Astrodome. It was Friday practice for the TT races and he was on the XS650 Yamaha. The next day he won the short-track race as a rookie expert and that was impressive. Kenny would go on to be one of the true legends of motorsport and would play a pivotal role in my own story. He was tough and hard and never suffered fools, either then or since.

I watched that first practice and noticed immediately that he was riding differently to everyone else. It was a lightbulb moment for me and I always paid attention when I saw someone doing something that was unique and an improvement. That technique was more efficient. It made sense.

The following year I was back there and it started to rain and sleet. It was so cold but I got up the nerve to stand there, shivering and waiting with my little book and pen. It would be the only time in my life that I asked for an autograph, but the person walked right past me. It was Kenny. Maybe he didn't see me. I just stood there not sure what to do. No one else, other than my dad, was there to see my disappointment but it left an indelible impression.

It was 1985, at the French Grand Prix, right in the middle of my assault on two world titles in one year. By that time of that season, my life had changed completely and I could not get from the motorhome to the grid on my own. Police were stationed outside the door waiting for when I had to go to practice. Every day fans would come over the fence and some would rip the licence plates off my motorhome. Inside I could hear the chanting – 'Freddie, Freddie' – that would not stop until I appeared.

Each morning and afternoon when I would leave my motorhome, the fans rushed towards me so the police would have to form a cordon around me. Once when I was walking down the paddock, out of the corner of my eye I saw the fans knock over a little boy. The fans were unaware of what had happened but I saw the boy fall. I stopped and took my helmet off. I picked him up and asked if he was okay. He was French and couldn't understand what I was saying, but there were tears in his eyes. I made sure he understood that he was to come back after practice and then I'd give him a signed glove as a souvenir.

Now, I realise more every day how Dad loved those early years too. One Friday night, when I was 13, we were racing in Benton, Arkansas and saw that there was a race in Sharpsburg, North Carolina, a tiny place best known for being a battle site in the Civil War.

Dad said: 'Do you want to go?'

'Yes,' I said.

So on that hot August night Dad got out the maps and, using the dome light, started studying it. That was not always a fail-proof methodology, but he said: 'We can get there by three tomorrow if we get going right after the race.'

So, around midnight, we headed east.

It was a hell of a journey and all we did was stop for gas. Tired and hungry, we showed up there at 4.30pm. Sign-up had started at 12pm, with practice starting at 3pm. Racing would begin at 5pm. We were very late and they were not going to let us sign in or ride.

'We've driven all the way from Arkansas,' Dad pleaded.

The man behind the sign-up desk fixed us with a look somewhere between wonder and pity. Why would anyone drive over a thousand miles for a race? I can understand why he would think that way, but we were extremely passionate. It was the adventure that inspired Dad and me, and I know my sense of purpose inspired Dad too. Like I'd told my mom when I was doubled up with stomach cramps: it's what I needed to do.

Dad never got angry. 'Look, my son is here, he wants to race, we've not eaten and we've driven all this way. Can you just give him a chance?'

The man frowned. Dad persisted. 'Just give him three laps of practice and let him race.'

I got two and went straight from there to the heat race. The green flag was waved. I popped the clutch and the chain came off. That was it. Our time in Sharpsburg was done. You got no second chances in those events. We loaded up the bike and turned around. Another thousand miles. Sometimes on those long road trips, late at night, after the races, I would roll down the window and listen to the noise of the road and the sound of bikes would echo in the wind.

When I was 13 and we were on the way down to Daytona, Dad said he was feeling tired. Dad was a resolutely strong man, who would lift outboard motors from the back of trucks without flinching, but he was feeling the miles that day.

'I can't drive any more, Freddie,' he said. He pulled over to rest, but we needed to drive straight through the night.

'Let me drive, Dad.'

'We can't do that.'

'But we can't make it in time if we don't.'

He knew the truth of that. It was an 800-mile trip to Daytona. We had to keep the miles up or we'd have no chance.

'Well, it's a straight road to Jacksonville. Just for an hour. Then you wake me up.'

'Okay, I will.'

I didn't wake him up and drove for hours. Dad was so tired and resting in the passenger seat and I just kept on through the night, staring at the road ahead.

Later they'd say I was a natural, but by the time I was 13 I would race 40 weekends a year in different categories. When I was even younger, between six and ten, and we got to within 40 miles of the track, I'd be so excited that I'd put on my leather pants and boots, even though it was 100 degrees Fahrenheit (38 degrees Celsius) outside. Dad rolled down the windows and turned the air conditioner off so I could get used to the heat. *He* thought it was a good idea.

The outlaw races

During my teen years, I raced on the dirt on Friday nights in two classes. We would finish after midnight and get up early the next morning and travel an hour to a road race for practice and heats in three to five classes. That would take us to Saturday evening when I'd have a dirt-track race. On Sunday I'd go back to the road race track for the main events. So many events, so many races with Dad taking care of up to eight bikes. It was great and I won a lot.

I was Texas and Oklahoma mini-bike champion in 1970. I'd switched to a big bike, a 100cc Yamaha, when I was eight and rode dirt bikes until I was twelve and got a 250cc flat-tracker. Titles, trophies and a bit of small-town fame followed. There is a faded picture of me receiving a trophy when I'm only six and you can see the blushes through the monochrome image as a girl hands over the cup and gives me a kiss.

You could make a lot of money at the outlaw races, put on by promoters who didn't want to worry about a sanctioning fee. That meant they had prize money. On Wednesday nights at Dallas International dirt-track events they paid out in silver dollars. To draw the best racers they paid a decent amount of prize money. It was the coolest thing as the silver dollars were put in old sacks like you see in an old western movie. I liked to count them over and over.

I could get $100 for a win in the 125cc class and $40 for the 100cc. I often went away with $140 a night, which was good money for a kid.

I used some of the money to buy Dad a Texas Instruments calculator, which cost $84. It was the first he had ever seen. I'd see him at the store with a pen and paper, doing his sums and then erasing them because he had miscalculated. I thought it would be nice. It was a thrill for me to give him something like that. Not that long afterwards I also paid for us to have air conditioning in the house. It was amazing to me how much money you could make from this stuff. It was a long way from the times when I promoted little bicycle races in our neighbourhood. I offered some prize money – a dollar fifty for a win and a dollar for second – but I made money by getting drinks from the store for free and selling them for a quarter. I made posters with our address on, even though everybody knew where it was, and there would be about ten kids from the neighbourhood and from Sunset Acres. Nevertheless, I felt like a real race promoter.

My parents pushed me to do other sports because they were worried I was becoming obsessed so I tried out for the football team in sixth grade. Dad took me up to Sunset Acres and dropped me off. He said he'd be back in an hour. That was a long walk for me on to that field. What would I say? I had the application form with Dad's signature on it and handed it to the coach. I sat down on the bench. I was so nervous, but once we started practice I actually enjoyed being part of a team.

Before long we were racing in Dallas so much that there was almost a groove in the road from Shreveport. After I graduated sixth grade in 1973 we even moved over there so it would be easier for my racing. We got an apartment in Garland and Dad got a store in Seagoville, a small town near Dallas County, but we kept the house in Shreveport. I was used to having so much space to ride and now I was in a small apartment. That meant going to a new school for six months before we all got homesick and moved back, which is when I started at Grawood Christian Academy, a small, private school in Shreveport. I could not get a good education and race as much as I wanted to if I was at a public school so the choice was simple. All I had to do was get the grades.

It was not that I was so focused on racing that I had no time for anything else, but I could tell people who were receptive to what I was doing and those who weren't. Adults were sceptical. This was the time of Hells Angels, the movie *Easy Rider* and a counterculture clad in black leather. Bikes were synonymous with the wrong kind of people. I had one teacher who told me I'd never amount to anything if I continued to race motorcycles.

The school principal at Grawood was Leonard Phillips and he was the one person who understood. He would get teachers, who didn't want me to take their tests outside of the scheduled time, to work with me and give me a chance. Years later, when I got my first letter from President Reagan, it was Principal Phillips who was one of the people I was happiest to acknowledge. I went back to those days sitting in his office and him letting me do the homework at different times to fit in with my racing and travel.

He did not let me have it easy, but he did let me have a chance when the common perception was that if you rode motorcycles then you must be crazy and have no future. Even if they didn't say that, I could sense it. There was no urge to prove them all wrong, but there was an urge to show the folly of that lack of acceptance. The last thing that you could say about me was that

I was crazy. I knew exactly what I could do and I knew where I wanted to go. It was totally sensible.

I was soaking up experiences and knowledge riding in my yard. I would get the garden hose and wet one corner of my little oval track around the trees. Then I'd ride round and round and adjust my line and trajectory lean angle. I'd drift the bike to certain points of the corner and wait for the nanosecond when I could accelerate again. That has always been my favourite thing – the *transitions*, those subtle moments. For years I would lie in bed at night thinking about it and it would come to me. Then the next day I would try it out and I'd continue to move forwards in understanding another bike and how to work with it.

It was when I was in the ninth grade that I met Mr Williams. He was the father of my first girlfriend Christi.

She lived in Keithville, which was 20 minutes south of Shreveport in the country, on Williams Road. I'd go out and pick her up in our van. I was 15 but you could get a licence in Louisiana at that age. My shyness meant the idea of going to pick her up was incredibly difficult, but we became like family. Mr Williams had great stories about how him and his brother Vern would get in a Model T and crank it up and go sideways down the Williams Road back when it was just dirt and they were kids. We had a mutual affinity for racing.

The first time Christi came to a race was in Arkansas. It felt odd to have someone else there with me and Dad. She asked how I was going to do and, trying to be cool and calm, I said: 'Usually, I do pretty good.' That night got rained out but the next weekend we went back and won.

Christi and I dated on and off in the ninth and tenth grades, but we grew up and became friends. I stayed in touch with her and Mr Williams, and he even built a track for me to practice on. Christi helped me out when I started going to Europe, coming to a couple of Grands Prix in that first year along with Mr Williams. Many nights I'd watch Mr Williams race at Hill Top, one of the many local banked dirt ovals where people had names like Slick Swain, an almost comic-book South.

The road trips continued. Dad and I covered 100,000 miles a year as we sought out races, spending 15 to 20 hours cooped up together. Imagine the amount of time we spent together, weekends and weekends, years and years, miles and miles.

The first time we went up east was to New Hampshire. On the two-day drive Dad and I noticed a stronger and stronger smell of gas, but he didn't seem too worried and we needed to stay on schedule. We didn't know the smell was coming from leaking fuel because the petcock, a switch controlling flow from the tank to the carburettors, had been left on. That meant the engine became full. When we arrived and tried to start the engine it was overloaded with fuel and wouldn't turn over. Dad's bright idea was to take out the spark plugs and have me hold the handlebars while he pushed me from behind. This would get the pistons moving and pump out the excess fuel. It was a good theory, apart from the fact the plug caps that give the engine life were still active.

Inevitably, flames gushed out in a puff of fire, singeing my hair and eyebrows and I dropped the bike.

Dad said: 'What are you doing?'

'What do you mean what am I doing?' I yelled. 'I'm on fire!'

'Stop messing about, Freddie.'

'I was on fire! My face is singed!'

The flames dwindled because it was a flash fire, but I was in shock. Dad and I did not fight about the incident and still raced the whole weekend. It was more embarrassment on his part.

The different tracks were fascinating to me and helped me become adaptable to changing conditions. I was always adjusting and I loved that part. Ross Downs was about carrying a lot of speed. Yukon, near Oklahoma City, was a hard-packed clay oval. As the race night progressed and the track dried it would get slippery. A groove would form and it would be very tricky. That required a lot of finesse and throttle control.

Yukon was also flat with short straights and tight corners. It was a track promoted by the McDonald family and their patriarch Norm. They supported countless local racers. People like them gave us the chance to hone our skills and sometimes to take those skills out into the world. It has to start somewhere.

One night in Yukon I finished in seventh place in the main event. I *never* came seventh in a main event. I knew I rode okay, so I wasn't too disappointed. To me it was out of my hands. Dad and I tried to figure it out on the way home and he decided he was going to get a new frame designed with a shorter wheel base and move the engine down and forward. The new frame would help get the power to the ground better next time. That conversation with my dad was my first real lesson about geometry and caught my imagination. My dad ordered a bike and built it. Suddenly, I could do so much more with the motorcycle. I won at Yukon and I won everywhere. It gave me far more agility. That seventh place helped me to win many more races.

Daytona was my exposure to the big wide world. I won amateur races there in 1973 and 1974 on my Yamaha TZ125. It was like the kid who plays baseball and goes to the Texas Rangers games; I would watch the greats like Giacomo Agostini racing and think that maybe that would be me someday.

I was getting so much experience, winning on the TZ250 when I was only 14, riding the Yamaha TZ750 at 15, the fastest road-race bike in the world with a top speed of 180mph. Dad bought one for $5,500, a lot of money, although I could not race it professionally until I was 18. The only other people who had them were pros. I was lucky. I was seen as a wunderkind to the older guys. I almost beat Dale Singleton, a rider who would take to bringing his pet pig Elmer to races, the same year he won the prestigious Daytona 200.

I had my first sponsorship contract in 1978. Roger Weston was the importer for Arai helmets and he approached me one day at a race and said he would like me to be their representative. My first contract was for $225 a month and a free helmet. I never wore another brand. It will be 40 years of collaboration with Arai in 2018. With that money coming in January 1978, on the way to a road race at Texas World Speedway, my dad and I stopped off at a Lincoln Mercury dealership in Dallas in October 1977 and bought my first car. It was a Mercury Cougar, chocolate brown with tan seats, just sitting on the lot. I drove straight off in it, making to TWS on time. I was 15 turning 16 and I loved that car. Now I was able to drive to school every day. I was on my way.

I won five WERA amateur road-race titles in 1977, the year Barry Sheene won the 500cc World Championship to underline his superstar status, and we had travelled far and wide.

Dad was obviously thinking about things. I did not know that there was some trouble with the store at that point. Dad would never talk about things like that, but I guess he had done the sums on his $84 Texas Instruments calculator.

We went to the Grand National Finals at a track called Mid-Ohio in Lexington and the only open spot to park was next to a gleaming white van.

I was 15 and riding in five classes in the nationals.

The WERA was the biggest amateur road-racing series at the time and they had invited Gary Nixon to come to race in the 250 class. He had almost won the coveted Formula 750 Championship the year before and was a bona fide star. I noticed someone sitting in the front seat of the white van and as I looked harder I could tell from the distinctive mirror shades that it was Gary. I had watched him so many times at Daytona where he raced factory Suzukis and Kawasakis. With him was Erv Kanemoto, the renowned tuner, who had helped him to the US Road Racing title in 1973. Also there was another rider, Randy Mamola, a young Californian who would be the next to follow Kenny to the Grand Prix circuit.

I don't think Dad had any intention of this happening, but it proved fortuitous. Looking back at all the races we had done, on all the bikes, jumping from one to another at events without even removing my helmet, it is clear the cost had added up and Dad had no more money left. It was going to hold me back.

Mid-Ohio had concrete strips where the outside wheel of cars would go. It made it really hard in the rain and it was impossible to get across those edges if the lean angle was too great. I was racing a 125cc against 350cc bikes. Mike Baldwin, a well-known pro rider, was on one of the bigger Ducatis and we went down the back straight, duelling in the pouring rain. I was looking at him and he looked across at me. We both crashed. It was almost funny. I tried to stop in the slick grass but that was impossible. I did manage to pick my bike up, though, whereas he could not get his started again.

The second race was the big 250cc showdown, and I won by more than a minute. It was raining but one of my greatest assets has always been recognising situations. Most people get a little bit tentative, but my ability to adapt would take only a lap.

For a long time afterwards I didn't know what had gone on at Mid-Ohio, but Erv had come up and congratulated my dad on my 250 race win.

'Really good job.'

'Thank you,' Dad said. Then he confided in Erv. 'I know my son has the talent and the drive to go places, but I've taken him as far as I can. His mother and I want only what is best for him. Can you help us to give him the chance?'

Erv said: 'That's why I walked over to talk with you Mr Spencer. I would really like to help in any way I can.'

It was an exchange that would have huge repercussions for me. My dad, who had been there every day from that first race

11 years earlier, was now willing to put his own wants aside for what was best for me. I know it wasn't easy for him. He was always the racer in the family. But he did it. And that was the beginning of my relationship with Erv.

Erv is one of the most humble people I have ever known and it would have been hard for him to broach the subject with my dad. It would have been just as hard for my dad. On 20 December 1977 I turned 16, so my very first race as a professional was in March 1978, and Dad saw the need for a change. It was the beginning of him walking away and the start of a new partnership.

Most people view anything spiritual as unpredictable, but for me it's the opposite. They view faith as a little bit out there, but Erv and I could communicate without speaking. He would intuitively know what the next step was. My dad was the same. Dad knew he had taken me as far as he could from our garage on Amelia Street. Our road trip was coming to an end.

Breeze, Louisiana, 2010

As I was sitting there in the hotel, looking at my computer, the two thoughts I had earlier, at the graves of my parents, came back strong. So I went online looking for 'Amazing Grace' and a few YouTube versions popped up.

The one that caught my attention was the LeAnn Rimes a cappella version recorded in a Mexican church. I played it and it was nice. I'd never really listened to her music before – nothing wrong with it, but I've always been more of a rock 'n' roll and pop music fan. As the song finished I looked to the right of the screen and saw LeAnn's song 'Strong' listed. After I listened to it I didn't go back to 'Amazing Grace'. There was something I sensed about 'Strong'. I just didn't know *what*.

This was not the first time I had experienced such a moment. In 1979, I felt exactly the same watching the Honda team on the ABC broadcast of the 500cc British Grand Prix from Silverstone.

I watched LeAnn sing 'Strong' and felt a connection to the music and the passion with which she sang. I could feel the song meant a lot to her. When she finished I sat there for a few minutes. I didn't play it again right away. I wanted to see if I ever got the feeling to press play again. It would be four days until I would listen to 'Strong' again and, this time, I would listen to every word.

Then I looked for songs by Faith Hill. I had not paid much attention to her music, as she is mainly a country singer like LeAnn, apart from that night in January 2001 when Mom and I watched the concert on TV. I put her name in the search box and a number of her songs came up. The only song I considered was one I'd never heard before called 'The Lucky One'. I watched the video and my first feeling was there was something about it that portrayed a side of Faith Hill that was sincere and real. I put it in my favourites folder thinking I would know what it meant at a later date.

Since I have been here at the Courtyard Marriott one of the strongest things I have sensed is a feeling of empathy. I am beginning to see that empathy is a cornerstone feeling essential to our connection with others.

Chapter 3: **THE DAY I SHOCKED THE WORLD (1978–81)**

IN THE summer of 1978 everything was going well. I had won every professional road race by then on my way to the AMA Novice title. There was always a bump in the road, however, and this time it came when some friends and I drove out to Bossier City to go water-skiing. We had borrowed Dad's pick-up with a trailer carrying a boat, but as we were crossing the Red River Bridge, heading to the freedom of the summer before our senior year, things literally came undone.

My friend Gilbert Little was there along with his girlfriend, Deb Shelton, and Christi. As I was driving across the bridge, Gilbert looked in the rear-view mirror and said: 'Freddie, we have got a problem.'

Sure enough, when we all looked behind us we saw that the trailer had separated from the truck and the boat had come off and was spinning in the middle of the two lanes. Then the trailer jumped the concrete median into the oncoming traffic. Cars had to drive under it as it flipped in the air. The girls started screaming. Three or four seconds passed and we were over the bridge and we took the first exit off I-20. We could no longer see the chaos in our wake but I imagined someone must have hit the boat or even driven off the bridge trying to avoid the trailer. Gilbert's face was drained of all blood. I decided I needed to call home. Fast.

As we got to the gas station my mind was a mess of worries. I said: 'Maybe we should just head to Mexico?' It was only half a joke. I honestly thought we had killed someone. I dialled the number and Danny answered.

'Danny, did you hook up the trailer? It just came off the back of the truck!'

I was talking so fast that all he said was: 'What?'

He did not believe me, but when he detected the panic in my voice and he realised I was serious, he said: 'Okay, I'll come out there.'

Everyone was talking. What should we do? I said: 'We don't want to be fugitives on the run.' Mexico was off the agenda. Reality bit and we needed to get back to the crime scene. I was filled with fear of what we might find but was amazed to find the traffic moving fluently in both directions. A wrecker truck had pulled the trailer and the boat off the road. The driver got out.

'Looks like you had a little problem here,' he said. The driver said he could winch the boat back on to the trailer. He may, literally, have been a lifesaver. I asked what we could do for him.

'It's my pleasure,' he said.

I breathed a sigh of relief and turned my attention to thinking how Dad was now going to kill me. I would never forget that day when four teenagers nearly took out everybody on the Red River Bridge.

It was not the only time I found myself in trouble as a teenager. At the start of 1979 I was excited because I was due to race in the Astrodome for the first time.

I was still playing other sports then. I was cornerback and safety on Grawood's football team and, while I was not the best player, I enjoyed playing. One Friday night we were taking on our rivals from Shreveport Christian Academy when Tommy Chandler ran straight through me and laid me out. After scoring his touchdown he picked me up and straightened my jersey.

'You okay, Freddie?'

They all knew the Astrodome was coming up, my first National Championship, and had bought their tickets. Tommy was concerned he might have taken me out. We still laugh about that today. I grimaced and said I was fine.

After football season, basketball season started. Basketball was a great way of staying in shape and I even had a signature move – whatever the situation I would go to the corner and shoot. Even if I was wide open and could shoot or lay-up I would do the same thing.

Unfortunately, it was raining so hard one night that the roof began to leak and the floor got wet. The game was cancelled, but a few of us stayed and started to goof around.

We started to showboat and got a chair. We recruited Darlene Hay, a sweet classmate of ours, to hold it as we ran up and used it to help us dunk the ball. She complained that our shoes were getting too close to her face.

'Listen, one more time and I'm letting go of this chair,' she said.

'Darlene, you better not.'

The next time I got too close. The laces of my shoe brushed her face. Instinctively, Darlene let go. The chair toppled. I crashed to the ground. I knew right away that my wrist was broken.

'Darlene, you let go!'

She had warned me. She was completely devastated and would always apologise when she saw me. Now I was going to miss the Astrodome. I shouldn't have been there goofing around. My friend and teammate Albert Moore, drove me to the hospital saying the whole time, 'Your dad is gonna kill us.' I kept reassuring him that it was only me he was going to kill.

After he did the surgery that night, Dr Goodman said he felt I would not be able to ride at Daytona as well as missing the Astrodome because that was only five weeks away and the wrist was completely displaced. But after four weeks the cast came off and I headed to Daytona for Speed Week. I was looking forward to racing Kenny Roberts for the first time, but he didn't make it because he had ruptured his spleen in a crash while testing in

Japan. I was second to his replacement, Skip Askland, in the 100-mile lightweight race.

I dominated the 250cc AMA Road Championship that year and, despite my football and basketball problems, opportunities arose. When Mike Baldwin crashed in a race at Loudon in New Hampshire in June, he hit a fire extinguisher on the edge of the track and broke his femur. That opened the door for me. The race-team manager from Kawasaki came up to me and offered me the chance to take his seat for the last three races. I won the first two.

Yet the most significant moment that year did not involve my races or injuries to me and others. It was not even the fear of fleeing to Mexico over Red River Bridge. It came while sitting on the sofa at my parents' house that August and watching the broadcast of the British Grand Prix on the TV. During the race between Kenny Roberts and Barry Sheene, they took a moment to show a video clip of some Japanese men watching their ailing four-stroke NR500. It was hardly the picture of success: stern-faced expressions fixed on perceived failure. Yet that image of Mr Honda, arms crossed and looking into the distance, kindled something inside me. I did not know why but it was the same feeling I had when I had walked into JW Gorman's Power Cycle dealership and saw that grainy image on the wall in his office. There was an unfathomable connection.

So when talk turned to contracts at the end of 1979 I kept putting Kawasaki off. They offered me a deal for 1980 but I needed more time. I didn't know why, since Kawasaki was a proven commodity and Kork Ballington had just won the 250 and 350cc world titles for them on the KR250 and KR350 twins for the second year in a row. Still I delayed.

In retrospect, I showed a tremendous amount of faith in my belief that it would just be okay. Others would call it foolhardy. There was no reason to make me think about Honda at all. Kawasaki made perfect, practical sense. Their Superbike was great – I had already won on it and Erv had already worked with them. Yet for some reason I kept putting them off. When they talked to Dad that October to find out what was going on in my head, Dad was as perplexed as anyone. After chatting with them, he said to me one day: 'You sure you know what you are doing?'

I said: 'I hope so.'

Dad never asked again. He trusted my judgement.

Kawasaki were offering what seemed like the earth. A salary of almost $50k a year, plus bonuses for race wins, podiums and the championship bonus. That was more money than my dad made in an entire year. I'd already bought a car with the money they had paid me that year. Both Erv and I knew I was ready to move beyond the National Championship. I would be 18 in December making me eligible to compete on the world stage in 1980.

In mid-November Kawasaki gave me one more week to decide. Then one day I was outside in the front yard washing the car when Mom shouted to me.

'You've got a call, Freddie.'

'Who is it?' I asked.

'Someone from Honda I think.'

I got a nervous but excited feeling walking to the phone.

'Hello,' I said into the receiver.

Dennis McKay, the general manager of American Honda, introduced himself. 'I know you've been negotiating with Kawasaki, but you haven't signed anything have you?'

I said I hadn't.

'We have a new Superbike team to race in the US National Championship and we already have three riders. We'd like you to be the fourth.'

It was not the hardest sell. It was a little less money. I was the fourth rider in. My goal was to be the youngest world champion but only Kawasaki were offering me a ticket to the Grand Prix circuit at that time.

I said yes.

I rang Kawasaki and they were shocked when I told them I was signing with Honda. They simply could not believe I was turning them down. Understandably, they were disappointed. I know it didn't make sense. I could not say I had sat on a sofa watching the British Grand Prix and had a feeling. But that did open the door for Eddie Lawson to sign for Kawasaki – a perfect match. I used the money from the deal to buy my first Ferrari, taking Danny with me to the dealership in Dallas. It was the same car Tom Selleck would drive in *Magnum P.I.* On the way back from the dealer we stopped and the driver's door was impossible to open. I called the dealer who said they had just had a telex and they needed to recall the car due to a fault. I took it back and got another one. The first was silver, the second black. This time we were close to home when the windscreen wiper came off. I had gone through two Ferraris in a day.

Part of me was not sure what was going to happen in 1980. I had a feeling from watching that broadcast of the British Grand Prix but there was no history to the American Honda team. There were no plans for Europe and the only things I had lined up were to race in the AMA Superbike Championship starting at Daytona and, first, to ride at the Houston Astrodome for the first time on the American Honda dirt-track team.

I was 18 and the Astrodome had huge significance for me. I ended up finishing fourth in the TT national on a Friday night in January. Kenny won. It was a dream come true to make the main event in the Houston Astrodome Nationals.

From there I went to Daytona. I walked in the garage that first day and the bikes were still being worked on. I got to meet Mike Velasco, an esteemed tuner. For me every day was a new chapter in this adventure and now I was finally to get a chance to race against Kenny Roberts in the Daytona 200.

I was lucky because Honda did not have a bike for the 200 and so they let me ride Erv's Yamaha TZ750.

I won my Superbike heat race on the Thursday and so I had

my first chance of qualifying for the 200 on Erv's TZ750. It went well. I almost became the youngest rider ever to get pole position for the Daytona 200 but one of the front brake discs warped going into turn one on my fast lap. I finished the session second to Kenny Roberts.

That Friday afternoon, aged just 18 and in my very first race for the brand-new American Honda Superbike team, I finished second to Graeme Crosby after a great battle. On Saturday I finished third in the 100-mile 250 race behind Anton Mang and Randy Mamola.

It was a great two days and a promising preamble to the 200. On that Sunday I lined up against Kenny, on his way to completing a hat-trick of 500cc world titles and the undisputed king of the track. Yet skill and circumstance narrowed the gap in top-class experience. He dropped out not long into the race. The 1978 winner was gone and I took command. Even when they stopped the race for a while, after the rain came and the wind blew sand on to the track, it did not interrupt my flow. After the restart I opened up a huge lead. And then, with ten laps to go, I felt the engine starting to slow down. The crankshaft was failing and the engine stopped. Patrick Pons, who a few months later would be killed at the British Grand Prix, took the win and I lost my chance to become the youngest rider to win the Daytona 200.

As I sat in the garage with Erv we were disappointed but proud that we had almost won our first Daytona 200. Perhaps Honda felt a tinge of satisfaction, too, that I had showed promise but not won for a rival manufacturer.

A man walked into the garage as we pondered all this and introduced himself. He said his name was Gavin Trippe and he was the promoter of the Trans-Atlantic Match Races that Easter in the UK. He had a problem. One of the American riders had dropped out leaving a slot unfilled.

'We'd like you to come,' he said.

It was a sentence that would change my life.

I asked Erv what he thought and he said: 'Let's do it.'

I said I would need to clear it with American Honda, but I thought it would be great experience for both of us. The Match Races were hugely popular Anglo–American races, the motorcycling equivalent of golf's Ryder Cup, and they captured the public's imagination and patriotism. At that point, we only had one more event at the end of the year. Erv had put his programme on hold to support what I felt I needed to do with Honda and I appreciated that.

A month later I was in London on my first trip outside the USA. I was barely old enough to ride in international races. At the Kensington Close Hotel, near to Buckingham Palace and all that historical splendour, I felt it was all moving in the right direction.

They took us to Brands Hatch in Range Rovers on Thursday afternoon. We were wearing neon red, white and blue jackets, which seemed the height of cool to a teenager, and fans spotted us and came rushing up as we emerged. I quickly realised they were not here for me. They marched straight past me to Kenny and Randy Mamola, the Grand Prix stars. I was just a young kid and I got out of the way.

I loved the Brands Hatch circuit from the first 30-minute practice. I loved the elevation changes and the technical precision required. I appreciated the complexity, but to me it was just a series of left- and right-hand corners that I learned in a very methodical way through my ability to focus and remember. I didn't use braking markers. I did it by feel in relation to my ability to judge distances.

There was a hierarchy in the paddock. The Grand Prix riders were stationed closer to the garage but the rest of us were outside. When I walked through the tunnel to the infield and came out of the darkness and saw the febrile crowd, thousands of fans spilling over fences, I smiled. Dale Singleton, another of my experienced teammates, asked me if I was nervous. I told him I wasn't. It was the truth. I was focused. Fourteen years of hard work had led me to that moment – emerging from that tunnel at an international event – and I felt this was where I should be.

Mike Hailwood was the British captain and Barry Sheene and Graeme Crosby were on the UK team. Our captain was Kenny. We sat down in the team meeting and he said: 'Okay, you rookies, the most important thing is not to make mistakes.' He said the British had been winning the series in recent years by filling up the middle-order positions. Riders got points depending on their places. We needed to be more consistent rather than just having a race winner and some also-rans.

'We need you guys to step up and do a good job,' he said. The words stuck. Kenny said he would put the rookies up at the front because we would need that advantage to get a good start.

The first race started and Graeme Crosby took the lead. I was second. In fact, that opening lap was the only one on which I did not lead. I passed Graeme coming into Paddock Hill bend. I had already decided where I was going to look back. With every lap I felt more and more comfortable.

Alan Wilson, the track manager who would re-enter my life in the distant future, handed me the trophy. I was on top of the podium. Mike Hailwood and Giacomo Agostini, legends who had duelled in the sixties, were there. It was an amazing sensation. Just the previous August I had been sitting at Mom and Dad's watching Kenny and Barry battle in the British Grand Prix.

Maybe it was a fluke. That was clearly going through many heads. I was a kid who had got lucky. The second race would sort the men from the boys and restore order. So they probably thought.

But I led from the start and won that race too. To this day people come up to me and say: 'I was there when you shocked the world.' That was the day. I may have felt it was almost inevitable, but I had been riding in my yard and racing in global backwaters beforehand. Now I was a new sensation. My cover had been blown.

When I got back to the hotel I was so excited because I now had the chance to call home.

Mom answered.

'How did you do?'

'Where's Dad?' I said.

Mom shouted: 'Fred, pick up the phone.' Dad picked up. 'We're both here now, Freddie.'

'How did you do?' Dad asked.

'Guess.'

Now Dad started asking the questions.

'You didn't crash or anything did you?'

'No, I'm fine. In fact I did pretty well.'

There was a pause as Dad checked his optimism. 'Did you finish in the top ten?'

'A little better.'

'Top five?'

Mom chimed in at that point. 'Did you come third?'

I had never teased them like this and, finally, Dad sensed what was going on.

'You didn't win, did you?'

'Yes!'

'Well, what happened to Kenny?'

'Nothing.'

'You didn't win *both* races?'

'I sure did.'

It was priceless.

On Saturday we travelled north from Brands Hatch to a circuit in the Midlands called Mallory Park for the Sunday races. I read the papers and winced as they called me 'The Next Mike Hailwood'. I called him Mr Hailwood and did not think the headline was fair because I had not earned the comparison yet, but maybe they saw some common bond through our relationship with Honda, even though I was actually on a Yamaha that weekend.

Some of the other press was not so good. Some riders muttered that I was riding over my head. I understood that, but I rode hard and was under control. Too much success too quickly bothers a lot of people. They feel you need to pay your dues. It irritated a lot of people that I had left America for the first time and won twice at a track that they said you couldn't learn so quickly. For my part, I knew the importance of having the discretion to know what you can do and the common sense of knowing how much you had to learn. I did not view the 'day I shocked the world' as anything other than a step in the right direction. I could hear Pop saying: 'Keep your feet on the ground.'

I didn't win either race at Mallory Park but I had some good battles as we moved to Oulton Park for the last leg of the Match Races. Kenny won the opening race there and I got second. That meant that if I won the last race then I would be the leading point-scorer for the series. And I wanted to show what I could do now because, since Friday, I had been listening to the debate about my riding style, and how the way I slid the bike proved that I was out of my depth and an accident waiting to happen. They didn't know that I had been doing this for years. I would show them.

For the first five laps of the race I am flying, breaking my own lap records on almost every circuit and pulling out half a second a lap. It is a beautiful day and I'm riding harder than I need to. I come to a left-hand corner. On the fifth lap I had saved a fall with my knee as I dragged the fairing through there. Not so lucky this time. And so I don't show anyone anything but I learn my lesson. I crash. On the long walk back to the pits all I think about is how stupid that was and how am I going to apologise to Erv. I've let ego and my desire to prove a point override my judgement. I get back to the pits full of emotion. I say, 'Erv, I'm so sorry.' We are not a factory team and I have wrecked the bike. I have proved their point. I did not need to ride so hard. I will never forget how this feels. I tell Erv it will never happen again. And it doesn't.

* * *

It was not the only reality check I would encounter during 1980. The oddest came at the second Superbike race of the year at a banked oval with an infield road course section like Daytona called Charlotte Motor Speedway. On the last lap I am leading from Eddie Lawson on the factory Kawasaki, and seemingly heading for Honda's first victory. But then I felt the rear of the bike begin to slide as I came down off the banking on to the flat part of the track. For some reason, I had a strong sense to jump off the bike. Had I thought about it then I probably would not have done something that seemed so illogical. I only had a split second to react. I did not know in those moments that a bolt holding the oil filter in place had sheared off. Now oil was being dumped on the track in front of my rear tire. I knew something was wrong and I had the strangest sense to do something that seemed so weird. An analogy is to consider sitting in the backseat of a car as you travel down the freeway at 130mph when, suddenly, you want to open the door and jump out. But that jumping off saved me from serious injury. All I could see was the ground in front of my shield as I bounced and rolled down the track. It seemed like it lasted for ever, but the key in those precarious situations is not to fight it. Instead you have to relax. I know that seems impossible but you can do it and you have to. I was alert the whole time as I tumbled down the circuit and finally came to a stop, sitting upright, Indian style, legs crossed, covered in spilled oil.

Eddie Lawson had to navigate the wreckage but he picked his way through and won the race. I checked myself over to see if I was okay, stunned but otherwise unscathed, and I noticed a figure running towards me. It was Dennis McKay, the AHM race team manager.

'Are you okay?' he puffed, panic written all over his face.

'Yes, Dennis,' I said.

A siren signalled the ambulance's arrival and they asked me the same question. By this time Dennis had gone white as a ghost and was doubled over, hands on his knees.

'I'm fine but I think Dennis is having a heart attack.'

They put Dennis in the back of the ambulance instead and gave him some oxygen. I had felt the peril and that had saved me. Some 23 years later Eddie and I were walking past each other at a race in Fontana, California where I was doing a broadcast. We had never spoken about that day at Charlotte, but he stopped and turned to me.

'You know I'll never forget that time in Charlotte when you jumped off the bike,' he said. He was as incredulous then as he had been back in the immediate aftermath. 'You can't imagine how strange that looked.'

Aliens

I was learning that looks can be deceptive. I found that when I went to Road Atlanta in a place called Elkhart Lake near Milwaukee for a new stop on the calendar in June 1980. I went to a radio station with Stuart Rowlands, the PR man for American Honda, to help publicise the event. Stuart had to leave to make a call and so I sat there in reception. A well-dressed man in a white shirt and nice tie came out two or three times and then said to the receptionist: 'There's supposed to be a motorcycle racer coming to do an interview. Have you seen him?'

She nodded at me.

He said: '*You're* the motorcycle guy?'

'Yes.'

'Where's your leather jacket?'

The man was Ron Swoboda of the Miracle Mets, the baseball team that had won the 1969 World Series, and he showed me that day's local Sheboygan newspaper with its front-page warning of motorcycle gangs coming to town. We did the interview, no easy feat for a teenager who had barely passed speech class, and Ron and the town came to love the motorcycle-racing community. It boosted the economy and there was never any trouble. In that time of black leather clichés it was easy to jump to conclusions.

The last Superbike race of 1980 was at Road Atlanta and, while leading with three laps left, the engine blew and more oil was dumped on the rear tire. To my relief I didn't hit anything and saved a crash. That was fortunate but it was a season of trials and tribulations and we were too inconsistent to win the championship.

But with Yamaha I had another opportunity to travel abroad, which was an incongruity that I am grateful for, a contracted Honda rider in the US given the freedom to ride for a rival factory in Europe.

After the Match Races I had met Paul Butler, who ran the Yamaha Europe programme out of Amsterdam, and he offered me the chance to race in a Grand Prix on a Yamaha-supported semi-privateer TZ500. I asked American Honda Motor and they gave me the okay to do another race on a Yamaha. It was another project for Erv because he was not involved with Honda at the time and the destination for this debut would be the Belgian Grand Prix at Zolder.

We drove from the workshop in Amsterdam to Zolder on the Wednesday and figured we might just get there in time for the first unofficial practice. As we crossed the border I looked out of the window of our truck and noticed some people waving.

'I think they were waving at us to stop,' I said.

We carried on but five miles down the road I was proved right as motorcycle border patrols pulled in front of us and made us sit there for an hour while they went through the paperwork.

When we finally got to Zolder we pulled in too late for practice but I could hear the beautiful sound of the bikes. My abiding memory when I close my eyes is that noise. We stopped and I got out of the truck and I ran to the control tower and climbed to the top so I could see. Then I looked down and it was like an Aladdin's cave. The first bike over the hill was the

Suzuki of Wil Hartog, the Dutch giant in white leathers, and then came Kenny on the black and yellow Yamaha. My respect for them was huge. This was different. I had raced at the Match races and done well, but I sensed the seriousness here. This was the absolute top of the pyramid. It was practice at the Belgian Grand Prix and I was there. That sense of history never left me.

I qualified okay for my first Grand Prix but it was not an auspicious start. It was my first ever push start and the bike didn't fire properly. That led to me being hit and, in turn, my knee struck the gas tank and dislodged the fuel line. I made a few laps before gas was leaking on to my boots and my race was over thanks to a broken valve.

My travels were changing from road trips with Dad to international jet-setting as a pro racer for Honda and Yamaha. In 1980 I made my first trip to Japan for the Suzuka 8-Hour race. I took my mom and, although she loved the experience, it was a culture shock for a woman from Blanchard, Louisiana. Even at the airport in Japan, when travellers were funnelled into two lines, she was shocked to see a sign for aliens.

'Who are the aliens, Freddie?' she asked.

'We are, Mom.'

We took the bullet train from Tokyo to Nagoya and then a local train to Suzuka City. We were the American Honda team but we were getting support and equipment from Japan. It felt a million miles away but a bit like home.

Armbands of different colours were given to each rider to distinguish their slots for the practice sessions. My teammate was Ron Pierce and, for some reason, our armbands got swapped. He went out for my session on the Saturday and broke his back when he crashed into the barrier. It pretty much ended his career.

Mike Velasco, our chief mechanic, and Steve McLaughlin, our team manager, were trying to find the crashed bike. It turned out the Racing Service Centre, the precursor to Honda Racing Corporation, worked to strict union hours. It was past 5pm and so they had locked the bike in their on-site workshop and knocked off. I will never forget the sight of Mike and Steve breaking into that garage. They kept asking whether they knew we were racing tomorrow.

Virginio Ferrari, an extremely charismatic Italian who lived in Monaco, was to be my new teammate for the weekend. He had almost won the 500cc world title in 1979 before breaking his leg in the French Grand Prix at Le Mans. I qualified second quickest but an electrical issue knocked us out of the race early on.

I soon had another chance to enter an endurance event, though, when we went to the Bol d'Or 24-hour motorcycle race at the great Paul Ricard circuit in France. This time Dave Aldana was my teammate. Dave had caused a minor storm a few years before when he had starting racing with skeleton leathers in the US. After crashing a lot he explained his method was to find the limit where he crashed and then back off a bit, a bone-rattling trial-and-error approach that summed up his idiosyncrasies. Now, five years later, he was paired with me and could not wait for me to arrive from Louisiana so he could take me down to the beach on the French Riviera because he knew the women would be topless. He wanted to see the look on the face of this 'conservative and religious' teammate.

We had the lead in the race when it came to my second stint, the third hour. I was wearing a dark shield on my visor but, by the end of the hour, the light was beginning to fade. I came in for the pit stop and rider change but Mike told me to get back out because Dave was off somewhere getting a massage. That made it tricky because I was now riding in the dark with a dark shield. I could not open it because I wore contact lenses and the turbulence would dislodge them. So there I was, going down the 160mph Mistral Straight, literally in the dark, with only the bike lights to guide me. I could barely see my pit board but I got through an hour like that and maintained the lead. It taught me that it is amazing what you can do with the right amount of focus. We led the race for most of the night, but early on Sunday morning we had an engine failure. The race was over.

Honda brought me to Japan in October to talk about where we were going after 1980. I had been third in the Superbike Championship behind Wes Cooley and Eddie Lawson. In the meeting, I recognised Shoichiro Irimajiri as the man who had been standing next to Mr Honda in that broadcast I had watched from the 1979 British Grand Prix. He told me they had come to the realisation that the NR project, with the same oval piston four-stroke engine that had been struggling in that broadcast, was not the future. He told me that if I could be patient they would create a company that would be up and running for 1982 called the Honda Racing Corporation. They were heading in a new direction and were going to build a new bike with a two-stroke engine. Mr Irimajiri explained that it was Honda Japan who had wanted me at the end of 1979. They had seen something in me as I had felt something about them. It was an unspoken, intangible bond traversing thousands of miles.

They knew I was getting offers and so they asked what they could offer me for 1981. And that was the beginning of Honda's 750cc dirt-track programme with Jerry Griffiths. Because the programme started so late in October 1980, it began using a CX500 V-twin bored out to get as close to a 750cc as possible.

And so I would resist the chance to go race on the Grand Prix circuit for one more year as I rode dirt-trackers and Superbikes. The following year the dirt-track 750cc programme got its first win at a Friday-night half-mile race at Ascot Park when Jeff Haney was first and I was second. It was our greatest day but it was a struggle that year. Later, Honda Japan built a purpose-built dirt-track 750cc engine that was amazing – the NS750. And four years later, in the fall of 1985, Jerry would rent the San Jose Mile track for one day so I could ride an NS750. That was a great day.

The dirt-tracking took me back to my roots and it was as tough as ever. I once came off on the last corner of the last lap in the prestigious Indy Mile. I had no broken bones but I was banged up and dirt had got into my shredded skin. I was taken to the local emergency room to be met by a real-life Nurse Ratched, the tyrant from *One Flew Over the Cuckoo's Nest*.

'You race motorcycles?'

'Yes, ma'am, I do.'

'Well, I need to scrub the dirt out. Normally, I put anaesthetic in there, but you're a motorcycle racer. You can take it.'

I'm sure she did that on purpose.

People may have referred to my choirboy looks and my callow youthfulness, but I was battle-hardened from my youth, tossed from frying pan to fire with a burnt arm and blackened innocence. I had been through the mill with only my dedication and belief getting me out the other side.

As 1981 wore on we were dogged by teething troubles. Daytona had been a grim portent. In the 100-mile race I came in for a fuel stop and the quick fuel filter didn't connect correctly. Unbeknown to me, some gas had leaked down the gas tank. I popped the clutch and the engine backfired at the wrong moment. That ignited the fuel. The flash fire was dramatic but brief and it cost me the race, although I still finished second.

Eddie won the Superbike Championship and deserved it. It was a transition period for me. Erv and I decided that he would go to work with Barry Sheene in 1981. It was good for him because he needed the work and it was good for us as a team because it meant he got to know the Grand Prix circuits and got an invaluable taste of that world.

We got a glimpse of our shared future on the Tuesday before the Superbike race weekend at Laguna Seca in July 1981. Even though Erv had his duties with Barry and was not contracted with Honda, I wanted him there because I knew we would be in this together. He flew in from Europe and I flew in from Shreveport.

We gathered in a conference room at American Honda in

Gardena, California. The only thing on the table was a 2x3 foot wooden box. Erv was sitting to my left speculating what it could be. Then Takeo Fukui and Mr Irimajiri came in. Mr Fukui took off the lid and we peered in. Inside was the three–cylinder engine. Erv leant into me and whispered: 'It's missing a cylinder.'

It was funny but he had a point. All the other manufacturers were using four-cylinder engines. The engine was also using reed valves, which was something everybody else had moved away from. It was the very first thing that the new HRC had created and we were not bowled over. But what did I know?

Erv went back to Europe to race with Barry. I focused on the race at Laguna and my first chance to ride the NR500. The Superbike Championship was not looking great but this was a chance for me to race against Kenny Roberts on his 500cc Grand Prix bike. With no American Grand Prix at the time, these were big events for the bike fans to get a chance to see their hero and the three-time world champion.

The clash came in the five-lap heat race on Saturday. We were both on the front row, but I got the better start and was able to fend him off. It was a little race but a significant win. My four-stroke had beaten his two-stroke. The last time that had happened was in 1975 with Phil Read. The Japanese faces reflected that. You would have thought that we had won the World Championship itself. They had spent tens of millions of dollars on that bike and technology and they finally had their win, in a long-forgotten heat race on a Saturday afternoon at Laguna Seca in July 1981.

In the next day's final, it broke after about ten laps like it normally did, but Honda came to me after the race and said they wanted me to race the NR500 in the British Grand Prix in two weeks' time. As I remembered sitting in my parents' house and seeing that clip from the 1979 British Grand Prix, I could only smile.

Two weeks later I qualified in the top ten. In two years the bike had improved dramatically. I was not used to the push starts, though, so Carlo, an Italian mechanic, took me out back on one of the unused runways at Silverstone when everybody else had gone and showed me how to do it. I was only around 135 pounds and Carlo was bigger than me. He took two steps and flung himself on to the bike, bump-starting it by hitting the tank with his chest. I tried it but it knocked the wind straight out of me. Two days later my chest was black and blue, but I had learned how to do it. I got off in the top ten when the Grand Prix started and was up to fourth before the engine broke.

The waiting was over. A lot of water had gone under Red River Bridge. The kid in the yard was heading to the biggest stage of all. I was still only 19 but I was on my way to the World Championships.

Breeze, Louisiana, 2010

Even though I have been around the world since I was 18, this was the longest I had ever stayed continuously in a single hotel. Just a while back, staying in a hotel away from home and family for even a couple of days was too long. But now it didn't bother me that I've been here for 21 days.

Sitting at a computer in the lobby, I heard a voice to my right.

'Hey, Freddie.'

I recognised the voice of someone that I have known for many years, Pastor Denny Duron.

'You staying here?'

'Yes,' I said. 'I was at my sister's for a while visiting but I left a few weeks ago.'

We talked a while and Pastor Denny went back to his guests having breakfast. I saw them getting ready to leave from the corner of my eye and decided I should go over.

'Hey Denny, it was good to see you again,' I said.

Denny turned around and said: 'I don't know if you heard but the Shreveport Country Club was donated to the church. Would you like to play golf with me on Thursday?'

I had a feeling that maybe there was more to it than just playing golf.

I said: 'Absolutely, that would be great.'

Denny picked me up that Thursday at 10am and we played a round. I saw another familiar face, Martin Stewart, who had been the golf pro there in the eighties. He asked if I wanted to come out tomorrow.

It had been over 25 years since I had been to the Shreveport Country Club. That was in October 1985 for a celebration of my last World Championship season.

I did enjoy those moments back then, because it doesn't get any better than being surrounded by family and friends, but why was it that I felt more content now than I did when celebrating my World Championship seasons?

When Denny dropped me back at the hotel, I stopped by the front desk and Tina, another staff member, said: 'Mrs Ada is looking for you.'

I said: 'Really?'

'Yes. It's about your laundry.'

I know I had a quizzical look on my face because I had put some clothes in the dryers that are available to guests and they hadn't finished drying when I had left with Denny that morning. I had asked Teresa if she could get them out when they were finished. I knew she wouldn't mind.

I went back to my room and had only been there a couple of minutes when there was a knock on the door. It was Mrs Ada and she had my laundry neatly folded in her arms. She handed the stack of clothes to me.

'If you don't know how to do your laundry right then I will show you.'

All I could say was: 'Yes, ma'am.'

That was the beginning of my education on how to do laundry with care and respect. They were some of my most cherished moments of the next few months.

Chapter 4: **THE CUSP (1982)**

I WAS on the cusp of what most people, from the outside, would think of as a dream. But like most dreams there were loose strands and bits that did not make sense, snapshots that burnt with an incandescent vividness and then faded to half-memories. Try to connect the dots from a dream and you end up frustrated as you search for meaning among the images and the perennial battle between the conscious and subconscious. I was on the way, sure, but where to?

That was one question. The practical answer was to the Grand Prix championship. I was going to what rookie baseball players in America's national pastime used to call The Big Show. I was heading for the big time – my time.

Erv came back to me at the end of 1981. That was always the unwritten deal. He worked with Barry Sheene for that year and gained valuable experience. He was with Barry when he won his last Grand Prix, in Sweden, the very last time a British rider would win a race in the elite class of what would become MotoGP until 2016. When I had seen Erv at Silverstone in July 1981 he told me that he was looking forward to Sweden in particular. 'Barry should go well there,' he said with his usual understated enthusiasm. Barry did go well and I was happy for him. He was a good guy. Flamboyant and cheeky, a magnet for press, fans and women, blowing on that cigarette through the hole drilled in his helmet but never blowing smoke up anyone else, a fast-talking, street-smart rival doing his TV ads and living to the max, he had a big heart and we enjoyed a mutual respect. I also admired his respect for the fans and how he spent time with each one so they knew the admiration mattered.

I had a three-year deal with Honda, unusual back then, and through that 1981 season it was always in the back of my mind that next year would be a Grand Prix year. By that time Marco Lucchinelli had won the Grand Prix world title. The Italian was a true maverick with a reputation for partying hard and chasing women as well as points. He signed to join Honda from Suzuki and so he and Takazumi Katayama, the previous 350cc world champion from Japan, would be my teammates for my debut season.

I went over to Japan to test at the end of October. The ill-fated four-stroke NR500 had been a hugely expensive and much-mourned project. Mr Honda initially hated two-stroke engines. He had faith in his engineers, even amid the mounting consensus that they were trying to reinvent the wheel. Yoichi Oguma, the Honda team manager, said they would have to commit hara-kiri if they continued. His forthrightness was anathema to Honda's ways, but he survived and thrived. It was as well he did, because history would mark down the four-stroke as an elaborate folly, but it was still one that I felt was a success in its failure. Mr Honda, too, still believed a Honda-engineered four-stroke could be successful. Now we had the hastily built two-stroke and the unique three-cylinder engine that we had last seen amputated and delivered to us in a wooden box like a museum artefact.

We were due to test at the Suzuka circuit. I took the bullet train again. It became my favourite train ride. I thought about my dad working on the railroads for Union Pacific and how he had liked trains too. I got off and was met by Mr Fukui, the boss of the three-cylinder project.

'Small problem,' he said. 'Test rider in hospital.'

'What happened?'

'Transmission locked in sixth gear. No testing.'

I sighed. 'Well, okay.'

Hindsight is always 20–20 and, looking back, the problem was in the design. Two-strokes always vibrate but especially so when you are dealing with an unconventional engine. The whole philosophy of the three-cylinder engine was that it would be narrower and lighter and that extra agility would make up for the reduction in power. Now the accident to the test rider just added to the unanswerable questions. We were only months away from the start of the season.

Disappointed, the next day I tested the oval piston NR500 for the first time. It was unique and faster than I anticipated. I did well in that test and I almost set a lap record for the 500s, but we had to cut it short because a typhoon was coming. I only did about ten laps.

I went back a month later. I got off the plane in Tokyo and this time I didn't even make it to the Suzuka circuit. Once again I was met by Mr Fukui. He had his poker face, but again there was no bluffing.

'Small problem,' he said. 'Test rider in hospital.' The poker face dropped and we both laughed at the irony of the situation. I checked into a hotel and flew back the next day, another long and this time worthless round trip from Louisiana to Japan.

December came and I had still not ridden the bike. Suffice it to say that was far from ideal preparation. In Japan they were working feverishly to rectify the problems that kept putting test riders in hospital as well as trying to make the bike as light as possible while maintaining reliability. They also felt bad about my two trips in deep winter to Japan and so they tried to find a track somewhere warmer, and closer to the US, where I could test the fruits of their toils. They landed on Laguna Seca in California, best known for its plunging, blind turn called the Corkscrew. It is not a high-speed circuit, though, and that suited the Honda chiefs given that the bike was already proving something of a health hazard. I appreciated their concern.

We arrived at the Laguna Seca circuit and there was a large truck with Budweiser Sports Car Team written on the side. I wondered who the driver was and I walked up the pit wall as the team car pulled in. The mechanics swarmed around it and were talking to the driver in their midst. The driver got out and took off his helmet. I recognised him. My thoughts flashed back to the late summer of 1969 and the movie I went to see with my parents at the drive-in theatre near the airport – *Butch Cassidy and the Sundance Kid*. And here was Paul Newman. He walked over to me and introduced himself.

I managed to mutter: 'I'm Freddie Spencer. It's a pleasure to meet you. Thank you, Mr Newman, for letting us share the track with you today.'

'That's okay,' he smiled. 'Where's your bike?'

The Honda engineers wheeled it out and I got on. This was the first time I had sat on it. That Laguna air was thick with what-ifs. Perhaps some of the Japanese crossed fingers and remembered the fate of the test riders. Paul Newman, a veteran of the Le Mans 24-hour race and now running his own race team, looked on with interest.

I went out and was immediately hit by how horrible this bike felt. I had been riding two-strokes my whole life and though I didn't have a lot of experience on 500cc Grand Prix bikes – only the NR500 a few months before and one race on the Yamaha 500 in 1980 – I got on this and knew straight away that it was nowhere near as good as it needed to be. The throttle response was like an on–off switch. It vibrated badly. That perfect poetic synthesis you crave between man and machine was absent. I rattled my way around Laguna, down the Corkscrew and came in.

They were all there as I came into the pits, waiting for me to tell them how great their project was. I was trying to think of what to say.

There was Mr Oguma and Mr Fukui, two men who would become stalwarts of Honda for many years. Both had their backgrounds in research and development. Mr Fukui was a young engineer recruited by Shoichiro Irimajiri when he formed the NR group in 1979 to carry out the NR500 project. Then in 1982, when Mr Irimajiri created HRC, he brought Mr Fukui in to manage the NS500 V3 programme. He would eventually become president of HRC and later president of Honda Motor Company. Mr Oguma was a good semi-pro racer in Japan and a Honda test rider who was assigned to the NR500 project and then became the boss of the field operations for the HRC Grand Prix programme. Those three were invaluable to our success in those first years, but that first day was not a great beginning.

I stepped off and shrugged my shoulders. The first eyes that met mine were Paul Newman's. He seemed to read my face well.

'First time you've ridden it?' he asked.

'Yes, first time.'

'Well, you know…' he said with an expression that said things could only get better.

I was not going to lambast or embarrass these brilliant engineers, but I had to get my message across. 'The vibration is so bad it's hard to connect to the bike,' I said. 'My hands are going to sleep!'

I might have told Erv a bit more, that it was even worse than the NR500 at this point. It was freezing cold and our breath blew little circles of mist. I reasoned that at least it had not put me in hospital and I had got to meet Paul Newman, so it was not a bad day all told, but they were 20 hard laps that did not bode well. They were just the beginning.

The clock was ticking but we had no baseline as to where we should be. This was the first two-stroke 500cc Grand Prix bike that Honda had built. They had been out of Grand Prix racing for 12 years, the gap between Mike Hailwood's bike failing at the Italian Grand Prix and the return with the NR500 in 1979. Now it was 1982 and we had a new company, HRC, and a new direction with a two-stroke V3 machine.

Two months later there was another test, this time with my two teammates, in São Paulo, Brazil. Shreveport was gripped by winter and a bitter cold that cut right through you. At home I was notorious for waiting until the last minute to pack, a habit that drove my poor mom insane, and it didn't even cross my mind to check the weather in Brazil or to think that it was located below the equator. At that time, devoid of the Internet and with only a few countries visited, I just packed my winter Shreveport clothes.

When I got off the plane it was at least 100 degrees Fahrenheit (38 degrees Celsius) and felt about the same percentage in humidity. I was dressed as if I was heading for the North Pole, with long sleeves and a thick jacket. I cut an incongruous sight. While checking in at the hotel I looked through the glass wall behind the reception and I could see the swimming pool where a man was reclining in a chair, wearing only trunks and large black shades, flanked by two gorgeous scantily clad women. I recognised him straight away and, swathed in self-consciousness, just hoped that they would give me a room on the other side of the hotel so I would not have to venture outside. No such luck.

'Here's your key, Mr Spencer. Just walk straight past the pool and your room is on the left.'

'Is there no other way to get there?'

The receptionist looked puzzled and, considering how I was dressed for the weather, spoke to me politely with a look that wondered just where I had come from.

'I'm afraid not.'

As I walked by the pool, sweat literally pouring off me, the man slowly lowered his shades to the tip of his nose. His gaze followed me with an expression of amusement and then, in that great Italian accent and with the certainty of a world champion, he waved his hand and said: 'Hey, Freddie, come here!'

'Hey Marco,' I replied. 'I didn't think about being below the equator.' Then, feeling embarrassed and self-conscious, I said: 'I know I look like a tourist.'

Marco ignored all this and hugged his two friends. 'Well, welcome to Brazil. Which one do you want?'

There was no front. He was blunt and brazen, and we were

very different, almost polar opposites, but I liked Marco from the beginning.

I said; 'I'm okay, Marco.'

He told me to get my bathing suit. I didn't have one, of course, but borrowed one and spent a couple of hours outside, enjoying hanging out with Marco and not realising I was getting incredibly burnt in that blazing Brazilian sun.

I didn't realise how strong the sun was near to the equator but I knew when I woke up the next day and had to ride. I was a Southern red lobster with a suit and helmet.

Interlagos is a very bumpy track and in the days before liners I had to pull leathers tight over my sunburnt body. The pain was severe, but at least the bike had improved. Right away I was quick, almost two seconds a lap better than Marco, the reigning world champion, and Takazumi.

After each session I came in and stripped to my ankles. I'd stand there, fanning myself. Erv joked: 'You're going so fast just so you can come in and pull your leathers down.'

I was miserable, but the more it hurt the more focused I became. All the things we had gone through in 1980 and 1981, combined with my unfailing belief that my partnership with Honda was in some way predestined, meant I expected this to happen – to be quicker than a far more experienced and successful rider; to be riding a bike that had put test riders in hospital; for Honda to cure the vibration problem. Marco didn't expect it, I'm sure. It was extremely difficult to find himself slower than this rookie.

The girls by the pool did not interest me. I had one of my own back home by now.

Sarie worked in a clothes shop at the St Vincent Mall in Shreveport.

We hit it off immediately. She did some modelling for them and her pictures were all over the walls. As soon as we started talking, I knew she was an amazing person and sincere in her heart. Over the next few years, as my motorcycling career took me to new worlds, she would be there, sharing in the highs and lows even though before me she knew nothing about the sport or that life.

One very important aspect of being self-sufficient is being able to clear your mind and focus at will on whatever the task is. It has to be immediate: anything less is wasting time and will interfere with your performance. That was why my extreme sunburn during that test at São Paulo might have been a distraction when I rode, but it had no effect on my performance. It was uncomfortable but I had to work around it. Along with Mr Williams, Sarie was a rock of support, but the bottom line when it came to racing motorcycles was that I had to rely on myself.

I was glad Sarie had her own interests. She had her job and she was a part-time model. Life was good. I had Sarie and Mr Williams and I also had Erv. He lived in San Jose and, although we occasionally spent some time together in the winter months, we were professional allies and kindred spirits. We operated by near telepathy and simple clear thinking. Words were not wasted, but we both knew that it was almost shocking how much better the bike was now. It meant we were going into the Grand Prix world full of realistic hope, but first there was the small matter of getting that boyhood monkey off my back and winning the Daytona 200, the most fabled and iconic race in a young boy-racer's head.

Daytona

The new Honda FWS 1000 V4 that I would get to ride was a real joy. Honda had learned from the NR500 and moved to more conventional and commercially viable four-stroke engine design. They were still pouring time and resources and a staff of around 70 into the four-strokes then. They brought the FWS to Daytona. It was a straightforward conventional 1000cc V4 and it had the most unique sound, a low, consistent drone that was like smooth and powerful uplifting music.

Kenny was also there on his Grand Prix bike, a 680cc version of the 500. Just as I knew the truth when riding that bike in front of Paul Newman, I knew this bike was good and fuelled by potential, but I never assumed anything because we were on a four-stroke and we were up against bikes like the two-stroke Yamaha TZ750 and the factory Kawasaki KR500, ridden by quality racers like Graeme Crosby and Eddie Lawson.

I won the Superbike race, Honda's first win at the Daytona Speedweek, and then came to the 200. From that year on the pace of the Daytona 200 would escalate dramatically. It is a marathon not a sprint, but that was lost in the competitiveness and so it became a marathon sprint.

Kenny led from the start but he could not get away from Mike Baldwin and me. The lead changed between the three of us and I could get past them under acceleration off the corner in the infield section. Eight laps in, Mike was leading from me and then Kenny. I came off the corner leading on to the back straightaway and I was tucked in behind Mike.

I was not staring at back of his bike. I was staring through it, but in my peripheral vision I noticed something fly off. Whatever it was had hit the windscreen and the top of my helmet. I knew it had come from the bottom and, as I looked I could see the chord of the rear tire appear.

Mike felt it too and slowed as we went into the chicane. I passed him and took my left hand off the bar and pointed to his rear tire. By the time I hit the front straightaway *it* hit me – I was on the *same* bike with the *same* tire. My bike felt perfect and there was not even the beginning of any vibration, but there was a nugget of concern. What if?

Mike came into the pits that lap. Nobody was expecting that because the plan was to do only two fuel stops with no tire changes and so he was coming in early. The team had a spare wheel ready just in case, but the bikes were not set up for a quick change of wheels. I came in the next lap and so there was a semblance of readiness in my pit stall. They changed the tire and I shot back out. Kenny always had rough luck at Daytona – from 1974 he had led every Daytona 200 at some point but he'd only won once, in 1978 – and now he dropped out again.

And here's the thing. Instead of getting discouraged, my mindset now changed. I now knew I had to manage that tire performance one corner, one lap at a time, with a lean angle and throttle control. There was no communication with my team like there is in car racing. They had no idea what I was doing or my strategy. So they didn't see that I was the kid in my yard in Shreveport, Louisiana, spinning my tire. They didn't see a six-year-old riding the Daytona 200, but I changed my lines and trajectory, ratcheting up my senses to a higher level. I could not do anything about the banking on the circuit but I could do something about how much my tire was spinning coming on to it. I understood implicitly that it was the movement, not just the spinning, which put heat in the tire and made it overheat until the tread would separate from the carcass. I innately understood how to stop movement based on the way I positioned my bike. It was a matter of fractions, degrees and angles.

I reasoned that the damage to Mike's tire was slightly off-centre, so if I could stay off that part of the tire as much as possible, then who knew? Graeme Crosby, the leader, was going to run one tire for the whole of the race and so inevitably his pace would drop, but his pit stops would be for fuel only. I computed all of this and formed what I believed to be a foolproof plan that might work.

I worked through the pack. I came in for my stop and they changed the wheel and, with a new tire, it was not that bad. More fuel was added. Seconds passed as hours. Races drag and stretch every ounce of drama and confusion from each moment. Speed commands you to appreciate the instant. Every man in that pit stall also did sums in his head, but they did not see what I saw. I had completely figured out the movement of the bike and how to stop the spinning by running an entirely different line into the banking. I'm rolling the throttle sooner but smoother to compensate and maintain my exit speed. I'm staying off the middle of the tire. I'm clocking faster lap times than at the start of the race when I had a mindset unaffected by the tire issue. I have figured all this out and I know I'm going to catch Graeme Crosby on the very last lap of the Daytona 200, the race I have wanted to win since I was eight years old.

And then with three laps on my board the words 'PIT IN' are calling me. I have to decide. I feel fine and my gut feeling and intuition say it's okay, but what if the team have seen a problem that I haven't when we changed the wheel in that last fuel stop? What if they now know why these tires are coming apart at the seams? I can see Graeme now. He is not far ahead of me. My plan is working. What should I do? I have to decide.

This is a crossroads. I am making tenths of a second every lap. Huge leaps of faith. I know exactly what I have to do to catch him and have done it. I know the cost of every delicate movement of the bike. It is a reckoning. I am putting everything I have honed in my yard into the greatest moment of the greatest race we have in America with the greatest handicap to overcome. I have to make up ground and save myself at the same time. I have done all I can.

Coming off NASCAR Turn 4 I can't wait any longer to decide and I come in. They add a splash of fuel to see me home. Graeme is one of those tough competitors who makes no mistakes and can ride anything. He knows I am there and then, in a blink, I'm not. He will win the Daytona 200 and he deserves it.

I go out and never lose second place but my chance of winning has gone. Mike doesn't finish. When I return after the cool-down lap the team are ecstatic. To come second with an extra stop, plus two unscheduled tire changes, is a huge achievement. There are smiles and nods of self-congratulation. I'm happy for the team but I feel differently. I feel I had it. They check the fuel and tire wear. I see the look on their faces.

'You had plenty,' Mike Velasco says. 'You didn't need the splash and go! And the rear tire looks the best so far!' And then I knew I should have trusted myself. It was my fault, my responsibility to know the situation, and I alone had decided to come in.

Reality dawns but the clarity of perspective gives that moment much more precision than was available at the time.

Was I disappointed? Sure. It was now three years where I'd had the chance to win the 200, the race I went to as a kid, riding through the tunnel on that morning of the first Monday of March, listening to the sound of the bikes and watching guys like Giacomo Agostini made mythological by the passage of time. Did I *show* my disappointment? Absolutely not. These guys were doing all they could for me. This was the last time I was going to see a lot of these guys because I was going to the World Championship now. There was sadness, but also a joy in experiencing the emotional, physical and mental sides working together in harmony as a team.

The willingness to change is a wonderful thing, but you need to recognise and trust it. I felt certain that day, just as I would all those decades later when I left my sister's house. I knew I was getting closer to where I needed to go even if I still didn't know why.

The team only understood the pace I was riding at. Over the years I'd come to view that race as my finest two hours of riding. What was the greatest race I never won? The 1982 Daytona 200. I should have recognised the perfect moment when all converges to show complete faith. I should not have come in for the extra fuel and should have trusted what was inside me.

The Big Show

The next time I went to South America in March I was better prepared in terms of my clothes and I hoped we had made progress with the bike. We were heading for Buenos Aires and the start of the 1982 500cc World Championships season. The line-up may have been daunting to some – Kenny Roberts, Barry Sheene, Marco Lucchinelli, Graeme Cosby, Randy Mamola, Franco Uncini – but after all the hard work I felt I belonged in this company.

The Argentina Grand Prix was held at Autodromo 17 de Octubre, so named in honour of Loyalty Day, when the masses demonstrated to free Juan Perón from prison. Every day we took a taxi from our hotel to the gates at the south of this beautiful city, with its breathtaking vistas and baroque buildings, and it was always an eye-opening trip. Our driver would pull out into the oncoming traffic and then start to pump the brakes at the first sign of needing to stop. It became very clear very quickly that he was not going to manage it in time. Erv and I winced at each other, but somehow he got away with it. The taxi driver would sit there and start laughing and apologise for the brakes. Then he did the same thing again before the next stop. They call racers crazy because of the risks we take, but this cavalier approach to well-being was something I had never experienced. 'It's safer on the track,' I said to Erv.

Suzuki and Yamaha had been at this since the mid-1970s. Honda had been out of the game for longer and had last won in 1967. Scepticism and suspicion abounded. We didn't have a history at HRC yet. We were just beginning. We had hope but the very first time out on track in the first practice I made it to turn one and crashed. I walked back and looked at Erv and shrugged my shoulders. 'Sorry. Too aggressive on cold tires.'

Erv smiled and said: 'Well, you got that over with.'

The rest of the weekend was good. I qualified the Honda in

second place to Kenny. I then led the race at various times, before having to slow my pace and settle for third place behind Kenny and Barry after suffering with an overheating engine. They had been there before and were expected to battle for the title but I was up there, doing enough to prompt commentators to call me the 'new sensation'. My memories are vivid – of the weigh-in and the look of surprise on Mr Oguma's face when the Honda, supposedly lighter and more nimble than the rest, was actually a kilo heavier than the Yamaha and Suzuki; of the Buddhist who came into the garage to tap bars over the bikes for Katayama; of the heat and the hay bales, the passing moves and the chances we had. Suddenly, the future looked promising.

Three weeks before the next Grand Prix in Austria I went to see Mr Williams and told him that I wanted him to come with me. Mrs Williams scoffed at that.

'Jere has not taken any vacation days for 25 years.'

That meant he had built up enough days for him to come over for six weeks at a time for the next four years, which is what he did. It was perfect.

The time we spent together was priceless. My life was changing. I now bought JW Gorman's second Power Cycle store. The dealership came up at the end of 1981 and I purchased it with my friends Steve Roberts, Perry Pringle and Ronnie Hampton, the man who had once looked at my van when I went to pick up his daughter Mary-Ann and asked: 'What do you think you're planning to do in that van tonight? And, by the way, why do you have a van and not a car?'

I had said I needed a van for going to races and Ronnie had said: 'Okay, but what are you planning to do when you grow up?'

I said I would race in the World Championship one day and he said: 'No, I was asking what you will do as a job.' Then he smiled. 'Oh sure, *that's* a job?'

Now I was maturing and getting a better reputation. Ronnie and I would actually invest in property. When I finally won the world title he would be the third person who hugged me that day at Imola. From questioning my intentions, he came to understand them.

'I guess you were right,' he would say.

That was a long way off but now Mr Williams and I were trying to navigate a route down an Austrian mountainside on our way to the Salzburgring. The motorhome was a deluxe beast that reflected my improving monetary status.

We had to turn around to go in the opposite direction and I was looking out of the back to let him know how close we were to the edge. When I suddenly could see nothing but emptiness below I knew we were too close.

We were like fish out of water, a 20-year-old from Shreveport and a middle-aged man from down the old Williams dirt road in Keithville. After we had nearly driven off the mountainside, we finally got to the track very late. Mr Williams looked at the tunnel that would deliver us to the parking lot and said: 'You think we can clear that? It looks kind of low.'

I looked at the numbers marked on the side. 'Sure we can.'

I did not think about the metric system, but when Mr Williams steered the motorhome down the dip and beneath the bridge, we quickly realised we had made a major error. The sound of cold, hard rock scraping on the metallic roof accompanied the blackening of the windows. Mr Williams hit the brakes. There was no way out of the door because we were such a tight fit, like an oversized dog burrowing down a rabbit hole.

Mr Williams reversed up. I looked out the back window and realised the ladder on top of the roof had been ripped clean off and was lying on the ground beside us. I got out, scooped it up and put it inside. Now, with the extra few inches, we could make it. It was a funny start to my first Grand Prix in Europe.

Two years earlier, snow had stopped everything at this track. Eventually they would stop racing in Austria in April, but now the show had to go on even if the sleet was cold and grey. I looked out of the damaged motorhome and said to Mr Williams: 'No way are we going to go out in this.' Sitting quietly in the motorhome there were 15 minutes to go until practice and I listened to the sound of sleet hitting the roof. Then came the announcement on the loudspeaker.

'*Achtung Fahrerlager*! Practice in eight minutes.'

I literally tingled in trepidation. The sleet hardened to hail. And then I will always remember Mr Williams saying with such calm, comforting authority: 'I guess we're going to go out.'

I escaped unharmed but after that session Erv came running to find me. 'Quick, come and check on Mr Williams!'

'Why, what's wrong?'

I did not wait for an answer and followed Erv out of my motorhome. We found Mr Williams with his bloodstained handkerchief wrapped around a finger. His face was pale. The story tumbled out. He had been helping someone put the bike on a stand when someone turned the wheel. His finger had been caught between the sprocket and chain and the tip had been severed. I looked at Erv, who was squeamish, and said: '*You're* the one who looks like he's going to pass out.'

There was no clinic so we took Mr Williams to the local hospital where they sewed it up. I knew how much that would hurt because of all the nerve endings in the tips of your fingers.

'Do you want to go home, Mr Williams?' I asked.

He said he didn't but he would if it was going to distract the team. We all said: 'Please stay.'

That was all the first day in Austria and it was a portent of things to come. I had my worst qualifying all year and was only twelfth and then suffered a broken crankshaft that put me out of the race. Look back at old footage of that race and you will enter a time warp and see a ridiculously dangerous track, shrouded only by hay and ancient guard rails, a throwback to the older days when riders said there were six deaths a year and you reasoned you had three crashes and so you crossed them off and hoped.

This was no place to crash, but such intimations of mortality were always in the back of my thoughts. All you can do is take precautions and move on. I was more concerned about seeing how Kenny went on his new Yamaha. I had got close to him on the straight and then he had just accelerated. I sat in debriefing with Erv and told him: 'We are in trouble if they ever get that Yamaha working properly.' Seeing Kenny disappear and fighting the instability, I could feel it was going to be him I had to battle with down the road. I just didn't know when.

Breeze, Louisiana, 2010

Lately, I've realised I was at my best when I was a kid and a young adult, when I trusted what I sensed and felt with openness and clarity. Somewhere, I lost focus on the spiritual side of my awareness. When I was riding in my yard, practicing on my mini-bike, from the first moments I would get in the zone. As soon as I began riding every day it was easy. No distractions, just focus. I was completely concentrated on all I could see, sense and feel, basically honing my ability to meditate at will.

On 31 August, I wrote that fear cannot control our path in life. When we face difficult decisions, fear can paralyse us. We will never get out of our comfort zone, even if we want to, when controlled by fear and doubt.

On Sunday 5 September, I called Chelee'. I knew it would not be an easy conversation. The kids had been at their grandma and pop's in Conroe, Texas, since school let out in early June. Chelee' had just moved from Las Vegas to Texas. It had been a few months since we talked and I wanted to tell her what I was doing. I had not seen the kids since 21 April, the night before I left, when I let them know where I was going. It had been an unbelievably hard thing to do.

I called her and told her I was sorry that I had to leave. Our divorce had been final since the previous December. My leaving was tough on everyone, but I had to go. It was a sense and feeling at the deepest part of my core, a drive to know more.

Chapter 4: THE CUSP (1982)

But what?

A few days after that conversation with Chelee', I realised how little we had actually talked over the 19-plus years we had known each other. Since I have been here in the hotel I have thought about how I knew I was going to ride for Honda and how we never talked about that. Until recently I had forgotten about it and the realisation said a lot about how far I had got away from who I was.

A week later I went to Holland for the Centennial TT event in Assen. The Dutch track had always been a favourite of mine, not because I did particularly well there when I was racing, but because it has such history in my sport. The fans are such enthusiasts and it was one of the few tracks built specifically for motorcycle racing, so I respect that.

It was raining from the moment I arrived in Amsterdam. All the memories I had of racing in the Dutch TT involved rain. It didn't matter. I was glad to be at the event. I finally arrived at the hotel and went to bed after a nice dinner.

Friday was an easy day, just a couple of appearances and interviews with Dutch journalists. It had been a long time since I had been to a European event and I had got divorced and closed my riding school in the interim, so I knew there would be some questions asked.

The first question out of the box was blunt enough. 'Did your divorce have an effect on closing your riding school?'

I answered it as directly as I could and, for me, that was a big step, because most journalists knew I rarely, if ever, talk about my personal life.

I talked about how they were separate events and that my divorce was difficult in every way you could imagine. My main feeling at that moment was for my kids. As much as I thought I understood all that happened, I was just at the beginning. As much as I thought I understood faith, I would soon realise how little I really knew.

I woke up on Saturday morning looking forward to getting out on the track and that has not always been the case.

I loved riding as a kid and I liked to race, but I had nothing to prove to anyone because riding was never about that for me; it was about what I felt when I was on the bike. It was a connection to the inner me. I just sensed that if I worked hard then someday I might know why it mattered so much. Then, as I moved into professional racing in my late teens, riding became a business. It was how I earned a living.

After breakfast, we headed out to the track and there was already a good crowd. These events are about nostalgia and tradition and they bring back fond memories for everyone.

The first bike I went out on was beautifully painted in the Rothmans Honda colours I used when I was the 250cc world champion, owned by a collector called Richard Grantham and his father John. The track was getting wetter with each lap. I was picking up pace and, for the tire I was on, I was not being as cautious as I should have been. I was riding well within my limits but the margin of error was still too small.

I accelerated through a right-hand bend that led to the hairpin behind the paddock. I came into the left a little faster than I should and came upon Tepi Länsivuori, a Finnish rider from the sixties and seventies. As I was moving up and around him, Tepi slowed and began to tighten his line. I had no choice but to try to slow and pass him on the inside because I couldn't miss him to the right.

All the choices I made were far too risky considering the conditions. To avoid hitting him I had to tighten my line with too much lean angle and speed. I did manage to avoid hitting Tepi and almost made it, but the rear tire lost traction and slid to the right. The bike's momentum began to make the bike stand up and I flew over what we call the 'highside' to the right.

But then a phenomenon happened. Everything began to slow down. I felt the bike's rear tire lose traction and slide right, but because I sensed and felt that, I was able to slow the transfer of weight by shifting my upper body to the left. I let go with my right hand but kept my left on the handlebar. By doing that I was able to minimise the damage to the right side of the bike. This all happened in a camera's shutter speed from one frame to the next, but being focused and aware had allowed me to react a split second sooner. Your mind is able to process what it sees and feels faster. I have been reacting like that all my life – *on a track*.

On Monday afternoon I took a plane from Amsterdam to London. I had a night at Heathrow before flying home to Shreveport. I decided to pass the time by reading, but for whatever reason I was unable to focus. I put the book down and leafed through a photo album I had with me. I was in talks about a coffee-table book about my double-winning season 25 years before, so I was slowly picking the best pictures.

There were some candid shots of Sarie and me. I had seen the pictures multiple times over the years, but as I looked through them I began to think how I had never really understood what had happened between us. It ended in October 1985, after three-and-a-half years. Sometimes people just grow apart, but I always felt there was something more than that.

I had never asked Sarie what had happened – she left Shreveport to move to LA afterwards – and we had never talked, because as much as I paid attention to things professionally, I did not do the same personally at that time.

I came upon a series of three photos. The first was from 1983 on the podium at the San Marino Grand Prix in Imola. Sarie was there, on the left, with a big smile on her face.

The next photo was from 1984 and we were riding together on a mini-bike in the paddock. We were waving to someone and, again, we were both smiling – but she was smiling a little less.

The last shot was from 1985. I am sitting in a chair talking and she is standing behind me in the background. I am smiling but Sarie isn't. I had looked at this photo before but now I was seeing something different – it wasn't just her not smiling; it was something behind that. It was the few seconds after that realisation that were the most powerful.

Two weeks passed and I woke up thinking about what I had experienced at the Heathrow Sofitel. I had been in Shreveport since 22 April and had not seen Sarie (who had come back to town in the early 1990s).

Mr Williams was going to come around at lunchtime and we were going to run some errands, which means 30 minutes of errands and then two hours spending time together; apart from my precious kids there is no one on the face of the earth I'd rather spend time with.

I was in my room when Teresa called and said, 'Mr Williams is out front.' As I walked by the front reception desk, Teresa was standing there with that smile on her face. She looked towards the front doors and said: 'I can just tell he's a sweet, kind soul.'

I said: 'They don't make them any better. Mr Williams and I went through many long weekend wars when I was racing in the World Championship.'

I got in the car and Mr Williams immediately handed me a section of that day's paper. It was the obituaries. I glanced at it but didn't recognise anyone I knew. Mr Williams pointed at a picture and it clicked.

It was Janine Joubert – Sarie's older sister. I was startled because Janine was only a year younger than me. My immediate thought was for Sarie and how devastated she must be. I felt I needed to talk to her anyway after going through the old photographs, but now that wasn't the first priority. I dialled the number.

Mother June
Alice Attaway,
circa 1949.

My dad Frederick Burdette Spencer
Senior on the first motorcycle he
had, circa 1945.

'Pop' Spencer and Grandma
Spencer, circa 1945.

Mom and Dad just
married with their
first car.

Pop Spencer,
Uncle Gerald
Spencer and Dad.
Uncle Gerald flew
bombers in World
War II in Europe.

The patio where I had
lunch with Levy C
and where my mom
would watch me
when I rode.

Grandma and Pop
Spencer in front of the
house in Sunset Acres.

My sister Linda, with Dad's
Harley-Davidson.

Linda with her go-kart smiling
because she beat the boys.

Danny and his go-kart.

Me standing on Dad's Harley-Davidson.

Me with my arms already holding the handlebars of my future bike.

Danny and me saying: 'I need a helmet!'

First row and ready to go. The helmet is still too big for me today! Dad is on my right and Danny on my left.

My first mini bike:
a Briggs & Stratton.

My poor sister having to chase
me around all day.

Me and my Yamaha 125cc flat tracker where I learned my style. I was 10 years old.

Riding in my yard.

On my 100cc Yamaha at Ross Downs on any Friday night. I was 9 years old.

My best year as an amateur road racer, 1977.

My first amateur Road Racing
Championship at Daytona in
1974, riding a Yamaha TA
125cc, wearing my Bultaco
Dirt Track leathers.

Danny and me, circa 1975.

Me at a local race in
Shreveport.

My first race weekend outside the US in 1980 for the American British
Match races, riding Erv Kanemoto's Yamaha TZ750.

Me and the NR500 in 1981 at the British Grand Prix at Silverstone. My first Grand Prix with Honda.

Paul Newman and me at Laguna Seca in December 1981.

Erv and me in Japan in September 1983 at the bullet train station.

Mr Honda and me in his back yard, the day I met him on 10 September 1983.

Chapter 5: **THROUGH THE HELLFIRE AND RAIN (1982)**

THE SPANISH Grand Prix was held at Jarama in Madrid. It was quite a sight, with 100,000 people cramming inside the circuit and thousands more parking up on the neighbouring freeway and standing on their cars to get a glimpse of further conflict.

I was going to new circuits and was being competitive from the start. The team was flush with ambition and desire. Parts and updates were coming every race but new frames kept breaking because they were trying to make the bike as light as possible; they were changing the light titanium pipes after every session; rebuilding engines almost every day in a time before rules limiting the number of changes. The engine crankshafts would last maybe two weekends and so there was a constant transfer of goods being hand-carried every week from Japan. It all looked promising, and then there was Erv and me, sitting down for hours and going through the endless sheets detailing transmission gear ratios and any way to improve our performances by thousandths of a second here and there around the track. Together, we were all dragging Honda higher and seeking constant improvement in every lap of every session.

I loved pushing the performance to the edge, but we had to figure out how to improve the way it was delivered from the moment I turned the throttle to increase the power to the critical moment when the rear wheel began to increase its speed. To compensate for our lack of acceleration, I would increase the radius of that corner so I could run a higher corner speed with slightly less lean angle. People soon noticed how early I was turning and then sliding the back of the bike around to help the bike change direction at a higher speed.

The bike had overheated in Argentina but that was resolved with a bigger radiator. We were getting the engine vibration worked out. Other problems would manifest themselves though, and it became a domino trail of trickle-down puzzles. The bike was like a hypochondriac – cure one thing and another issue would rear its head. And the crux of the problems was my yearning to always have more power and go quicker with less effort. Racing is a journey of constantly correcting imperfections.

A coil wire broke when I was leading in Spain so I had to retire. Kenny Roberts won the race and Barry Sheene came second. I made the podium at Misano in Italy for the Nations Grand Prix behind Franco Uncini. Graeme Crosby was third. What I have never talked publicly about is what happened before that race.

On that Sunday morning in Italy I was listening to some music. Christi was there with her dad and we were goofing around as we would, not thinking about anything. I was jumping up and down on the sofa when I caught my ankle on the edge of the heater vent. My ankle turned inward. On landing I felt it pop. Immediately, I knew.

'Oh no!'

'Oh my God!' Christi cried. 'What happened?'

'I will be fine.' I felt that panic you feel when you don't know what to do.

I tried to stand up and could not put weight on it. My face said it all and Christi's eyes grew as big as saucers. 'I'm going to get Dad.'

I told her not to tell anyone else and try to act as if everything is okay – as if nobody would notice the look on her blood-drained face.

A few minutes went by and then it got worse. Mr Williams rushed through the door into the motorhome and he tripped on the step. He hit his head on the corner of the kitchen table and it started to bleed.

Christi looked at us and said: 'Are you guys trying to kill yourselves and give me a heart attack?'

I started to laugh and I asked Mr Williams if he was okay. He was dazed and started to laugh too. What else could we do?

'Christi, go get your dad a towel.'

After she left Mr Williams asked what was wrong with me.

'Mr Williams, I don't think I can stand up. I heard a pop. I think I've broken my ankle and I have to push-start the bike. What am I going to do?'

Christi came back and I told her this was worse than the time I'd injured my heel in Dallas one night when I'd crashed at Ross Downs when I was 15.

'You remember that? That hurt but this is worse.'

She began to laugh.

'It's not funny. And this is a little different to being at Ross Downs!'

Erv then came in and looked confused at seeing me holding my ankle and Mr Williams holding a towel to his head. He put his hand on his forehead and began to smile.

'What happened?'

Really embarrassed, I tried to stop Christi from explaining. My ankle was swelling up like a balloon and I thought I would struggle to get a boot on and zip it up as they were skintight.

'Okay,' said Erv. 'I've got to get the bike to pre-grid.' The look on his face was tinged with disbelief.

Mr Williams murmured that he would go looking for an Ace bandage or something to wrap up my ankle.

I said: 'And find a Band-Aid for your head too while you're at it!'

They both left. Ten minutes later the door opened again and the first person in was Kenny Roberts followed by Mr Williams with a first-aid kit.

'What did you do?' Kenny said.

I was shocked to see him but told him I'd tripped. He cut me off with a slight smile and said: 'I don't want to know. Just give me your ankle.'

He took out an Ace bandage and began to wind it round my ankle.

'That's tight,' I moaned.

'It needs to be tight to stop the swelling and give you the support you need.'

I just nodded my head. 'Okay.'

I thanked him and he left. I found out that Kenny had seen Mr Williams walk by with 'a serious look on his face'. He immediately said: 'What happened to Freddie?'

It showed the camaraderie between competitors that would often go unspoken, which gave an interesting angle on what happened between us the following year and the bitterness that lingered for decades.

I was able to get my boot on and I made it off the starting line well enough. Once going I tucked in behind Franco and finished in a strong second place.

Franco was just too strong for us that day, but we learned some valuable lessons. One: no jumping around the motorhome on race weekends. Two: after following Franco for 40 laps I realised I still needed to work around the character of our bike and find ways to compensate for the weaknesses. Those lessons proved invaluable for 1983.

After Misano we went to Assen, a circuit I had been looking forward to visiting all season.

The track in north-east Holland is known as the Cathedral of Motorcycling and the race uses public roads, hence the official race title of the Dutch TT, standing for tourist trophy. The circuit has been developed since then – it's very safe for a street circuit – but it was still long and unique. I'd only seen some footage while at the Yamaha workshop in July 1980 and I'd marvelled as Jack

Middelburg, a Dutch racer who would be killed in a road race in Holland two years later, and Graziano Rossi, the wild, hirsute and uber-cool father to Valentino, duelled with Kenny Roberts on those long, sweeping stretches.

Once you got through the trees at Assen at the beginning of the lap, it was endless esses. The track has since been shortened and, in my opinion, ruined to a degree, but back then it really was the sport's cathedral, a place for leather-clad pilgrims to congregate with religious fervour. Being run on public roads, it was a narrow track that required precision. If you were late on your preparation to a section of corners it would screw up your rhythm and momentum. I was thrilled to be there, but went out in the first practice session and crashed at the first-gear hairpin. It was my own fault, too much throttle and excitement.

I shook my hand in the hope it would alleviate the pain. It didn't. I went back to the motorhome and told Erv: 'I've jammed my thumb.'

Erv looked worried. He said we should get some ice.

'It's already swelling up,' I said.

It was not a great precursor to such a demanding race, but I qualified on the second row with my sore thumb and trusted adrenalin to numb the pain. I'm glad I made it because this was the race in which I got a true motorcycling lesson in realising just how talented the opposition really was.

I got a good start and was with the lead group, but as the pace picked up I was just hanging on. Jack and Boet van Dulmen, his compatriot, and Kenny, Barry and Franco set a mindboggling pace. It started to rain after a few laps and so the back part of the track was completely wet, but these guys were on slick tires and were not slowing down much. After almost crashing twice I had to back off.

What I did not know then was that Assen has a tremendous amount of grip in the wet but I loved watching these guys ahead of me. One of the beautiful things about motorcycling racing for me was the appreciation I developed for the human and mechanical connection. The motorcycle does its job, and if you do yours by being able to adjust, then together it is symbiotic. It is a harmony created by the practical assistance of the motorcycle combined with the awareness, sense and feeling of the human pilot. And in those horrible conditions those great riders rose above the circumstances and elevated each other to a higher plane. It was as good as it gets, wonderful in fact. People say we must be crazy but that's not why I was there. I was not there for speed or an adrenalin rush. I was there for the love of the human ability to adapt and these rivals were doing that sublimely.

Down the back straightaway it was raining so hard that my vision was severely distorted from the water on the face shield. It was like driving down the freeway in a storm at over 100mph with the wipers off. I was trying to stay with the others, but their superior experience was paying off. One lap before the officials put out the red flag, I came to the first-gear hairpin and I saw a flash of red and yellow. In the pouring rain I was barely able to see it but I veered left just in time and, to my amazement, I looked over at Kenny Roberts' bike on fire. He had come off and was ignoring the flames to lean in and pick up his burning bike. The contrast of images was jarring, the grey and the white, the fire and rain, the triumph and disaster.

I managed to stay on two wheels through all the hellfire and rain and then the red flag came out to stop the race that lap. I then suffered a moment of huge embarrassment as I got to the front part of the track and crashed myself. As I slid along I was almost laughing at the irony of having made it through so much only to crash after the race had been stopped.

The crowd was clapping at the curious sight of a rider bouncing along with his bike, going past after running off the track on the grass. I had the fastest lap of the race but also a crash and some indelible memories. When the race was restarted after a short delay, the weather had cleared, but my steering damper was broken. It was too late for us to repair it. My race was over.

Audri was my new motorhome driver from race to race and became an invaluable part of the support system. He was going to take us to the airport in Amsterdam ahead of the next race in Belgium. I clambered into my bed in the back next to the window. I pulled the curtain to and drifted off.

I fell asleep instantly after a dramatic day and it seemed like only minutes before Audri pulled to a stop. He came back and said: 'We're here.'

Wiping the sleep from my eyes, I noticed a warm amber light shining through the curtain.

'Already?'

Audri looked at me and pointed out of the window towards the light. 'We're here,' he said again in his broken English.

'Okay,' I shrugged. I pulled back the curtain and was greeted by the sight of a neon-framed window and a woman in her skimpy underwear sitting in a chair staring back at me. She saw the shocked look on my face and laughed. I pulled the curtains back shut. It took a few seconds to realise Audri had parked my motorhome in the heart of the red-light district. The warm glow had been the lights from the store fronts.

I looked at Audri and said: 'I wanted to go the airport.' I made an airplane with my hand and tried to communicate by semaphore.

'Oh,' he said with a look of confusion. 'Not here?'

I think he had assumed this is where I would want to go, but with his rudimentary grasp of English and my Southern drawl we had failed to understand each other when planning our journey.

'No thank you,' I said. I had my girlfriend at home. We laughed about that for many years.

Spa

If I had been looking forward to Assen, Spa was different altogether, although I was not sure what to expect. On the first night in Belgium, deep in the Ardennes forest, we found a small family-owned hotel. I still go back there to this day for when I attend the Spa Classic event, where the little girl who used to bring me my meal is now the manageress. Right away I loved the place.

Immediately, I felt connected to the circuit, the way the corners were laid out, how the circuit fit the elevation changes. It was exactly how I would have built a circuit in my dreams. It also has my favourite two corners of any track I have ever raced – the double left leading into the esses down the bottom of the hill. The way they build momentum was just perfect. When you got that entry just right the rest fell into place, but if you were impatient at the beginning you would have to readjust and lose time.

It was not a perfect weekend, though. We were struggling to keep up, especially accelerating out of the high-speed corners. Barry still has the highest average speed at the old course, a crazy 135mph set in 1977, a feat I could remember reading about in the *Guinness Book of World Records*, and although the track was cut from nine miles to four miles in 1979, it was still lightning fast and had some dangerous sections of public roads.

We worked hard and studied the gear ratio charts and finally came up with a way to solve the conundrum through compromise. I qualified in second. Jack Middelburg was on pole and the only man to break 2 minutes 40 seconds. I knew I was getting faster every day. I did not get a great start but now I was picking people off, one by one. Everybody was improving their lap times, but I improved mine by a massive three seconds from my best time in qualifying. It was simply comfortable and enjoyable as I went through those lefts and sampled the thrill of the famous Eau Rouge section.

Tires played a part in this too. The great tire wars would really start the following year with my Michelins versus Kenny Roberts' Dunlops, but that was the genesis and they were hand-building tires and giving us new ones every day during race weekends.

The long, sweeping corners enabled me to counteract our lack of acceleration. It was the perfect storm of track and bike and rider. I was almost four seconds clear of Barry by the end, with Franco third.

As I celebrated I got distracted by all these people running towards me on the track and I dropped the bike. Barry came down the hill. He was the first person to hug me.

'Great job,' he said.

I had huge respect for him. A month later he passed me in one of the first practice sessions on Wednesday at Silverstone. He was flying. He was faster than me and I marvelled at his speed and skill. A few minutes later he had his famous crash and it was over, but the joy I felt for him at seeing him riding so well was reciprocated at Spa. With Kenny, who crashed on the first lap, it was always a bit different. It was not a lack of respect at all, but I'd been watching him since I was 11. It was why I had been so surprised to see him in my motorhome in Misano, although in truth I was not yet duelling with him for the world title.

It was 4 July and even though I expected to win, nothing can be taken for granted in this sport. The most overwhelming feeling was one of relief. And the first win is priceless. And I was the youngest-ever winner of a 500cc Grand Prix race. And I did it at the greatest place.

A few hours later, I walked out of the paddock and to the hotel. I signed a few autographs on the way, but I was looking forward to this part. It was time to call home. I had got used to the challenges of that from my time in Argentina when we had gone to check out and the manager had said my room bill was $500 dollars but my phone bill was $3,600. Those long, late-night calls to Sarie had stacked up. I was with Stuart Rowlands, and he pointed to the armed military guards in the lobby who were staring at us and told me to keep my voice down. It was a few days since the British had invaded the Falkland Islands and he told me that I should just pay so we could get out of there as fast as we could.

This time the call was short and sweet. Mom and Dad were happy, of course. Mom knew there was no going back now and knowing that I ended the day being safe was what she cared about most; maybe Dad thought back to all those thousands of miles with me and the little TV with the rabbit ears, that day I crashed Danny's bike, the leaf fire and the cost of it all, and perhaps he thought about how he had taken his son so far and then stepped aside to let Erv take over his role.

Franco won the Yugoslavian Grand Prix race and I was fourth, a good effort but our inconsistency meant we were never really in contention to win the title that first year.

I was 20 and getting an education in the world. In Yugoslavia I saw the Russian ships out to sea and the Communards with their machine guns at the airport. The dinar was almost worthless and I would take the 800,000 start money home and use it as Monopoly money for years afterwards. There was only one hotel with a phone and where I could make myself understood. I would go there, call home and then go and eat a slow dinner because it would take at least an hour to connect. Finally, they would come and get me and I would rush to the phone and say: 'It's okay Mom, I'm fine.'

I was appreciating the contrasts in the places I was going, understanding the differences to what I was used to in Louisiana. It was a privilege.

The fallen

Silverstone is an old high-speed circuit, very simple-looking. It was beautiful and poetic in a way. But that Wednesday in 1982 they decided to send all the bikes out together for practice so the 500cc bikes were there with the 250s and 125s. That would never be allowed today. Unfortunately, Barry would be the bearer of the lesson.

As Barry went past me that day, he waved to me. Of course he had famously done that to Kenny on the last lap at Silverstone in 1979. That two-fingered sign had caused a ruckus. It just made me smile. I loved it. Now Barry was flying and then he disappeared. I came in and Erv asked what was I smiling for. I said that if Barry rides like that he could still win the World Championship. I knew I could not run with the combination of that V4 and a fired-up Barry. He had come in and spoken to Erv and, while I was not listening, I knew what he could do. And then the red flag came out and word filtered through that Barry had crashed. He had hit a stricken 125cc bike at 160mph. Someone said it was his legs, but at least he was alive. I was so disheartened. I connect things. I knew what he had gone through in 1975 when he had crashed at Daytona and ended up with broken limbs, shredded skin, an 18-inch metal rod inserted into his leg and instant fame. He had ridden into the hearts of the public between those two savage dots.

I had a job to do and so 45 minutes later I was back on the bike. It is the practical side of being a racer. Some people have that ability to switch off more than others, but it is a learned thing too. I had done it way back when I had seen that kid go through the wooden planks at the track in Dallas. Do you think about it? Sure, you do. I had it the next year too when Michel Frutschi was killed in front of me at Le Mans. He was sliding but I was watching him and he was fine. And then he hit a bump that changed his trajectory and was sliding on his back. His helmet struck a pole. What are the chances of that happening? How can that be fair? It is one of the things that make it hard for people to believe. For me it showed the uncertainty of physical life and why we have to strive to appreciate it in every moment. If it can happen to Michel Frutschi, who had won the French Grand Prix in 1982, or to Barry, or to that kid at Dallas International, then it can happen to anyone. But the tragedies have no effect on the purpose of our existence and we should keep faith.

I wished I had gone to see Barry in hospital but I didn't. I got word to him and saw him a few months later when he came to San Marino. I avoided hospitals like the plague for the same reason a lot of riders don't go to funerals. There is a line from the film *Days of Thunder* which is sort of silly but rings true: 'You get a driver to a funeral before he's actually dead and you've made history.'

By the British Grand Prix, Barry was probably the only rider left who really had a chance to beat Franco that year. The rest of us knew how hard it was going to be to win. But life has to go on. So as Barry recuperated from his horrific crash, Sarie and I stayed on in London at the Park Lane Hilton. We ate at the original Hard Rock Cafe around the corner and went to a show in Piccadilly Circus. It was lovely.

There were no mobile phones then and nobody knew where we were so we could escape and just be two 20-year-old kids hanging out in London and loving life. It was bliss.

Being incommunicado meant we were oblivious to the storm bursting across the sea in Sweden. The next Grand Prix was in Anderstorp the following Sunday. We were meant to be out on the track on Wednesday, but I got my days wrong and I was still in London. The Italian and British Press had a field day and the headlines were all about a young American racer not turning up. So the headline was 'He's so cocky'. We showed up on Wednesday afternoon, embarrassed not to have made it on time, but determined to make up for it on Thursday.

I went out and, within five laps, was the fastest rider on the track. That enhanced my reputation as a fast-learner of circuits, but it hadn't been intentional. I qualified on pole for the race and was leading until I had an electrical issue like in Spain. We did all we could, it just wasn't our day. I was happy for my HRC teammate, Takazumi, who won the race and that tempered the disappointment.

A few weeks later I was sitting in the Piazza della Signoria in Florence. This was the first time I fully appreciated the power of architecture and history. What a place! The San Marino Grand Prix was taking place some 30 miles away in the Tuscan countryside at Mugello. I looked around at the majestic buildings and really appreciated all that had gone into creating this. It made a lasting impression on me. Sitting in that square, built purely from the power of the human mind and hands, I understood the limitless possibilities. Strength of imagination and will were the key.

It was a few miles and a world away from the blinkered Grand Prix scene and its own battle between perfection and imperfection. I was soon sucked back into it. The weekend was hot. Franco had wrapped up the World Championship a race earlier. Now he came into the pits with heat exhaustion. He did not finish the race. Of those that did a lot of them collapsed afterwards. I was a kid from Louisiana who had grown up in the steamy, oppressive heat of the Deep South racing on days just like this one, so it suited me. I won the race by 17 seconds.

A mistake by Franco proved costly for me as my debut season climaxed at Hockenheim in Germany. Franco was too consistent for any of us, but I could still finish second in the championship if I made up four points on Graeme Crosby.

I took off into the lead and had the race under control, and with Graeme crashing on the fifteenth lap, the runner-up spot looked almost assured. But it's not over until the chequered flag waves. I had a 2.2-second lead going into the final lap. The rpm had been dropping but I still felt I would be fine.

At that time the number shown on the pit board when I came by on the last lap was actually from the previous lap. Now it is much more accurate with high-tech data, but in those days it was done by a stopwatch and a clipboard. Normally, I would look behind at some point too, but Hockenheim is such a high-speed circuit that there was no time.

So in reality my lead was actually half what I thought, but this is racing. You live in the moment. There are no mirrors to see behind you.

I loved the last part of the Hockenheim circuit, the long straight going out in the German forest through the big sweeping right-hand corner, heading back towards the stadium in the distance. Just me and the bike, the wind buffeting us, the engine vibrating, the sound muffled by my helmet. I can close my eyes and relive that lap. It felt great at more than 180mph.

I begin braking for the corner leading into the stadium. I can see most of the 60,000 people begin to stand up in my peripheral vision. I am completely focused on what is happening in front of me. Just Sachs Corner, a short straightaway and then a double right and the race is mine.

Then a blur of colour and a jolt to the system as Randy Mamola passes me on the inside of Sachs. I try to follow Randy and I do not even see Franco who is following. He hits me so hard I go down and am briefly knocked out. Then I hear the faint sound of bikes and voices getting louder.

'Freddie, we have to get out of here!'

Ken Vreeke, a journalist from the USA there to write one of the first stories on me and who would become a good friend, has jumped over the perimeter fence and pulls me off the track.

There are three-and-a-half corners to go. And now I'm sitting in the back of an ambulance as I hear the American national anthem. I am concussed and have a broken collarbone. They start to cut my leathers off.

Breeze, Louisiana, 2010

The last time I had seen Sarie was at the Louisiana Sports Hall of Fame in 2009. I was the first motorsports person to be inducted and I had flown down with my two kids. Having them there was great. I had some other family and friends come and support me, but the two people who had been there during all of my World Championship seasons were Mr Williams and Sarie.

After seeing the obituary about Janine, I called Sarie. She said: 'I was just thinking about calling you.'

'Sarie, I'm so sorry about Janine. Mr Williams just showed me the story in the paper this morning. Is there anything I can do?'

She said: 'Mom and I would really like you to come to the memorial service on Friday.'

'I was already planning on it.'

As we were about to hang up I told her that I had been contacted to talk at the Breakfast Business Meeting at the University Club. I was due to appear that Thursday morning.

I said: 'If you feel like it then maybe you'd like to come by?' Then I added: 'You might enjoy what I'm going to talk about.'

I could tell she was intrigued. 'I'd like that,' she said.

Sitting at the desk in my hotel room I thought about how you never know, how life is fragile. We have to make every second count. And then the feeling comes over me about how much time I had spent to get here. And I realised there are many moments that it doesn't seem like much is happening. I have spent a lot of time waiting.

Waiting for what?

I didn't know until I arrived here at the Courtyard Marriott. And I still don't exactly know. I may never fully know. But I do know that inside I've never felt more complete.

No emptiness.

No doubt.

Just like I felt as a kid.

Mary Lynn Stewart – Martin Stewart's wife – was organising the Breakfast Business Meeting. She told me: 'You can pretty much talk about anything as long as it's about 20 minutes in length and doesn't include politics or religion.'

I had no plans to talk about either. The tough part for me would be keeping it under 20 minutes. With all my years doing commentary on TV, I could reduce comments to fit into 30-second segments, but that's not my life.

At the hotel, Lorraine was busy in the kitchen. She had been here for as long as Teresa and cares about two things – her job and her bowling league. I've been talking to her about her struggles in games during her Tuesday matches. She said she starts off strong and gets in the zone, but then she starts thinking about how she's in the zone and going to get a good score – and she finds she can't see the game out.

I really like the passion she has to do well for her team. I've noticed that quality in each of the folks I've connected with at the Courtyard Marriott. So, talking to Lorraine about what she enjoys doing mattered to me too. And I knew with all my years in racing, training and competition that maybe I could help her.

Once she gained confidence in what she felt she should do then she would stay trusting that. Then, as the pressure intensified, she could stay in the zone and not get in her own way.

I told her to stay in the moment. Be patient. Clear your mind as you step up to get ready. Take three deep breaths, in through your nose and out through your mouth. Focus to your core to open up what you sense, feel and touch. That will allow you to be completely in the moment.

The day before the Breakfast Business Meeting at the university I realised I didn't have any clothes to wear. I have always liked nice clothes, but when I left Las Vegas on 22 April, I left with only two carry-on bags. I had more in storage but I hadn't really needed any more than I could fit into those two bags – until now. I talked with Martin and Mary Lynn and went to Stein Mart to buy a sports coat, shirt and pants for my talk and for Janine's memorial service the next day.

Chapter 5: THROUGH THE HELLFIRE AND RAIN (1982)

On the drive up to the University Club at 6.30am, Martin asked me: 'What are you going to talk about?'

I said: 'Mary Lynn gave me two rules: keep the talk to 20 minutes and don't talk about politics or religion.'

Martin smiled. 'You should listen to what she says. She knows the crowd.'

Heading to the university in my new clothes I didn't know exactly what I would talk about yet. But I knew for sure that it would not just be about racing motorcycles. Finally, my slot came. Be patient. Clear your mind as you step up to get ready. Take three deep breaths. I stood up and began

'When I seemingly had it all, I realised I had nothing.'

Chapter 6: **WHEN WE WERE WARRIORS (1983)**

I FLEW home from Germany, battered and bruised and with my arm in a sling. Mom was there to pick me up at Shreveport Regional Airport and she looked at me kindly and said: 'Well, you've been lucky all these years, Freddie.' It was what I needed to hear. Her understated manner was comforting. As I rode back in the car to the house on Amelia Street to rest up and get some of Mom's home cooking, I was back in the drama of those last few laps at Hockenheim. The contrast of the two things and being in her presence was as comforting as it had been when I was six and she would walk me around the Ramada Inn for as long as I needed for my stomach cramps to go away.

My other great maternal influence was a different personality entirely. When Pop once had a heart attack, Grandma Spencer went to the hospital and said they needed to get him out of there fast. 'He's got work to do,' she said with a wink but still kind of serious. Pop had a pacemaker fitted but it kept causing infections so Grandma made him a sling so he could wear it outside the body with the wires attached while the wound healed. He single-handedly built a garage like that.

I loved being around Grandma for different reasons to my mom. She was small, outwardly determined and certain in her action. She was as tough as nails. Mom had an alcoholic father so scarcely had it easy, but it didn't harden her at all; she was strong in a quiet way out of necessity. My grandmother grew up in Oklahoma, out on the farm, surrounded by her brothers, only four foot eleven but with a giant personality. She was just strong. Sitting in her living room as we talked over my crash, she was clear about what was required. 'You have to beat that guy who knocked you down.' I told her that it was just one of those things that happened in racing and that nobody was to blame, but her mind was made up. 'You've got to come back stronger and more determined, Freddie.' That was Grandma, that little girl in the buckboard wagon going across the Oklahoma plain, the woman who made me my first set of leathers and spelt my name 'Freddy' because that was how she thought it should be.

When she was 90, she told me that when she turned 100 I had to make sure she had a nice party. She started having little strokes in her late nineties but, sure enough, she made it to 100. There would be about 70 people at her party, mainly family friends because most of her peers had died many years ago, but she stood up there and, although she was a little confused, started talking away in front of everyone. It was almost impossible to understand what she was saying because of the strokes, but *she* knew what she was talking about and that was what was most important. It was about being there for her. I'd smile at that and admire the sheer will and determination of this woman who had seen the first Model T Ford and the Wright brothers fly their plane at the state fair and then moved into a new age where I showed her how to use a laptop computer. She stayed true to herself but moved with the times, adjusting to the present, traits I shared that would become invaluable for me as I faced 1983.

There was a lot on the line and I could feel the pressure everybody was under from Honda. They had created HRC, this grand racing corporation, even though there had been little recent success to build upon, and they were still dealing with the wounds from the fate of the NR project. Now they were in a rush to see the fruits of their labours and it felt like now or never.

I also knew that this could be Kenny's last season and so he would be riding like never before. He was always a combative, rock-hard opponent, a man with absolute belief in his riding and his ability to control the outcome through his strong will. I had seen that and understood it completely when I saw him ride when I was 11. Now I was the one standing in the way of a grand farewell. In addition, I added to the burden on myself because my personal goal had long been to become the youngest-ever 500cc world champion and take the record from the great Mike Hailwood. This year was my last chance. And so the pressure was immense on both HRC, this new division of a great company, and on my team and me.

Times were changing and lap times were dropping. We had made a huge leap forwards in terms of the bike's power, performance and stability and my own improvement as a world-class rider. The dramatic speed increase from 1982 to 1983 was of a scale you would never see now, but I found a beauty in the constant change of that era.

The first time I got back on the bike was at the Daytona tire test with Michelin in October. I had won the Superbike race there that March and declared that I was done with racing Superbikes. With 30 minutes left on the last day of the test they asked if I'd ride the new Honda Superbike. They said they knew I didn't want to race it but it would be good to get some feedback. It was an all-new 750cc V4 prototype called VF750 'Interceptor' and I went out for five laps, came in and said: 'I'll race this.' It was an amazing, extremely stable bike on which I ended up winning at Daytona for the next three years.

That New Year's Eve Sarie and I went to Hawaii and we stayed at the Kapalua Bay Hotel and Spa on the island of Maui. We sat in a restaurant with the pink sun setting in front of us and I asked her to marry me. She said yes. It was perfect. The plan was to get married at the end of the season. I had total trust in my team. Mr Oguma and Mr Fukui were in charge and there was Mr Miyakoshi, the V3 engine designer, who had a book in the back of his car called *The Land of the Rising Sun Shall Return*. These were true old-school warriors and I appreciated and respected them. But as is the case in Japanese hierarchy, they were almost faceless as it was all about the team.

They were feeling the heat too. I went to Daytona and won that Superbike race on that lovely machine, but then watched Kenny win the 200 as if to provide cast-iron proof that he was going to be a warrior that year too. Our NS500 V3 was too fragile to run a 200-mile race.

By the time I got to South Africa for the first Grand Prix of the year, the intensity had been cranked up. I had to deliver, and at Kyalami I did. The other Hondas – Marco, Takazumi and now Ron Haslam – were actually battling with Kenny too, but I was clear of them all. It was the perfect start. Our three-cylinder performance was strong and it needed to be.

Apart from power, the bike had one major change, which was the addition of exhaust valves as a response to Yamaha's own system. It was almost an arms race between the manufacturers as they sought to reduce the advantage held by others and eke out gains they already had.

I told Erv that it was vital we got as many points in the bag in the early part of the season. The first three races would be key. Yamaha always improved as the year wore on and, of course, Kenny was never going to go quietly.

Le Mans was a horrible weekend. It seemed appropriate that the weather was chilling as two racers, Michel Frutschi and Iwao Ishikawa, were killed, a rarity in the modern era. The horizontal sleet made the grid shudder as one at what was unfolding both on the track and up above. At least Erv and I combatted one issue by getting hold of some surgical gloves that I wore under my leather ones. It was a simple thing but made such a big difference. My hands actually sweated while riding. I won again. This time Marco and Ron got between me and Kenny, who had a problem with his exhaust. Two races, two wins and Kenny was struggling.

I had an even deeper sense of purpose now. We arrived for race three at Monza on Thursday and walked out to look at the most famous corner of the Monza circuit that is not used any more, the Curva Grande. It is part of the original banking, like at Daytona, and I pictured the history. It was where Jarno Saarinen and Renzo Pasolini lost their lives at the Nations Grand Prix in 1973. I came back to the present and said: 'I feel like I'm going to win on Sunday.' I was slightly embarrassed and shrugged my shoulders as if to acknowledge it was only a feeling.

This was a circuit that did not suit us. Without question, it should favour the Yamahas and then there was the fact I had never even been around it yet. Erv looked at me with a faint smile, tapped his head for luck and said: 'Well, I hope so.' I realised that what I had said had made him nervous.

Monza was one of the few tracks – Spa and the old Hockenheim were the others – where history seeped down from the stands on to the asphalt and I loved it for that. As Erv and I walked back to the paddock we talked about how big and fast it was. I had decided that the Ascari section – the esses leading to the fast back straight – was where the race would be won or lost. I had a simple philosophy when it came to plotting my way around a new circuit – high-speed corners were the places to make up time and the slower sections were for surviving because they could tempt you into being too aggressive for not much benefit. The preparation for the first part of Ascari determined everything that came after it. Like a great song, the intro was the passage to the middle section, the verses, the soaring chorus and refrain. Get the intro wrong and it just didn't work. I knew I had to understand that corner if I was going to be close enough to Kenny so I could stay in his draft on the long straight leading into the last curve – the Parabolica.

I qualified second quickest and from the start it was a ferocious battle. I got out in front with a good start, but Kenny caught me after a few laps, as was the normal pattern. I knew his Dunlop tires had a longer window of performance but the truth was we both had only around six laps and then they began to fade. Our bikes were fragile, and the speed advantage we had in South Africa had been reduced already. It became a battle of wills and machines.

I could stay with Kenny up to Ascari but was hanging on, right on the razor's edge, by the time we hit the Parabolica. I made my mental adjustments and realised I needed to give myself some room on the entrance to Ascari so I could get a run on him and build momentum. For me, it seemed like these calculations took place in slow motion, but they were actually done at more than 100mph in a few thousandths of a second. However, the movie playing in my head did not foresee the plot twist and I will never forget what happened next.

With three laps to go we are doing the same dance, but I am closer now. Going into the Parabolica, Kenny can sense I am there, but he does not know that I am hanging on by the tips of my fingernails. It's taking everything I have to stay ahead of the bike's movements. I have no more anticipation, no more control, I have nothing left to give. I am on the edge.

And then, as we enter the Parabolica like we have all race, he begins to run wider and wider until he runs off the outside edge of the track. To this day I can see it happen like it is in slow motion as he goes off line. I cannot believe it, then and now. He goes off the edge and, as I go under him and he tries to come back, his front tire hits the lip of the asphalt and he falls. 'Brain fade,' he says later. He remounts and then runs out of fuel before the end of the race. I win the race by eight seconds from Randy Mamola. It is a huge moment. Pivotal. I had told Erv I was going to win, but would I have done so had Kenny not made his mistake? Who knows?

Thousands of people swarmed on to the front straightaway. I caught the eye of George my mechanic as they suddenly parted.

'Where's the bike?' George asked.

I muttered: 'I thought you were the one who took it from me!'

George was perplexed. 'Well, I don't have it.'

All soon became clear as we looked behind and saw some fans running down the pit lane with my bike. George began to give chase and I smiled at the scene, a diminutive engineer running after some Italian petrol-heads in a sweaty mass of humanity. I saw George catch them and they handed it back. They patted him on the back, all smiles, but George did not think it was funny. I looked around me and felt the priceless enthusiasm of the Italian crowd. It was unbelievable, even better than I had imagined.

Three wins in a row, but as quickly as I felt the elation of that I sensed the reality. Later, as we left, I turned to Erv again. 'This is going to get tough,' I said. He nodded almost imperceptibly. We knew Kenny was going to be steaming and was not going to let anything like that happen again. His brain would never fade again and nor would his title challenge. The stage was set for our greatest duel.

Spanish Grand Prix

I was quicker than the rest by a lot in Germany but we had a pipe issue in the race that weekend and I ended up being thankful for the rain that brought a premature end to the race and enabled me to settle for fourth. Kenny won. The lead was trimmed.

I was now a world away from my roots. I was attracting media from beyond my normal confines of the *Shreveport Times* and *Cycle News*. Sam Moses, one of the lead writers at *Sports Illustrated*, the premier national sports magazine, was coming over to Spain to do a story. I knew he was primarily writing a feature on Kenny but events would overtake that brief and his piece became about the two of us.

Sam would write:

It's the classic American shootout. Here's Kenny Roberts, the rowdy, lionhearted 'old' cowboy from Modesto, Calif., going up against the kid from Shreveport, La., Freddie Spencer, for the 500cc motorcycle road-racing championship of the world – the most coveted title in the sport. Though only 21, Spencer has 15 years of racing experience and is the most sensational young rider road racing has ever seen. Since 1978, Roberts, 31, has won the 500cc championship three times. Now King Kenny and Fast Freddie are going head to head for the '83 title.

There hasn't been such superb and breath-taking duelling between two riders since the days back in the sixties when the legendary Mike (The Bike) Hailwood of England and the dashing and daring Giacomo Agostini of Italy were racing wheel-to-wheel.

Roberts fits the European stereotype of the American racer: often loud, always cocky, sometimes profane. And spectacular on the track.

Spencer is Mr Clean at 11,500 rpm. He's mature, courteous and unassuming. He doesn't say provocative things, much less use four-letter words. He's engaged to Miss Shreveport 1981, Sarie Joubert, and he emphasises the word fiancée.

Spencer is a lanky 5'10". Kenny is a bowlegged 5'6". The physical differences are magnified when they straddle their bikes and lean them through the turns, dragging their knees on the pavement. Roberts crouches over his machine as though he were a wrestler throwing a full nelson, and he sometimes actually slides in the turns. No one before Roberts had ever slid a road-racing motorcycle, at least not deliberately. Spencer sits more upright, as though he were trying to push the machine away.

And Spencer hardly ever falls off. Maybe it's his reward for clean living. His attitude toward racing's risks is based on a religious conviction, which borders on fatalism: If God wants me He'll take me; if not, He'll protect me. Says Roberts, 'It's nice to put your faith in God, but I know damn well that if I go into a turn without shutting off, I'm gonna fall over.'

That paragraph would leap out at me when I read it. The images Sam created and quotes used enhanced a perception about me that was far from the truth. I often felt I was put in a box, with words like enigma, religion, and introvert bandied around.

But Sam captured the excitement well. It was the first time Kenny and I had really sparred with each other during a race and it would be my greatest battle. I got out fast and Kenny caught me. We swapped places two or three times a lap. The day was hot, the asphalt old, and as our tire performance began to decrease as normal, that left only pure racing ability and mental agility. Managing degradation and maintaining speed was both an art and a science, and every corner of every lap saw us make adjustments. You either have the awareness and skill to do that and to be able to focus on the race craft or you don't. That's what Kenny and I did that day in the Spanish Grand Prix. We applied those skills to the nth degree as Mr Williams stood on top of my motorhome with Sam. As the race neared its conclusion, Sam seemed sure that Kenny's superior knowledge and experience would win out.

'It looks like Kenny's got it under control now,' he said.

Mr Williams responded with his absolute belief in me. 'No,' he said calmly. 'I don't think so.'

Sam would tell me that was one of his most treasured moments – just standing there with this man who loved me unconditionally and had this unfailing belief.

Race day this year was gorgeous, and the fans were high on sunshine and red wine and paella. They pressed past the barriers to the edge of the track, undaunted by the guardia civil patrolling the circuit with submachine guns. Roberts had a typically slow start – a weakness he blames on his short legs, for the riders must push-start their bikes. Spencer led until the ninth lap, when he slid coming out of a turn and both his feet flew off the pegs, flapping in the air as if he were a cowboy fighting to stay with a bronco. Roberts soon slipped past, and Spencer pursued, staring at the tips of the Yamaha's exhaust pipes poking out of the back of Roberts' seat like tommy guns. Through an S turn they weaved – left, right, as graceful and rhythmic as slalom skiers around gates, their knees dragging against the pavement, eventually rubbing holes through the leather to the padding underneath. Spencer would sit upright and ease his Honda down until his knee touched, his large round eyes wide in the window of his helmet watching Roberts. Roberts would hang off the motorcycle to one side, the back of his knee hooked over the edge of the seat, his buttocks completely off the bike, and then shift the bike into the right-hander and hang off the other side, a balancing act so swiftly executed and so precise it was as if Roberts had swallowed a gyroscope.

With just two laps left we were lapping everybody. We came up to Jack Middelburg who was actually in eighth place.

There were two rights before the front straightaway and this was the moment that decided the race. I was just ahead and decided to buck conventional wisdom and go round Jack on the outside. Normally, I would pass him on the inside. The inside track was the way to overtake on the entrance to this corner, but I went around him and Kenny saw his chance to go on the inside. Then Jack turned in sooner and that blocked Kenny's line so he had to slow down more. That gave me the momentum I needed and I got my best drive of the race on to the straightaway. I had taken the riskier choice and it had paid off. Now there was one lap to go.

From the roof of Spencer's motor home in the paddock, a friend [this was Mr Williams] said, 'I's a dawg faght.' And indeed, the way the two bikes peeled off for the next turn, they did look like banking fighter jets.

One lap to go but I feel spent. And yet, with no grip left in the tires, I basically had no brakes, and with the bike drifting on every corner, I used the curb to stop the slides. I ignored the physical emptiness and set a new lap record. It was the epitome of the greatest duel. I came in and am mentally, physically and emotionally spent. It would be the greatest individual race of the year for me. That lap was as perfect as I could ride. I had dragged the momentum back our way.

As writers like Sam plundered that duel for all its dramatic worth, nobody knew that Kenny was in my motorhome less than an hour later. It may shock some even now, given what was still to unfold that year, but he came over and grabbed a beer while I settled down with a Dr Pepper. Two fighter pilots, chalk and cheese, the rodeo rider and Mr Clean. We didn't really talk about the race and he made no attempt to cover up his arm problem. Kenny was fighting through that problem as his body battled to withstand the years of toil – it would become a chronic condition – but there was no need for cloaks and daggers. Kenny understood what it had taken for me to beat him on that last lap because he had been there flogging himself in that Never Never Land between the edge and the unknown. In return, I had been there too and I knew that injury was not going to weaken him one iota. We were in deep and, in that respect, we were warriors, and no one understood that more than him and me.

Sitting there with him and with every passing moment and spoken word, I knew that Kenny was trying to figure me out. He was used to people acquiescing and perhaps he thought that if he got to know me he could gain an advantage. Later, when I read Sam's piece and saw Kenny's quote about God being unable to help him in the white-knuckle rawness of a title fight, I realised how different we were. It was not religion for me, even though everyone thought it was, but a faith that could not be dependent on the outcome. If faith fails when things begin to go wrong then it is not enough. I sat in my chair and watched Kenny watching

me and, while it felt uncomfortable, I knew this was my last
chance and nothing would dent my desire.

He was to depart that night for the next race, in Austria, along
with Sarie. Roberts saw them off with a hoot and a wisecrack
and then went to a restaurant fit for a peasant and got rowdy
and made everyone in the place laugh for the rest of the evening.

The rest of the team followed in a convoy 1,400-miles to Austria.
There was Mr Williams and Audri driving my motorhome and
Henk driving the HRC bus. Mr Williams and Henk made an
unlikely couple, this postman from Williams Road in rural
Louisiana and a tall, skinny Dutchman with a wispy moustache
and perennial cigarette. They somehow found a way to
communicate beyond language barriers and there was a comedy
to their union, not least the night Henk came over complaining
to Mr Williams about the shower and claiming that he had been
electrocuted. 'Maybe I explode,' he said in his staccato English.

Mr Williams nodded sagely and with a slight smile said: 'Well
Henk, take me and show me. We'll fix it.'

There were vans for my team, Taka's team, Marco's team,
a truck for all the spare parts. We were a modern-day circus
travelling around Europe and beyond to entertain. People even
called it the continental circus.

Sarie and I checked in at our little hotel overlooking the picture-
postcard village of Hoff. I slept for 12 hours, which showed how
tired and comfortable I felt. To this day it was one of the best
sleeps I ever had. I allowed myself to relax as I knew that last lap
had been the life-long culmination of my drive, determination,
ability and adaptability, allied to good fortune. I had held my
nerve, stepped out into the void and pulled off the most delicate
of balancing acts.

But this was hard and Kenny, with his arm and his poor starts
and his attempt to see inside my head, was a bloody-minded

bundle of igneous will. He may have felt exactly the same sense of purpose and expectation that I did, so something would have to give. And then those thoughts turned to reality that weekend when the crankshaft on my bike failed and Kenny won convincingly. The lead was down to six points.

Now the season has changed. Two of the last races have seen us suffer with mechanical problems and the early races have segued into lap-for-lap little wars. The outside world looks at every little detail to make sense of this. People note that Sarie does not sleep in my motorhome at races and journalists say this is down to my religion, but it isn't at all. It has more to do with my respect for Sarie and knowing that beating Kenny is going to take every fibre of my being and focus. So no distractions.

I go home and feel the weight of knowing that this is only the start, but the pressure does not get to me. The feeling I have is identical to the one I had walking under the tunnel at the match races in 1980 when Dale Singleton asked me if I was nervous and I said, 'No, I'm ready'. I am comfortable with this because I know it means this is as good as it gets. I have a belief that it will turn out all right but I can't be complacent. I remember the bit in Rocky *when the tone changes. Rocky knocks Apollo down and Apollo knocks Rocky down. It is only the beginning.*

Breeze, Louisiana, 2010

'When I seemingly had it all, I realised I had nothing.'

That got their attention at the Breakfast Business Meeting. I was about to talk about my journey. I went back and started my story with the leaf fire when I was two years old. The 20-minute deadline approached. I began to wrap up but nobody had left and nobody seemed fidgety. I could tell by the look on their faces they were enjoying hearing my story.

I explained my first statement at the end, how I had strived to understand why I knew to race. I had acquired all the accolades and material possessions from these accomplishments, but I hadn't reached that place of knowing what it meant for me. So that awareness that comes from that part of the subconscious was telling me it wasn't all I was supposed to know. So the 'nothing' is the difference in the value of material possessions versus knowing with certainty what matters: the true purpose of your life, my connection to you and the universe that leads to the knowing and the enlightenment that we share.

After 40 minutes I was finally done. I apologised for running over and opened it up for questions. That lasted another 20 minutes. When I had finished everyone stood up and clapped. I had talked about the spiritual side of life and nobody seemed to mind.

I felt good, more than good. I didn't know until I went up there where the talk would lead except for the first statement and the explanation, but I did know it was going to be more personal and intimate than any speech I had ever given.

Sarie had said she wanted to come but had to make a last-minute business trip to Dallas. More than anyone else in the room I knew she would have understood what I had been through.

The next day I got dressed and went on my usual 5am walk. I waited around for the sun to come up. It was a beautiful cloudless day.

Martin came by at his usual time of 6.30am. I told him I'd be down in a few minutes. I wanted to spend a little extra time writing down some thoughts about what today was about.

I knew I wanted to talk to Sarie about what I had experienced that Monday evening after the event in Assen, leafing through those old photographs, but only when and if it felt appropriate. What mattered most was to be there for her and her family as they remembered Janine.

As we were driving to the club I said to Martin: 'I really appreciate you coming by the hotel to pick me up every day. It means more than you can know.'

I really appreciated that sincere enthusiasm he shared with Teresa too. It's easy to miss those moments. They are often overlooked or forgotten because they lack drama. It's like the difference between the feeling you get from a gentle breeze and a stormy wind. I have learned to never confuse drama and perceived importance with a true moment of connection. That is a solid foundation to build on to move in the right direction.

After Martin and I arrived at the course, I went out and hit some balls on the range. I thought about how hard today was going to be for Sarie. She would be organising the service and would be getting up to say something about Janine and her life.

I had a quick scrambled egg sandwich and went back to the hotel to get ready and headed for Broadmoor Methodist Church.

When I walked in I saw Sarie's sisters, Moya and Danielle, and then Sarie's mom. It had been 25 years since I had seen Mrs Bryson at the Shreveport Country Club to celebrate my two world titles. I gave her a hug and said: 'I'm so sorry about Janine.'

As I let go from the hug, we stepped back and she looked at me for the longest time. She said: 'You look great.'

A little embarrassed, I said: 'Thank you. I've never felt better.'

For me, this comment meant so much. Even in her moment of grieving for her daughter, Mrs Bryson noticed that about me. It was considerate.

Sarie walked up. We hugged and I said: 'I'm so sorry.'

We kept holding each other. I kissed her on the cheek and she said: 'I am so glad you are here.'

I smiled. 'Me too.'

The service was starting. After Sarie's eloquent eulogy we all went back out to the foyer. Sarie was busy talking to each of the guests and I wasn't sure I would get the chance to talk to her before I left. I certainly didn't want to interfere with her responsibilities.

After a while some people started to leave. Sarie freed herself and said: 'I'm sorry that I couldn't make it to the Breakfast Business Meeting yesterday. How did it go?'

I said: 'Great. I really enjoyed seeing a lot of people I knew from a long time ago.'

'What did you talk about?'

I said what I felt inside. 'About how in November 1985, when I had everything, I realised I had nothing.'

I could tell from the look on her face that I had really surprised her. She had a quizzical expression.

'That as good as I was at paying attention to what I sensed and felt while inside my racing helmet, I did a poor job of paying attention to what I sensed and felt in my outside personal life. For that I am truly sorry, Sarie.'

The look on her face changed and, with a little smile, she said: 'You finally realised that after 25 years.'

I said: 'Well, it's not quite 25 years.'

She said: 'It's like that movie, *For the Love of the Game*.'

I knew the film, about an ageing baseball player who pitches the perfect game while reflecting on his relationship with his girlfriend. I knew what she meant. Billy didn't realise what he had until Jane was leaving.

Even though we had seen each other numerous times in the past 25 years, this was the first time there had been any discussion or true understanding about what had happened between us. I was given that understanding that night at the Heathrow Sofitel. I didn't question it. I didn't dismiss it. I gave it the respect and appreciation it deserved.

Sarie went back to her hostess duties, but as she walked away I could tell that she understood too. We didn't get another chance to talk. When I hugged her as I left it felt different but in a good way.

Chapter 7: **SOMETHING TO SLEEP ON (1983)**

EVERY END has a start. This time it came in Austria when I struggled with a broken crankshaft for the second year in a row and retired from the race. Kenny won. Now the lead was not trimmed, but cut to ribbons. Six points.

I went home and drove out to Ronnie Hampton's lake house with friends and we messed around on my wet bikes, a cross between jet skis and motorcycles on the water, and waited. My thoughts were centred on what was next: what choice do you have? I had learned not to worry. Worrying interferes with awareness. Instead, I focused on mental preparation, making mind movies and then replaying them with different endings. Whatever happened I wanted to be ready for it, but while I was acclimatising myself to every possible situation, the one thing I felt sure about was that it would not be easy.

Spain had shown that. 'The hardest race of my life,' I told a journalist. It could have been different too. After the race they would start the bikes to listen to the engine but mine wouldn't start. It turned out the main bearing had failed. I was maybe a lap away from the engine locking up. Was it good luck? Perhaps, but I didn't look at it like that. For me it was just a fact. If something goes wrong you can curse the heavens or fate, gremlins or fortune, but for me it just produced the same result. It inspired me – the next time I would work harder.

Kenny and I were now being cast as polar opposites but I knew our contrasting personas were being deployed on common ground. I did not see us as being so very different and my respect for his abilities was immense, however, Sam Moses and the others would dramatise our relationship. I saw the supreme effort that Kenny was putting in and I reasoned that things could go his way just as easily as they could go mine. This battle was on a different level from the ones he had fought between 1978 and 1980. I am not diminishing those championships at all, but this was a changing point in the evolution of Grand Prix motorcycle racing and it began with Kenny and me. It was also the equipment. Honda and Yamaha and Michelin and Dunlop were now pushing each other and had two pilots capable of using each and every improvement with two different styles. It made for dramatic racing.

Heaven, fate, gremlins or fortune, the tide turned a little in Rijeka in Yugoslavia. One of the ways that I could detect Kenny's level of confidence was by his body language. I knew that if he jiggled his left leg then he was more nervous than normal. On the grid I looked over and, sure enough, I could see the leg moving. Kel Carruthers, Kenny's crew chief and a former world champion himself, was there and talking to Kenny. They were going back and forth. They started to lift the fuel tank and I said softly to myself: 'It's over.' I knew that meant Kenny wanted to make a change to the setting on his rear shock. I caught Kel's eye and he gently shook his head. He knew I knew. That shock adjustment meant the heat escaped from the engine when they lifted the tank up. I knew the Yamahas were sensitive to that engine heat and needed it to start properly. The quirk of motorcycling is that key events sometimes take place at rest, away from the cut and thrust of high-speed sparring. Those decisions can go either way. The change meant that when the flag dropped and we all pushed off, I got away in the top five while Kenny was dead last going into turn one; in fact, the start photo shows Kenny still pushing as he is passed by the chase car.

I took advantage and won the race but there was further intrigue in my wake. Kenny got through the field to fourth place with his teammate Eddie Lawson ahead of him. There may not have been any team orders, as such, but there were unwritten guidelines to manipulating results. Kenny, racing for the world title for Yamaha, clearly expected Eddie, on another Yamaha, to slow down and let him pass and thus gain another two championship points. Instead, Eddie either ignored the signs from the pits or didn't see them and he kept racing. Kenny was far from happy with that, or so I heard, and the team was locked behind closed doors to turn the air blue and then clear it.

I experienced something similar in the next race at Assen. Even though it was dry in Holland for a change, I struggled. I don't know why, but from the first session it took more effort to get my rhythm and I felt out of synch. Since I was a kid in my yard I had always been able to flip a switch in my thoughts and get to that place, the zone, so I was always in front of what I needed to do next on my bike. But not that weekend, in any practice or qualifying session or in the race.

As well as race winner Kenny, my teammate Takazumi was quicker than me. I was a good way back and, while I did not expect Takazumi to ease up, in the heat of the moment and with tiredness and adrenalin merging with disappointment, I came in after the race and expressed my feelings to Erv. I told him Takazumi had got in my way, but beyond the griping the reality was it would not have made any difference. Another hint at my mental state came when I snapped at a reporter for the only time that season. As I made my way to the podium I saw a writer who always seemed to favour Yamaha. He asked a question and I reacted. I don't even remember what it was but I sneered: 'Well, you wanted Kenny to win anyway.' Pretty quickly I realised the folly of my ire. It was never about the need to act or be perfect, but I knew that if my mind continued down that path then I was going to end up exhausted from all the negative thoughts. Anyway, it went against my core beliefs of how to treat others.

It had been a traumatic weekend. Franco Uncini ended it in a coma after a truly awful accident. A crash left him stranded on the circuit. Kenny and Jack Middelburg managed to miss him, but Wayne Gardner didn't. Franco, the reigning world champion, was in the wrong place at the wrong time. A wonderfully consistent rider, he was struggling in 1983 due to the improvements of the Honda and the Yamahas. He crashed and tried to crawl to the edge of the track and safety. He never got there. Wayne, riding in his first Grand Prix, hit him and Franco was spun around like a rag doll. His helmet came off. Wayne would say he had been waiting for this race all his life but it ended up being the best and worst day of his career. That was effectively the end for Franco; he recovered and rode on until 1985 but he was never on the podium again. It was over for him.

I went home to Shreveport after that race and the intensity increased. I was looking forward to going to Belgium next because it was now my all-time favourite track, and also because Dad was coming to see me race in a Grand Prix. He was scared of flying, which came from the war, but this time I was going home to get him. I left Holland on Sunday and we were back in Belgium on Wednesday. It was a quick turnaround for me, and tiring, but it would be the only Grand Prix Dad ever went to. Dad would still go to watch when I raced at Daytona, but he had now been on the sidelines for years. He had passed on the baton to Erv and others and now stood off to one side in the tent, his respect for the team palpable. He never interfered with us doing our jobs.

I qualified on pole, a lap record, my time a full four seconds faster than the previous year, but the same went for Kenny and everyone else. Kenny and I were dredging each other's core for skill and spirit on that route snaking its way through the Armco barriers. By now Kenny and I were not waiting until the race; we would go out and every qualifying session would be a swinging pendulum for every minute.

'There's nothing else I can do, Erv. Any wider on the exits from the corners and you're going to be pulling hay out of my exhaust pipe – or worse.'

The average person would look at that and say it was going beyond what is reasonable, but I was pragmatic and, given the stakes and opposition, it was a calculated risk.

Spa was beautiful and technical in the way it rewarded precision. If you get in a groove it becomes just you, the track and the bike. Kenny and I were in that groove, like a needle in vinyl throwing up little symphonies, but he had something more, and I had a front tire issue from pushing so hard early in the race and trying to build up a quick lead over Kenny. It cost me. I pushed too hard. Yamaha were providing new parts at that point in the season and Kenny was a man of many parts himself. He was clear of me by the end and the lead was five points with Silverstone up next.

I was painfully aware that the British Grand Prix would be very difficult, but the practical side of my mind took away the doubt and fear and made me try harder to bridge the gap. I was a little discouraged and on Friday I could not get within a second of Kenny which meant I had no chance of beating him unless he had a problem.

Now I'm feeling it. Not only is Kenny going to be an issue but so are the other four-cylinder Yamaha and Suzuki bikes – Lawson is Steady Eddie and is emerging stronger, Randy is always fast at Silverstone. There are ten minutes left in the afternoon qualifying session. I am feeling resigned and have my head bowed in thought, as I sit alone in the back of the garage. The team are off to the front, working away, leaving me in my thoughts because they know how hard I am trying and can see the strain on my face and tiredness in my body language. Suddenly, I feel two hands on my shoulders. I can still feel their reassuring warmth. I look up and see a face I've never met in person.

'Do you know who I am?'

'Of course I do, Mr Surtees.'

'Just call me John,' he says with a slight wave of his hand. Then he puts it back on my shoulder.

He smiled at me. I had never met John Surtees but I knew who he was. He was the man who had won four 500cc crowns. After the last one in 1960 he switched to four wheels and then won the Formula One World Championship with Ferrari in 1964, a double that has never been equalled and is never likely to be.

'Listen, it's going to be okay,' he said. 'I know you are riding beyond what the motorcycle can do and what the tires can do. I see that. But you just keep doing that and it's going to be okay – because you *can* do that. Not many can but *you* can. I know that and you know that. Okay?'

He kind of winked at me and then walked off. I have never forgotten those words. They were exactly what I needed to hear. We were connected via those hands on my shoulders and a shared knowledge of the cost of racing.

'Thank you,' I said as he moved away.

I still needed to go out and execute my plan, but now I felt encouraged. And it was in these circumstances, beneath the threatening sky, that I felt most alive and it was because of the incredible degree of trust involved in what we do.

It would be the same sitting in a car with Mr Williams outside the Courtyard Marriott in August 2010 as it was in the garage at Silverstone in 1983; it is the trust in other people in the situation that is such a life-affirming part of being a human being, and it was trust that led to one of the most remarkable moments of my career.

I am still struggling to match Kenny. The team know it. They know we need more power. With seven minutes to go in practice I am barely hanging on to second place. On every lap I am on the edge and sometimes a little beyond.

Jean Hérissé, my Michelin engineer, is a dear friend. He has that insatiable belief in what Erv and I need and fights for us. With a few minutes to go he comes to us and says: 'We have a tire that should be better.'

I say: 'In what way?'

It has a softer compound that should help the edge grip. More traction means more corner speed.

'Okay, but can we use it for the race?'

He looked at me and kind of shrugged. 'Not sure.'

The Michelin men had turned up at lunchtime on Saturday and the chemist, himself, had brought a hand-built tire from Clermont-Ferrand. The intriguing part of racing is everything I do with throttle and lean angle is based on my belief in what the tire is capable of doing and the trust I have in my feel from it.

I go out and do one warm-up lap. I begin my fast lap on the edge. I have to push it now. There is no time to wait. The only reason I would ever do this is because I have been told there is more grip on the edge of the tire. But it is not okay and on the first corner of that fast lap it breaks traction more abruptly than the others. And now the bike is sliding. I am on my knee and if I can get it up quickly then I can slow down the rate of the inevitable highside and crash. This is not ability now. I am at the mercy of my instinctive reactions, the mechanical forces of energy and forces out of my control.

My body is thrust up and my head goes through the windscreen. I am almost thrown over the front of the bike. Somehow, impossibly, I save it. My shoulder is almost pulled from the socket but I haven't hit the ground. Somehow I didn't crash; it is over in an instant.

I tootle around the rest of the lap and come into the pits. The session is over. My heart is racing and I am livid. I take Jean and the chemist to my motorhome to find out why this happened. That is where the chemist admits in his understated French way: 'Well, we thought it would have more grip being a softer compound – but maybe we were wrong.'

It is such a candid admission that it makes me laugh. I'm not even angry any more. I think, 'Well, that's honest.' I look from him to Erv and Jean and say: 'Guess we won't be using that tire again.'

The job the Michelin chemists did to create a tire comprising more than 300 different ingredients and getting it right most of the time was amazing. I was extremely fortunate. The championship could have been over in that instant if I had crashed and been injured, but I wasn't so I could put it out of my thoughts.

The next day was race day. Erv and I communicated largely by facial expressions, but he came in for our final briefing before the race and had a sheepish smile and a few words. 'Well, we have the bike as good as we can get it.' With that it was up to me.

The race was dramatic for many reasons and the first part was the tragedy. Norman Brown was slowing and heading for the pits when he was hit by another rider, Peter Huber. Both were killed. The detritus of a disaster was littered on the tarmac, but we kept circling, waiting for the red flag that did not come. Eventually it did and we pulled in. Barry Sheene was the first. Belatedly, the race was stopped.

We had only done a couple of laps so that meant we had a complete restart. I was trying to hang on to the back of Kenny's Yamaha as best I could, knowing that Randy and Eddie were right behind me on every corner. I could not make any mistake or I'd lose ground on Kenny. After a few laps Kenny was pulling away and I was in my own battle with Randy and Eddie. I couldn't keep up this pace for much longer and a crash could mean the championship was over. Then I saw the first rain drops on the windscreen and my visor. Glancing around the sky, I saw the clouds were dark. Another lap, more drops. Randy and Eddie eased their pace. A few more laps and the rain came and they red-flagged the race. Because I didn't slow my pace as much in the changing conditions I had built up a 1.8-second lead over Randy and Eddie.

After the rain stopped and the race restarted, Kenny disappeared in the now dry conditions and won the race. I was second. That 1.8 seconds was the difference after combining the aggregate times from both legs. I was thousandths of a second ahead of Randy and Eddie. And now the lead was two points. It meant I had to win in Sweden to be able to go to Imola and finish second. That would be enough.

I left Silverstone exhausted, but what gave me a boost and a smile was my meeting with John Surtees. I wondered how he had made that transition from bike to car and had to wait until November 2015 to get my answer as he drove me from his house to the train station after having dinner together. In the middle of the night, on a road with no lights, this 81-year-old man's precision was absolute perfection. He anticipated every movement, just as he had in 1964 and 1983. As the race for the title, the pressure from Honda and the need to beat Mike Hailwood's record coalesced into a purity of motive, I replayed his words in my head.

'It's going to be okay.'

I'm sad to say that John passed away on 10 March 2017. I will miss him as he was an inspiration to me and many others. I am privileged to have called him my friend.

The hand

Sweden would change everything for Kenny and me. It would sour relations and lead to festering disgruntlement that lasted for several decades. Fittingly, given the way we had fought so hard for so long, it would be a matter of inches that would cause such a lengthy disagreement.

Sarie and I again spent time in London before the race. We walked around Hyde Park. Coming from America I have always had an admiration for Europe's respect for parks and open spaces. At home we sometimes build on every square inch of land, so an anomaly like Central Park is revered. In Europe it is a given. We went to the Hard Rock and went to see a comedy show. Coming from America, I only understood half the humour, but it was great fun.

Anderstorp is a ramshackle, overgrown sort of circuit formed from old airport land, but I knew the bumps in the road would affect the power of the four-cylinder bikes. Then there were the banked corners that helped my bike's steering issue. There were two races left and if I could win here then I would only need to finish second in the last race in Italy to be the world champion.

I'm comfortably quickest in practice and I get my customary good start. But Kenny is also away quick and is with me. Then he gets past and picks up the pace. Suddenly, it hits me. He has been sandbagging in practice. I had assumed he was struggling to get the power to the ground with his four cylinders but it wasn't so. He was just waiting to surprise me in the race. In the slow corners I'm hanging on. On the faster banked corners, where I might expect to have an advantage, I'm not close enough to make a pass.

I figure that the only choice I have is to make a pass at the end of the back straightaway on the last lap. At every other place he is so quick that even if I get past him he will get back past me immediately. And he will not hesitate. Period.

So I begin to set up my last corner move with three laps to go. I have one chance. One lap. The last lap. As we go through the corner on to the back of the circuit he holds the inside line. In his keenness to block an overtaking move, he takes the tightest entrance and has the most lean angle yet. I swing out and carry more speed. He has blocked me from passing on the inside but the price is he gets his worst drive on to the straightaway. I get my best. As we hit second, third and fourth gear I get up next to him. In sixth gear we are matched, the differences in the bikes levelled by the raw speed. I'm now on his right side coming to the right-hand corner.

This is the corner of the championship. In these few seconds a million images flicker and fade – the leaf fire, Levy C, the protective sock, the outlaw races, races against the cops to Pop's backyard, Dad and Mr Williams, Mr Honda's photograph and Kent Andersson's grainy picture in the back of Cycle News. *I* don't think about them but they are there, coursing through my veins and sparking snapping synapses in my brain. Dot to dot, these are the building blocks that have lifted me to the most important, controversial and brutal corner of my life.

It is now about braking and blinking. You know someone is going to brake by the movement of the body. This is standard fare. You know your own braking zone. You have markers. Or you do what I do and for 90 per cent of the time you go by feel.

I know that we are close enough that if I brake a little later then I will have the inside line. In these nanoseconds I have a tremendous amount of responsibility and I am vividly aware of that. I have to do all this but retain a tiny margin of safety because the last thing in the world that I want is to take us both down and out.

I rely on my peripheral vision. Kenny and I have trained our brains to pick up wider and wider portions of the big picture. I am looking ahead but paying attention to what Kenny is doing on my left. And that is when it happened. For the first time I felt an urge to look across at Kenny's hand. I have never done this before in all our duels, but now, yards from the climax, I feel the need to look away from where we were going. In that moment things begin to speed up dramatically. From being almost tranquil at blistering speed to a rush of action, it is all on the line. Kenny sits up as if he is going to brake, but I am looking at his hand and it has not moved. He is still at full throttle. In that split second I realise he has tried to trick me. He has faked to brake. Then he squeezes the brake and I do too.

This is all happening at 70mph with thousandths of a second changing everything. We are now both deep, deep, deep. No way are we going to make this corner on the right line. He can't turn in because I am there. We both run towards the edge of the track. He goes off and I slip by for the win.

It looks like I pushed him off the track and that is what Kenny believes too. He is extremely upset.

I'm feeling lots of things but I'm not happy either.
'I can't believe you did that,' he tells me.
'Kenny, you would have tried exactly the same thing.'
I don't say you head-faked me. And I don't apologise. I know
what happened.
'Where were you when I was in the dirt?' he quips. I tell him I
was there too. We were both in too hot. Too far gone. I understand
his frustration. He knows it is a defining moment.

The press did not see it like that and I was pummelled. It was very negative towards me. Even though Kenny had come through his rivalry with Barry Sheene, Britain's most iconic rider, he was the king and I was this young kid who a lot of people did not understand. I was referred to as an enigma because I didn't fit into an easy template. Added to that, a lot of people were anti-Honda at that time because they were coming into the sport and were spending a lot of money.

The truth was Kenny had a little more margin for error than me because the Yamaha was more stable on the brakes. Where he was braking initially was my maximum, but when he didn't brake I waited a fraction longer too. That's where the skill starts and ends. After that we are at the mercy of the bike's ability to handle how much weight has transferred forwards. We subjugate ourselves to our bikes' stopping power. I was trying to maintain my line without crashing because if I crashed he was going with me.

Our relationship became more serious. For my part I would say Kenny was the best at mind games, just as Valentino Rossi would become the best in his era. I don't begrudge him that; I just know it. What transpired on that corner did not make me feel good at all, but I know I did everything I possibly could to keep my position while staying safe. For the next 30 years he was deeply unhappy about it.

Of course I wish there had been more room. But if I could rewind through all those years and approach that corner one more time, shedding all the decades of anger, would I do the same thing again?

Absolutely.

It was all I could do.

Endgame

I had a month after Sweden until the final race, the San Marino Grand Prix at Imola, to think about the situation. I needed second place if Kenny won to clinch the title. Eddie Lawson would be more than happy to boost his standing at Yamaha by being the meat in a title-deciding sandwich. And Yamaha looked to field another factory bike to aid their chances of derailing my hopes.

I was most nervous that first week at home. The closer I got to the event the more focused I became. That was relaxing for me because I had trained myself that way. I became more practical and less emotional. As each day passed I knew exactly what I needed to do. I would go over the eventualities in my head. I knew the bike and tire characteristics from the beginning to the end of the race and I had years of experience and a season of duelling with Kenny to draw on.

Then, ten days out from Imola, we got a call at the house saying Pop had gone to the hospital. He had a sinus infection. This is the man who had shrugged off his heart attack as well as the time his chest was crushed when a car he was working on collapsed on him. We thought he would be okay but he deteriorated. It became more than his nose.

Now it was his heart again. This time he did not just shrug it off and build a garage. He passed away and we were devastated. I very rarely saw my dad cry but I did then. I was due to fly out on the Monday and went to see Grandma on the Sunday.

'You know Pop would want you to go and win the championship,' she said.

She knew what Pop meant to me. He had built me ramps and cut off my crusts and been a compassionate ever-presence. I looked across at Grandma as we sat in her kitchen and asked her if I could write the eulogy.

'I think that would be exactly how it should be,' she said.

I was nearing the end of my journey to win my first championship and I admired Grandma's will. She never let anything deter her. There was always hope through strength and courage and perseverance.

I wrote the eulogy and spoke about what Pop truly meant to me, what he had overcome and the way he did it, without hurting anyone and with consideration and care. Then I had to leave them all. It was tough missing the funeral but it had to be and I carried him with me, words on the page copied into my head.

Sarie was with me in Imola. So was Ronnie. The talk was about what Yamaha might do to help Kenny. They needed him to win and to get another bike between him and me. The main candidate would be Eddie but they also asked for help from Carlos Lavado, who had already wrapped up the 250cc World Championship. He was told he had to go out and beat Freddie, but he crashed in practice and never got to race.

I usually ran on my own in practice, but this time I circled with a couple of Yamahas to see their strength and weaknesses. That Saturday evening, Audri and I were in the car on the way back from my daily call to Mom and Dad with the window down at a stop light. There was a pub on the corner and the door was open. You could hear the chanting. One group singing 'Go Kenny' and then a group would say 'Go Freddie'. I looked at Audri and we both just smiled because tomorrow only one group would be happy. The air was thick with tension, of what had been and what was to come. The long hard season, one that would be remembered as among the very best in the sport, wound a familiar circuitous way to this finale.

Kenny was on pole, I was second. I got out quickest, he caught me. And then the tactics shifted dramatically. Instead of trying to outsprint each other, wringing the last scraps of power from our bikes to eke out the slenderest of leads, Kenny slowed. In fact, as he came to the first chicane, he nearly parked his bike. He would do the same in all five of the chicanes.

I knew that he was trying to slow the pace so others could catch while simultaneously disrupting my flow. I also knew I was going to pass at Tamburello, the fast flat-out corner where Ayrton Senna would suffer his fatal crash in a decade's time. Kenny did all he could to bring others into the race, but ultimately this year had been about the two of us and that was how it ended.

I pass him and he passes me. Five laps from the end he appears to accept that his tactics are not going to work. We are in another zone to the rest. He ups the pace and, once he does that, I stop trying to pass him. He is trying as hard as possible now but I am staying with him. I don't need to continue at this pace. I slow to be more cautious.

Eddie is not close enough to have an effect on all this and then I come on to the front straightaway for the chequered flag and the first person I see standing on the track is Barry Sheene. I get second place. That is enough. I am over the line. This is literally my entire life's work. I see Ronnie and, remembering the time I had gone to pick up his daughter in my van and he had questioned motorcycling as a future, he smiles and says: 'I guess you did okay.'

There is a mocked-up photograph with me sitting on a throne and Kenny holding my crown. It is not something I am comfortable with but Kenny does not seem too reluctant and I appreciate him going along with it after losing the title by two points.

We stand on the podium and it feels blissful. I had understood Kenny from the first time I had seen him 11 years earlier. After the anthem has played, we are walking off the podium and Kenny says just one thing to me.

'I gave it all I had.'

I know it was not easy to say and I appreciated it. We had been selected for random drug-testing and so we sat in a room for 45 minutes, drinking water, dehydrated and exhausted, trying to make ourselves able to urinate in a cup. It was not so much awkward as resigned. After that they took us around the circuit in an open-top car. Kenny's son, Kenny Junior, later the 500cc world champion himself, was sitting between us. The fans throbbed around us and filled every inch of track. Thousands climbed over the fence. It took us an hour to make a lap as people desperately tried to get close and touch the car. It was insanity. People even tried to pull Junior off the car and so Kenny and I ended up grabbing his arms and holding on.

Eventually, I made it to the motorhome and sat on the bed. All the glimpses I had noticed – the photographs of Mr Honda and Kent Andersson and the unfathomable faith I had in riding for a Grand Prix team that had not even been created – had actually come true.

I needed to call home but it took an age to get away from the track to a restaurant that had a phone booth. The team was there in the background, wearing the 'Freddie Spencer – world champion' T-shirts. I had two calls to make.

Mom answered and Dad got on the other line.

'I did it, Mom.'

She was happy and relieved. 'Oh Freddie, that is just great. Well, we are so proud.'

I dialled the second number. 'I wish you could have been here, Mr Williams.'

'Me too, Freddie. I'm so happy for you. It's what you deserve.'

Then Mr Williams uttered the words that had become a saying between us, a little mantra that was not intended as a slight to anyone but as an affirmation, a truth that showed how a great racing duel takes place in at least two heads.

'I guess you gave them something to sleep on tonight.'

I said: 'I guess we did Mr Williams. Thank you.'

It was as good as it gets.

Breeze, Louisiana, 2010

I woke up to another beautiful October morning. My friend Jeff Manhardt was coming for a couple of days. With all the rumours and speculation about me since my divorce and since I closed the school two years earlier, he wanted to come to Shreveport to see how I was doing. I appreciated the thought. Jeff and I have been friends for a long time – he was director on the Speed Channel broadcast of the AMA Superbike races. We're going to talk through some ideas I have about a motorcycle-training DVD.

Jeff got in about lunchtime on Saturday and we went out to the Shreveport Country Club to meet Martin and Mary Lynn Stewart to have a bite to eat. I wanted him to meet everyone out there and treat him to one of Shreveport Country Club's best homemade egg salad sandwiches that I'd been telling him about. After lunch we went into the pro shop and visited Martin and his son Marty. Martin asked if we were going to play golf that afternoon, but I said: 'No, today we are going out to Keithville to see Mr Williams.'

I also wanted to show Jeff one of the possible locations for when we shot our 'on the road' segment for the DVD.

'We'll play tomorrow after lunch,' I said.

On the road to Keithville I took Jeff to the section of corners I was thinking would be perfect to show the different types of bikes and their characteristics from different camera angles.

At the end of the right and left corners there is a house that has a big oak tree. Hanging from the branches are all kinds of rocking horses, all different sizes, shapes and colours. When the breeze kicks in, it gives the illusion that they are floating in the air. Sometimes they move right then left and sometimes left then right, and when the breeze catches them they will all go round in a circle like a carousel. I was used to seeing this but Jeff wasn't. He talked about that tree on and off for the rest of the day.

Once we turned on to Williams Road, I pointed out a corner right before we arrived at Mr and Mrs Williams' house. When Mr Williams was a teenager, this corner was where he had accidentally shoved a man in an old Model T Ford pick-up off the road while trying to push-start him with a tractor.

Mr Williams had never lived anywhere else. He was born on this road. He grew up on this road. He was now living in this house his mom and dad had built. He would live here, on Williams Road, until it was time for him to go.

I had always liked that continuity in Mr Williams' life. The simplicity and routine were comforting, probably because my life was not like that at all. When we pulled into Mr Williams' driveway, Jeff said: 'This is what you would imagine a traditional country house to be like in the South.'

The house was built in the 1940s. It is an old-style, raised-roof wooden house, about 900 square feet. The house sits on about ten acres, just the right amount of property to keep Mr Williams busy, but not too big that he can't take care of it. And it's just down the street from Keithville Baptist Church where Mr Williams and his family have been members their entire lives.

When they saw us drive up Mr and Mrs Williams walked outside to greet us. I introduced them and we walked into the house. Mr Williams offered us some of Mrs Williams' sweet tea. Every time I drank some I would think of coming out here as a teenager after school and visiting – Mrs Williams would always have some sweet tea made or ready to brew. Years later she would give me that simple old teapot that had raised so many smiles.

It was reassuring to me at a time when I was competing at the top level in a sport that is anything but comfortable.

As soon as we sat down with our glasses, Jeff said: 'Mr and Mrs Williams, I feel like I already know you. Freddie has talked about you to me for years.'

Then Mrs Williams spoke right up and said: 'Has Freddie told you how long he's known our family?'

Jeff said he knew Mr Williams had been out to races with me back in the day.

Mrs Williams continued: 'So he didn't tell you he would call out here to talk to Christi and if I answered he would just hang up on me?'

Jeff looked at me smiling and said: 'No, he didn't mention that.' I was shaking my head very slowly and turning two shades of red.

I defended myself the best I could. 'I was a really shy kid, plus Mrs Williams would always say before I hung up, "*I know this is you, Freddie.*" I have to admit that did scare me a little.'

Jeff laughed so hard. 'So you could ride a motorcycle at over 200mph and race in front of thousands of spectators, but Mrs Williams scared you?'

'Yes she did,' but then I quickly added, 'but not any more of course.'

Mr Williams winked and, laughing with that great smile, said: 'I'd have hung up too, Freddie.' Then, boldly, he added: 'See what we had to deal with all these years, Jeff.'

As I was sitting there, drinking my tea, all these memories flashed through my mind. In my late teens, when I had just signed for American Honda to race Superbikes in the US, Mr Williams built a dirt track for me to practice on. And then I remembered funny moments from the first year in Grand Prix racing in 1982, when we knocked the ladder off the top of my Foretravel motorhome going through that tunnel in Austria. I thought about the quaint little hotel outside the Salzburgring and how I was amazed when I walked into it for the first time and read the hotel was established in the fifteenth century.

As we all reflected on some of those moments that Mr Williams and I shared in those first years, Jeff asked him: 'Which Grand Prix do you think was the best?'

Mr Williams mentioned the Spanish Grands Prix in 1983 and in 1985. He told the stories and Jeff was agog. After Mr Williams had explained the drama of 1985, I looked at him and said: 'What a day! But we got through it.'

He said: 'Oh boy it was not looking good.' He smiled kindly.

Before long we needed to head back to the Courtyard Marriott. We said our goodbyes and Jeff thanked Mrs Williams for the sweet tea.

As we got in the car Mr Williams was standing on the porch waving goodbye. Jeff said: 'I really enjoyed that. I could sit there and listen to Mr Williams tell those stories for hours. Thanks for bringing me out here.'

'You're welcome. I thought you'd enjoy meeting Mr Williams.'

What we experienced together is priceless. It's what it's all about. I've always understood that on some level, but now I'm realising it in a much deeper way, every day with everyone.

As we were backing out of the driveway on to Williams Road, Jeff asked me which way we needed to go to get back to the Courtyard Marriott. We could go either way but I smiled and told him to go right. I knew Jeff would want to see the rocking-horse tree one more time.

Late in the day, driving back from Mr Williams' house, the sun was setting in the west. It was a beautiful fall. It's easy not to notice how pretty the sun's rays are as they shine and reflect through the trees. Sometimes we forget we are privileged to have these experiences.

Chapter 8: **THE MAN WHO TENDED FISH (1984)**

BRIGHT AND early on Monday morning, we were on an Aeroflot flight from Milan to Moscow. It was the same weekend that the Russians shot down Korean Airlines flight 007 killing 269 people. At this time, the Cold War was still festering and the wall was still to come down. It seemed trite to be enjoying a personal high alongside the carnage and mass killing in the wider world.

There was huge relief that the championship was over but Erv was feeling the tension, so when all American passengers were told to walk into a room in Moscow his face turned ashen. 'You'd better not be carrying anything,' I joked. He did not smile back. They let us go after an hour and we boarded the flight to Japan where I was due to ride in the All-Japan Championship race the following weekend at Suzuka. It was to be a celebration and a thank-you note. I was relaxing in my JAL first-class sleeper cabin upstairs in the 747 when there was a knock on the door and Mr Oguma stepped in with his ever-efficient stride.

'Freddie-san, we have a surprise for you. We did not want to say anything until now. On Wednesday we will go for lunch at Mr Honda's house. Okay?'

I said: 'Doumo arigatou.'

Mr Oguma turned and walked out. I watched him go down the stairs. This was the destination I had been heading for even when riding round in circles in my yard.

After the long flight from Moscow to Tokyo we headed straight to the Sunshine City Prince Hotel in downtown Tokyo. I was looking forward to visiting the Honda office to celebrate our victory together and finally meeting Mr Honda. As usual, the first night I tossed and turned due to jet lag and spent most of the night waiting for the buffet breakfast served at 7am.

Then, at 10am, I got in the car with Erv, Mr Oguma, Mr Fukui and George. We drove and drove through Tokyo's mesmerising vista of metal and glass, block after block pushed close together, and then finally we came to a never-ending stone wall. It was noticeably different from all the other structures.

This was it.

My senses were soaking in every moment. I wasn't nervous. That self-consciousness I had felt on the plane was gone and I felt this was supposed to be. This was the endgame, the destination I had been searching for ever since I saw that picture on the wall at Power Cycle Honda in Shreveport 15 years earlier.

On arrival, I met Mr Honda's son first, Hiro, who had his own company called Mugen, which developed high-performance parts. Then Mrs Honda walked in from the kitchen and she welcomed us with a polite smile. As is the custom we all took our shoes off before entering the house. There was a dining table to the right, a sitting area with some chairs, and large glass doors leading to the backyard that housed a beautiful, manicured Japanese garden with a stream tended by a workman who was down on his knees.

All of sudden the hub of conversation stopped. All eyes turned to the glass doors where the workman had stopped tending the stream. He stood up and patted his cap against his side. He turned and began to fill the silence by walking towards us. I realised this was no ordinary worker. This was Soichiro Honda, the 76-year-old son of a blacksmith and a weaver, the innovator who had made an empire despite his first factory being flattened by a US bomber and then razed by an earthquake.

Nobody took their eyes off him as he moved with such purpose through the doors and across the floor. His gaze was fixed on me and, as he neared, I could see that he had tears in his eyes. Then he put his hands on my shoulders, nodded and said: 'Thank you.'

I just smiled and nodded. 'You're welcome, sir. Thank you.'

And in that moment I knew that all the things I had thought about, all the snapshots of something more, the victories and the crashes and the nagging doubt, all of it was for this moment. It was as if a jigsaw had been completed right then and there.

He nodded to everyone and walked to the dining table where he sat to my right at the head of the table. He did not talk about the glory of Sunday. In fact, the first thing he said was: 'I have these fish in my backyard. They are the most expensive fish I could find, but I'm not sure they're worth it. Yet each day I go out and take care of them. They are fragile and special. They are a challenge.'

I told him it was a beautiful yard.

'When I started in my garage I worked on engines. I thought, "How can I showcase that?" The only thing I could afford was a bicycle and I put an engine in it.'

As he said this it reminded me of my dad working in the garage.

'I had two dreams when I started my company – one was to get to the Isle of Man TT. That happened a long time ago. You gave me the second dream on Sunday.'

We talked more and then lunch was served. Mrs Honda brought out a tray full of sushi for the guest of honour. All I could do was stare. I don't like seafood, much less sushi. This was the greatest day when all that I did before made sense. But it could also be the worst day because there was no way I could eat anything on that tray. After a few moments, Mr Honda began laughing and I realised he was joking with me. He knew I would not eat the sushi. Mrs Honda brought out a cheeseburger for me. We laughed and I was relieved.

When I got back to the hotel I went back over the minutiae of the day and the decades that preceded it for the first time, and

I realised that everything I had experienced was not just about me winning races – it was about being in that room and that dewy-eyed gratitude. He was a Buddhist and I was from the Deep South, half a world and half a century separating us, but we were brought together for a purpose. I remembered the picture of him on the wall at JW Gorman and standing with his arms crossed on that TV broadcast from 1979. His ethos was never give up. We had a common bond.

There was no talk of the future that day. He was not involved in the company any more and his position was an honorary one. He had not come to a race in two years, but now I understood why: it meant so much. And he still remembered that first race back in August 1979 and all the disappointment.

Now it was on to the Japanese Championship round at Suzuka. The race went well. The riders were good and the crowd was huge, but I qualified two seconds quicker and won pretty easily, as expected. I was there for the Japanese fans. On Monday I flew home to Shreveport where a band of close friends and family were there to welcome me. Mom, Dad, Danny, Linda, Mr Williams, Grandma Spencer, Grandma Mason and Sarie all gathered for me. It was humbling. Mom, Dad, Sarie and I went to one of our favourite restaurants. I ate white bean soup and breaded veal cutlet in cream gravy. It was the dinner of champions.

The accolades kept coming. Hal Sutton, a professional golfer from Shreveport, won the PGA Championship that year, one of golf's professional majors, and we were both honoured. It still staggers me how many elite sportsmen and women came from the Shreveport/Bossier City area with a population of only around 260,000. At one point we had a string of NFL quarterbacks, including Terry Bradshaw who threw for nine touchdowns in four Super Bowls, and we have produced a rich seam of football, baseball and basketball stars, literally topped off by seven-foot-tall Robert Parish who was voted one of the NBA's all-time 50 greatest players.

We went out to Shreveport Country Club one day to take some PR photos for the banquet the city was giving for Hal and me in early October. We goofed around, me posing with his clubs and him sitting on my bike, and we valued our home-town appreciation. It was at that banquet where I looked out into the crowd and saw my brother and felt a sadness. It was difficult, knowing how I was surfing this wave of goodwill while he went down his different path.

There were some good things that came from winning the title. I began to sponsor a bunch of guys I grew up with who played softball. Four years later, my great-nephew Beaux was diagnosed with juvenile diabetes. Doctors kept believing he had a stomach virus but did not take blood tests and it was a while before they recognised the problem. At various times he was close to not making it, but he is still with us today, a father and a talented country singer who travels around Louisiana and Mississippi singing from his soul. I started hosting a softball tournament to raise awareness of the cause. Beaux's struggles mean he is in touch with the preciousness of life and that is a message for all of us.

I was also invited on to *The 700 Club*, a Christian TV progamme hosted by the evangelist Pat Robertson. Ben Kinchlow, his co-host, interviewed me as Sarie sat and watched. It was a fascinating experience. I remember a little of what I talked about and how it felt limiting. I felt there was so much I didn't know.

The state fair in late October at the Hirsch Memorial Coliseum added 'Freddie Spencer Day' to its usual roster of pig-racing and livestock shows. As I was leaving the coliseum that evening a woman walked up to me. It was one of my old teachers.

'You remember what I told you.'

I shrugged but my facial expression said I did. She went on and said: 'I told you pursuing motorcycle racing would never amount to anything. I said it was a waste of time. Well, I was wrong. I'm sorry. I should never have said that to you.'

I kind of hugged her and said: 'Thank you.'

I did not want her to feel bad. It was nice of her to say that, although the legitimacy of judgements on people's aspirations is not dependent on the outcome.

The support for me felt nice, though. I was proud of my roots and felt like I was showcasing Shreveport to the world. I felt accepted. The recognition and support from everyone, the city of Shreveport, the council and the community, was humbling. It was great to be home.

After all the attention I took a break that fall and went out on my dad's boat on Cross Lake in Shreveport. It was an idyll for me and a place to meet up with friends, relax and refocus. This was special as Dad took me out on his speedboat. It was something he was doing for himself after all the things he had sacrificed while he was ferrying me around the country from 1966 to 1978. I wanted to give back now. I had the wealth and fame and so I started to give my parents money to make sure they were comfortable, but time was more important. His tinkering with that two-stroke engine on that stripped-down, lightweight machine was his new pride.

The boat was a simple thing – steering wheel, seat, controls and gas tank. He had asked me to go out with him for months and now that racing was over I could.

'Where are you going to sit, Dad?'

'Oh, I'll be okay on the floor. I'll hold on to the gas tank.'

I would have asked how but knew there was no point in arguing. So I said: 'Okay, hang on tight.'

It was as if he was back in his garage again, all those years ago, tuning up the engine on my bikes. 'I tune them and Freddie rides them,' was his saying. He could not wait for me to get it up to maximum speed and tell him how great and fast it was. It was at almost top speed and as fast I wanted it to go when he said 'Trim it out', meaning get the boat hull out of the water even more to lessen the drag.

'Trim it out!' he repeated.

I felt the boat starting to move and buck from side to side and that made it less stable. I have raced bikes at around 200mph so speed does not scare me, but the lack of control I had when riding that boat compared to my Grand Prix bike was a world of difference. I was at the top of my game in terms of what I could feel and anticipate, but I did not like this. And yet my dad did not tell me to be careful. He just trusted my instincts and judgement. He knew this boat which was moving around. I didn't.

In a boat, 100mph feels like 200. Every bump from the waves resonated with aftershock. Feeling out of control is a frightening thing. On a bike I felt in complete control. I was out of my comfort zone.

But after a couple of runs up to maximum speed I could anticipate its movement and I relaxed more. I thought about how the critical part of riding is knowing when to get in the game, when to take control and when to let the bike do its job.

Motorcycling had taught me to do things simultaneously – to be completely in the moment while looking ahead. It is about paying attention and constant awareness. At the start of 1984, I had a world title in my pocket and more money and material things than I had ever imagined, but things were beginning to change.

The next step? I had joined the dots from the picture of Mr Honda to the flesh and bone of Mr Honda in his own house. I had my own company, my own Honda dealership, I was engaged to Sarie, everything was smooth, but this was my time of transition to becoming too practical. I was getting more distracted by life, my businesses and the profit-and-loss statements. Ask me today if that was the beginning of the end of my racing career and I would say yes, but it's easy to see it in the rear-view mirror. I didn't know it then. It was also the beginning of my journey to understanding what I now know and that is priceless.

I had based my career on what I could sense and feel. If it had been just about what already existed and the money, then I would have signed for Kawasaki. I did not get to Honda because I wrote letters or made phone calls or promoted myself. It was the only way I knew. It was all organic. But now it was changing. Now I had the responsibility of being the world champion. Now, instead of having teammates like I did in '82 and '83, it was just me and the brand-new NRS500 V4 with its unconventional design.

I know how it looked from the outside – you're the youngest world champion riding for the biggest motorcycle manufacturer and best-supported team, your home town has just thrown a 'Thank You' party and you've just got a letter from Ronald Reagan, the president of the United States. It was incredible and I was thankful. Most people would have thought this would be enough. Isn't this is what it's all about?

Wheel of Fortune

Kenny Roberts had retired from the Grand Prix scene but he was going to race in the Daytona 200 for the last time. It was also the last time they would use the original road course layout so my goal was to get pole and a lap record so that it would stand for ever. And to beat Kenny, of course, and win the Daytona 200.

There were lots of important subtexts to that final clash with Kenny. I got pole and I won the Superbike race on Friday, but now I wanted the 200. I knew it would be a 200-mile sprint between the two of us because of the speed difference between our Grand Prix bikes and 80 per cent of the field.

Part of my strategy was how to manage the pit stops. They were a crucial part of the race. Mine were near perfect. I felt as if history was reaching out from those grandstands and grabbing me. And then, with about five laps left, I realised from the changing engine sound that one of the pipes was splitting. Kenny caught and passed me and I was clinging on, just trying to finish. The pipes were right under me and above the frame and I could smell the fumes and see the exhaust burning a hole in the top of the fibreglass tank. The pitch of the engine was changing every lap. A death knell. The top speed was being slowly reduced because of the power lost through the pipe. And this time the bike did not want to come down on the exit from the steep banking. Instead, it moved further up that 33-degree wall. Even as the speed was reduced it refused to hold the line. I tried to keep my head back from the nauseating fumes and just get to the finish.

Somehow we survived and finished second in the race. In the debrief I told Erv and Jean Hérissé that I felt there was maybe something wrong with the rear tire. The cracked pipe and petrol fumes were one thing, but the way the bike kept changing lines as it was coming off the banking on to the straightaway seemed odd. Something did not feel right.

There was little time to rake over the last race with Kenny before we flew to South Africa for the first Grand Prix of the season, now on a four-cylinder bike as Honda realised the three-cylinder had reached its potential. The V4 was the future. It would not be as reliable as the 1983 bike, but it started well and I was quickest in the first qualifying session. The performance we had shown at Daytona was continuing.

Eddie Lawson was in second, relentless and consistent, steady by nickname and style, and I needed to continue improving in the second session. Erv and the crew put a new tire on for my second stint out on the track. I went out and I was trying to stay off line to get a little heat and grip into the cold tires.

After only about half a lap I was going around 30mph in second gear. I looked over my right shoulder and I saw Barry Sheene. The last thing I remember was taking my left hand off the bar to wave him through. Then I was on the ground and looking at a hay bale. It happened so fast. I started to stand up when I heard Barry's voice. He had seen my bike drop absolutely and the violent aftermath of the crash. He had stopped out of concern.

'Crackers,' he said in his London accent. 'Look at your bike.'

'What happened?'

An ambulance came and took me back to the paddock. In the garage the guys repeatedly asked me how I was. I was feeling stunned at what had happened but came back with the refrain: 'I'm fine, I'm fine.' But I wasn't. My feet were starting to hurt now. I took off my boots and the pain intensified.

'Are you okay?' Erv said again.

The shock was beginning to wear off and I confessed quietly: 'My feet are hurting bad.'

'Which one?'

'Both of them,' I said.

His eyes showed the concern and I knew then that this was more than just another accident. I still clung to the hope that it was not as bad as it felt, but Erv had seen the bike when they brought it back. The garage door had been slammed shut.

After about 10 minutes Erv came over to where I was sitting.

'You remember at Daytona when you said there was something wrong with the tires in those last few laps?'

'Sure,' I said.

'It wasn't the tire. It was the wheel.'

That was a devastating admission. It was the first carbon-fibre wheel built by Honda and put on a race bike. It was built from the same material used on the Space Shuttle tiles. They had tested it endless times at the factory's research and development unit, but there is no way of replicating the oval banking at Daytona in a science lab. And so, when I felt the bike moving up the banking, it was the wheel flexing. It taught us a lesson about how carbon fibre is very strong but also brittle. We were just at the beginning of fully understanding the way the fibres were laid over each other and the range of use and performance reliability. It had wrecked our first race as world champion and now I had broken my left foot in 14 places and my right one in 16. My feet had been caught beneath my body and the ground and had been shattered, and the only saving grace was it happened at 30mph on a warm-up lap rather than 180mph in the Daytona 200.

Sitting there, an image of what could have happened briefly went through my mind and it was sobering. I understood people's perceptions about someone who might be willing to risk themselves in a profession that most would deem so risky, but for me it was a risk I was willing to take. I recognised the gift I'd been given as the foundation of my purpose. I trusted what I could do and what I have always known. It was an unspoken agreement between the universe and me.

I listened to the doctor at the hospital and I thought, 'Well, today's Thursday, let's see how I feel by Sunday.' I sat in my hotel room for three long days and nights, just in case, consumed by boredom, crawling to the bathroom on my hands and knees. It was irrational to hold out any hope of riding with 30 fractures, but I had never been hurt much in all my years riding. I had fallen from a tree and landed on a root once and then there was the incident with the chair and Darlene Hay when I was playing basketball. I had broken my wrist three times, but never on a motorcycle, and the only racing injuries I had suffered were a broken collarbone and a thumb. This was off that scale, but I sat there on Friday and thought that if the swelling went down I might have a chance. And the forecast for rain might help us if I could walk.

Of course, I had no chance. I was still in my hotel room when Eddie won the race in the rain on Sunday afternoon, the first of many he would win in an illustrious career. That night I was pushed to my flight in a wheelchair, not exactly how I'd imagined my first race as world champion would end. The plane was heavily laden with fuel and could only take off at night because the air was so thin because of the altitude of Johannesburg. We would have a similar altitude problem because the engine was struggling in the thin air. A two-stroke engine runs on two things – air and fuel – and we had a problem with the heat and V-configuration of the engine, with the pipes running over the top of the engine tank and thus putting them in close proximity to the carburettors.

The engine needed to breathe and we were finding out that, when we hit the heights, the power would be reduced due to the lack of cool, fresh air. It was a frustrating situation. One for the engineers to figure out.

There was a month to Misano. We had some time to fix the issue, I hoped, and thankfully I healed up pretty quickly. I hoped. Dr Billy Bundrick, my orthopaedic surgeon at home in Shreveport, told me to be careful as he waved me off to Italy.

Some good news was the fact Misano is at sea level and had some big corners that suited our bike. With my broken feet not 100 per cent healed, my concern in practice wasn't my pace. That was okay. The main issue was the start because pushing a Grand Prix bike takes some effort. With two broken feet I knew it would be a very painful experience. I woke up on Sunday morning dreading having to do that.

At the start I steeled myself and waited for the flag to drop. I took the first step and my eyes began to water. The second step was worse. I let the clutch out as the engine fired and threw my leg over. Going into turn one I was in the top five and relieved, but I could barely see through the water in my eyes, which clouded my contact lenses that I had been wearing since I was 14. A few corners later my eyes cleared and adrenalin took over and I would take the lead, on my way to winning the Italian Grand Prix at Misano.

It looked easy but was anything but. I got the win and Eddie was second.

The Match Races were the following week. The transatlantic duels had become huge occasions, with national rivalries adding to the fervour of the packed crowds, but this was the last year of the heyday. Instead of being held over three days at different circuits, financial problems meant there would be six races over two days at Donington Park in the centre of England. The top riders turned up and if anyone won all six races they would get a £150,000 bonus.

Randy Mamola did not have a ride at the start of the season because Suzuki were curtailing their factory programme in 1984, so starting at the Match Races we gave him my two three-cylinder Hondas to use. He went well and won the first two races. I joked with him about how much he was going to pay me to let him win the others, but it was light-hearted talk and I took the next two. It was all going well and I was leading the fifth race but going into turn one I crashed when the bike folded beneath me. When I stopped tumbling I immediately knew what I'd done.

'My feet again!' I couldn't believe it.

Sitting on the edge of the track I felt only disbelief. In the medical centre they told me they would fly me by helicopter to a London hospital. I was angry at myself because I thought I could have done something different. I knew I wasn't over-riding – I was taking it easy and only going as fast as I needed – and I knew I was comfortable, but I hadn't caught it before the front got to the point of no return.

Sarie said: 'We need to get you to the helicopter.' She was going to push me in a wheelchair or get some crutches, but I stopped her.

'No, I can do it. I can try. Please.'

It was maybe only 50 feet but I had to do it. I didn't want to let anyone else know how bad I was hurt. I was embarrassed. And the other thing was this.was a non-championship race. I had been the one who wanted to ride here and give support to the series that had exposed me to the world in 1980. And now I'd crashed.

With my mind a mess of competing thoughts, and thinking it might somehow assuage the seriousness of what had happened, I was damned well going to walk to that helicopter. So I steadied myself for the longest 50-foot walk I'd ever had.

At the hospital in London the doctor confirmed that my feet were indeed broken again. The left was particularly bad. The metatarsals were not only fractured; this time they were completely displaced.

'We need to operate and put them back in place with pins.'

Sarie looked at me with concern.

'What do you want to do?'

I did not hesitate. 'Call Dr Bundrick. Ask him.'

Sarie had to go to the director's office to make the call. Eventually, as I tried to wish away the obvious, she came back.

'What did he say?'

'He said pack your stuff and come home. Don't let them do anything.'

'Okay. Let's go home.'

This time I gave in to the wheelchair. I had broken my feet twice in a little over five weeks, but I refused to believe that the season might be over, or even in jeopardy. In Shreveport, Dr Bundrick studied the X-rays and decided that we should let them heal on their own. Going in would create more problems. I needed intense physical therapy every day, and so they fixed me up with an electronic stimulation machine.

I would miss the next race in Spain. I was not even fit enough to use crutches at first and so, for the first time in my short Grand Prix career, I missed a race. Eddie won in Spain. I sat in my parents' house with my feet up, talking to a Spanish journalist on the phone as the race was happening. It was a lonely place.

When I did make my comeback, at the Salzburgring in Austria, I needed a win. The bike had performed well when it was upright, but there was just no consistency. The Austrian Grand Prix would be a depressing affair. Again, the race was held at altitude, up in the Austrian Tyrol, and so the engine problems were magnified. I could barely use sixth gear at the top of the back straight. No matter what adjustments we made, there was no solution to the power conundrum.

In the race I was hanging on to third place but drifting further back. It was a horrible sensation of powerlessness, but as the race wound its way to a seemingly inevitable conclusion on the last lap, Randy slowed. He let me pass to a chorus of disapproval from the massive crowd. Salzburgring is an old-style amphitheatre and the boos rained down and seemed amplified. Randy would have seen from his pit board that I was behind him. There were no team orders, as far as I was concerned, and it was not something I had either wanted or expected. Perhaps he felt obligated after we had helped him out with the V3, but the jeers and whistles were deafening as I stepped on to the podium.

'I do appreciate it,' I said to Randy, 'but please don't *ever* do that again.'

The two of us have never been close, but I was not close to any of the other riders at that time. Randy had been a top-class racer and was second in the World Championship on four occasions, but at that point in his career, his ability did not prevent him from being without a ride.

When we got to Germany for the next round this relationship took another twist. We were still struggling to get the V4 working consistently from lap to lap, let alone race to race. It was a design issue. I was still smarting from the previous round and my mounting sense that we were in trouble with this bike. The Nürburgring is also relatively high up and so the same problems looked sure to rear their heads. It made for a sombre mood for the team, but a new day always brings hope.

After the last practice on the Friday, I decided I had had enough. I told Erv I wanted to ditch the V4 and go back to riding a three-cylinder machine.

'We gave your V3s to Randy. We could ask?'

'No, no, no. I can't do that. I'm already getting booed after he let me through in Austria. If I take one of his bikes and then he needs his spare and can't ride, imagine what it will be like.'

Erv started thinking and the conversation carried on and ended with me saying to the team: 'Find me a three-cylinder. I don't care where. I'll ride anything.'

I left the team to their head-scratching and went to a welcome party for riders and car racers who had competed at the old Nürburgring. This was to be our first time on the new course and so they marked the baton-passing with a function for a timeline of legends. It was a tribute to the history that I respected so much.

One of many racers there was Niki Lauda, the Austrian Formula One champion best known for duelling with James Hunt and for the horrendous crash and fireball at the Nürburgring in 1976, and then the bravery of his comeback. He was seriously scarred, lost some of an ear and had his eyelids burnt off, but he had survived and then thrived. I had got to know him at the 1982 Austrian Grand Prix when he came over and sat in our tent. There was a resoluteness and real sensitivity about him that I liked. He was at the end of his racing career and I was at the beginning of mine.

Niki had promised to take me round the old Nürburgring in his car for a lap on the Thursday before the race. As he took me around, the precision showed that he was a master in his element. The transitions were seamless, something we are all looking for in every way. There was no waste of movement at all as we navigated the circuit, but of course my mind was wondering where he had suffered the crash that left him in a coma some eight years beforehand. As if on cue, he interrupted his commentary and, with a quick point, said bluntly: 'That's where my accident happened.'

We continued to speed by. It was so matter of fact. He never missed a beat. Suddenly, I was in a car with Niki Lauda and he was talking of the crash that almost killed him, just over there. It was a powerful moment.

On Friday night we gathered at the welcome party that the organisers threw for past winners of the German Grand Prix. I was talking to Niki when a gentleman walked up to me, never taking his eyes off mine.

He said: 'Freddie, you don't know who I am ...'

Before he could finish I cut him off.

'Of course I do, Mr Andersson. You're part of the reason I knew I would race in the World Championships one day.'

It seemed like fleeting images from the past were filled out into something real and tangible.

I went to bed that night thinking about the struggles we were having, not realising all that had transpired since I had told my team to get me a three-cylinder bike a few hours earlier.

After that meeting, Erv had sat down with the Japanese crew and gone over ideas. The one they came up with was outlandish and would not happen today. They reasoned that Marco's old 1983 chassis was still back at the workshop. The only trouble was the workshop was near Brussels about two hours away. So a few of the guys made a midnight flit and drove to Belgium and back, literally pulling Marco's bike off the lobby. The only problem then was the 1984 engine would not fit in the chassis so they found a spare 1983 engine on a shelf and used that.

The next morning Erv came to my motorhome and said: 'We've got you a three-cylinder but there are some restrictions. We don't have spares so you can run only six laps in the morning practice and four to six in the afternoon session. Then there'll be no warm-up.'

He grinned and said that should be enough.

'Okay, that's fine,' I said.

I assumed I had a new 1984 engine so I was surprised I seemed to be down on power. I came in and said something might be wrong to Erv.

'It's fine,' he said. It was all he kept saying that day every time I voiced a concern. He knew full well why the bike was not as powerful but he was not going to tell me. Not yet.

The first session was fine and in the afternoon I needed only two laps to get pole. I won the race. In the circumstances, it was some effort all round. The safe option would have been to ride the 1984 V4 bike – I had won a Grand Prix on it after all – but I was not content with a probable third place.

It was nice to win at the Nürburgring and to meet Kent Andersson and, later, to find out just what my team had been through to find me that bike, but things were becoming a struggle on and off the track.

Although the victory in Germany had been a triumph and an amazing experience, it was unsettling too. I had won the race by looking backwards and I knew that moving forwards is essential.

I was spending less time with my friends back home. Everybody was getting older, making the transition from late teens to responsible adult. Even Sarie and I were changing, although I was blind to that.

Ronnie and I bought 152 acres near Pine Road. I became part-owner of a Ford dealership and drove a new Bronco, one of the first SUVs, as part of the deal. I was doing a lot of stuff but I didn't feel settled. Just like when I took control of Dad's boat and he shouted 'Trim it out' over the roar of the engine, I was not comfortable. I was doing all these things because they are the things you were supposed to do. I wasn't asking why or what would make me happy. I didn't stop to think of Mr Honda patting his hat and tending his stream and asking whether the most expensive fish in the world were worth it. I was the world champion and I was growing complacent.

Breeze, Louisiana, 2010

As usual, right after I woke up, I took a long, brisk walk from the hotel. Even though it had been a few years since my feet had stopped hurting, it still amazes me.

Jeff and I had breakfast. Lorraine was there and, of course, we talked about her bowling league. Mrs Reine was making her delicious egg omelettes as she does on the weekends.

After breakfast we went and visited Denny's church with Mary Lynn. Then we went to the Shreveport Country Club to meet Martin and have brunch. After we ate we hit some balls and then headed out to play nine holes.

Later that evening Jeff and I sat down to really focus on a format structure for the first motorcycle-training DVD. With our years of experience in our respective fields, we were able to come up with what I felt was a good first hour for a series. The films were aimed at the first-time buyer who needed some direction on how to start their riding adventure.

I said: 'Running my school I noticed an increase in the variety of types of bikes that people owned and rode – sports bikes, cruisers and sport tourers. Too many riders were getting into trouble from not knowing the differences in each bike's handling and performance. Each of these differences affected the time and distances it took to make the radius of the corner. It depended on the bike's weight, wheel base and geometry so the riders had to change accordingly. To be able to make the right adjustment the rider first has to be aware of those differences.'

I said I could ride each bike through the same corners and we could shoot from different angles. Then we could line up the bikes next to each other in a static shot. I could talk about each bike's design differences and the adjustments needed when riding them because we are creatures of habit. We try to ride each bike in the same way but it doesn't work that way. It is what I've been trying to figure out for 15 years: how to show that in a visual way so it is easy to understand for the rider. I just hadn't figured out how!

'That would be great,' Jeff said.

We ate dinner and had a nice talk about being at this hotel. Jeff could see I was doing great. 'I understand why you would want to be here.'

'Jeff, it's where I am supposed to be right now. It's not the hotel or the club; it's all the people. It's what I feel inside.'

He left early the next morning as I was heading out for my walk. I got up earlier than usual because I wanted to spend some more time with Mrs Ada. Her mom, Lou, had passed away a few days earlier. I had grown close to Mrs Ada and we'd had a few laughs about my laundry ever since she decided I wasn't doing it any more because I didn't do it the right way – the Mrs Ada way with love and care!

I walked down to the laundry room at about 4.30am, about 10 minutes after Mrs Ada usually arrived. At that time there is only the night-shift staff up and around. Usually Danny or Ms Bernice would be on the front desk and Mrs Ada would be in the laundry room washing the linens.

I wasn't allowed to wash or dry anything, but I could help fold. And I was open and ready to become, maybe not an expert linen and towel folder, but at least somewhat proficient at it. Most importantly, I was spending time with Mrs Ada.

The day after Lou died, Mrs Ada was at the hotel making sure all was well for the staff she oversees as well as the guests. And she also checked in on me and my laundry situation because that is what she did. I understood why she was there that day. It was her distraction. And so when I walked into the laundry room, I just walked over to Mrs Ada, gave her hug and we started folding. She had to explain what I needed to do differently if I was ever going to make it as a qualified towel folder and, as I do, I followed her direction.

The fact I could ride a Grand Prix in the rain through a 120mph sweeper, drifting both front and rear tires, does not count for much right here on Monday, 11 October 2010 at 4.30am at the Courtyard Marriott with Mrs Ada folding linen.

And that is just perfect.

Getting into the rhythm of picking up the towel and folding it in the same way and then stacking it is a process. I would do the same with my riding. From the moment I would get my gear on preparing to ride my race bike in the morning practice session, no step would be skipped. I even approach getting on the bike from the same side every time. I climb on the left and grab the right handle first. It's not superstition. It's about a consistent approach, a mental procedure that allows me to focus on what I am sensing and feeling. Watching Mrs Ada go through the same step, every time, made me smile.

At that moment when I had looked up and seen the Courtyard

Marriott the only thing I had to do was believe and have absolute trust in what I sensed and felt at that moment. That's what this was about for me.

Mrs Ada stopped folding for a moment and said: 'I miss my momma's strength. She was the one who always made us feel better. She was the one who always knew what to do.'

I said: 'I know you can do it. I believe, Mrs Ada, that when we have faith in ourselves then we are showing belief and trust in where that comes from. And I sense that in you.'

'Really?'

'I do. You know I wouldn't say it if I didn't believe it.'

I finished my pile of towels and said: 'I'm going to go for my walk, Mrs Ada.' I gave her another hug and left. The most powerful feeling I had on my walk that day was that the more I understand, the simpler it becomes to see it.

Chapter 9: **FINE LINES (1984)**

IT SOUNDS strange, given that I was still world champion and the title was not settled, but the Dutch Grand Prix in 1984 was when I started looking to the next season. I could feel it. I had won the next Grand Prix races in France and Yugoslavia, and now had four wins on two different bikes to Eddie's three, but there was something that was not right.

I had got a three-cylinder bike of my own, not Marco's cast-off, but used the four to qualify on pole. It was still struggling and so I switched on race day, whereupon Giacomo Agostini, now part of the Yamaha team, brandished the rule book and made a complaint. I understood his actions, watching out for his team and rider. The upshot was I had to stick with the bike I'd qualified on. That mindset was born from the days with Dad when he would react to problems by saying, 'Well, we will make do with what we have.' I had a good lead after around a third of the race when the engine suddenly went off song, running on just three of the four cylinders. It turned out a 25-cent cap came off a spark plug so I came into the pits as it got worse. George stuck his hands under the exhaust pipe and burnt his arms as he tried to force it back on, but I just had this feeling. 'It's over.' I meant both the race and the season and would tell the press that it was slipping away.

It was the defining moment for me and, as I circled that circuit in Holland, it came to me. I should do something different. Next year I wanted to win not one but two world titles. I wanted the 500 and 250 double.

I got everybody together in my motorhome as Randy celebrated the victory. Eddie was fourth, his lowest position of the season, but he was relentlessly consistent whereas I had not even started or finished three races.

Erv, Mr Oguma and a few others were there.

I said: 'We may not win the World Championship this year if we continue to not finish races. If so then let's win two next year!'

There was scepticism. There was no factory Honda 250 at the time. Joey Dunlop was racing a 250 but it was basically the street production-based engine with a nice Grand Prix chassis and little support.

The man who was on my side from the start was Mr Oguma.

'Okay,' he said.

I appreciated that. He was a good man to have with me, but I had some influence too. There were no PRs or agents or managers between us. I dealt directly with HRC. By the time everyone left my motorhome the double challenge was definitely on its way to happening.

Kenny Roberts had tried it in 1978 when he won the 500cc title and was fourth in the 250, but nobody had pulled it off. As this season ebbed away into a sea of uncertainty, crashes, broken bones, exploding wheels and now a rogue spark-plug cap, I was looking ahead.

It was not a case of needing to prove that I could do it, but I felt it was something I should do. They gave the task to design the 250 to Satoru Horike. He had a blank sheet of paper and he designed and built a 250cc Grand Prix bike from paper to testing in three months.

My friend Butch came out to Spa for the Belgian Grand Prix. That was great and the victory meant the gap was a not insurmountable 20 points. There were still three races left, but before that denouement I had a date with Kenny.

He had declared that the race at Laguna Seca in California was to be his last hurrah on the race track and a huge crowd turned up to pay homage. I was looking forward to being a part of it with him. With all that we had been through together – the battles on the track, the mind games off it – I was looking forward to being there for his last race as well as riding in front of the west coast fans as world champion. As it was not a Grand Prix, the pressure was reduced and our goal was to go out and put on a good show for the fans. Of course we wanted to win, but the main goal was to get through the weekend unscathed.

It was a crystal-clear July day with a big blue sky for that Saturday qualifying session. On my fast lap I shot up the hill to the Corkscrew, that blind, coruscating drop, and was trying to keep the front end down while accelerating up a slight rise, no easy task. I was leaning to the right and at the last moment on the entrance to the Corkscrew I squeezed the front brake. The lever came back to the handlebars. I had no front brakes. It was like a whirlpool as I was now not in control. I had no choice but to lay the bike down. It cartwheeled away as I slid along until I came to a stop. Moments passed and I felt fine, so I got up, ran across the track and started heading for the pits. I had my helmet in my left hand and slowly my fingers began to tingle. Initially, I thought nothing of it, but it worsened as I talked to Roxy Rockwood, the former highway patrolman turned stadium announcer, and listened to his familiar baritone.

'I'll be back tomorrow, Roxy,' I told him. 'We were lucky.'

Roxy wished me well and I walked on but now the pain was rising. When I was out of earshot I turned to Butch.

'Go get the car.'

Butch looked puzzled. 'Why?'

He could see the expression on my face.

'My shoulder is starting to go numb.'

Butch drove me to the hospital near the track where the doctor took an X-ray. When he flipped on the light and I saw the tell-tale black line dissecting my collarbone, I knew I had broken it.

I could have had a plate put in, but chose not to. That fuelled the gossip that had begun to surround me. People wrote that I had turned down an operation because of my religious beliefs. There was a lot of untruths and speculation but the reality was the doctor told me this was the best way. It would heal better and stronger on its own. Ultimately, it was my choice. There were only five weeks left until the end of the season and I felt it was slipping away, over the blind entry and down the dusty turns of the Corkscrew, along the wrong line on the track and the black line on my X-ray.

I missed Silverstone and Sweden and, although I went to San Marino, I didn't race. Eddie was the new world champion. I had been resigned to that for some time but now had bigger fish to fry. I had the double to think about. That was already circulating around my mind when I took the plane to Japan for the end-of-season race there again. But this time I got off the plane and didn't make it out of the airport. Some Honda people were there to greet me and had a collective grave expression. 'You need to call home. Your father has had an accident.'

I rang the hospital and Linda was hysterical. Dad was in intensive care.

Mom came on the phone. 'You need to come home, Freddie.'

I knew then that it was serious because Mom would never say that to me. Her attitude was always that I should focus on my job and everything else would be fine. When she said those words, I knew Dad was in trouble. He had suffered terrible injuries after crashing his boat. It hadn't been his fault, but the truth was they did not think he would even make it through the night.

As I boarded the next plane home, I had hours to think about the past, what was happening at home and what might now be, all the great memories, sacrifices, struggles. In my comfortable first-class seat I closed my eyes and in my thoughts I said, 'Please help him make it through the night.' Why only one night? Because we had to take it one day at a time and to get better had to start with those few hours. It was the longest flight of my life. I got off the plane at Los Angeles Airport and rang the hospital. He had survived the night – there was hope.

I also thought about that boat, which I had felt so unnerved driving at the start of the year, coming apart at the seams at over 100mph on Cross Lake, the deck literally splintering and sending Dad spiralling into darkness.

He had almost been killed and the motor nerve had been ripped from his arm meaning that, even if he made it, he would be paralysed on that side for the rest of his life.

Dad, being Dad, did not give up. He fought on and became stable and then, eventually, he left the hospital and came home. He was out of danger but the physical injuries included a permanently paralysed left arm. It was traumatic for my mom too, but he was okay and so she told me to fly back to Japan. I had missed the race but I needed to be there because this was where we were going to test the first ever HRC factory two-stroke 250cc Grand Prix bike.

Riding that 250cc bike for the first time was amazing. We connected right away. I picked up every sensation on every corner of every lap and formed a new union with this new machine. On just my fifth lap, as I was going through the fast downhill right-hander in fourth gear at well over 100mph and at maximum lean angle, I hit a wet spot. I didn't see it until it was too late. I went sideways and should have gone down but, before I knew it, the bike had corrected itself.

I came in and Erv was expectantly waiting for my verdict.

'What do you think?'

'Erv, that bike has just saved me. More importantly, it's already great.'

I felt so blissfully comfortable on that bike. It had an intangible quality. I loved the fact that it needed different lines and a different riding style to the 500cc. By the end of the morning I was running quick lap times and believing. I had hope.

Later that week in Japan we went to HRC and I sat down with Mr Fukui to negotiate a new one-year deal.

I reasoned that if I was doing two classes I deserved at least a 50 per cent raise. We both wrote down numbers on a piece of paper, but I did not even get to show mine before he shoved his across the table. That was a game we played – who could get their paper across the table quickest. I looked at it and was disappointed. He could see the concerned look on my face and hear the tension in my voice as I smiled. He was not offering a raise of even a tenth of my salary for riding the 250. It was all geared towards wins and championship bonuses. My paper remained unread, but I did not complain and I did not ever think about going anywhere else. Honda knew that too. Only they were able to back this audacious plan and commit the resources needed to pull it off.

If I was to do the double I needed to be lighter. I was tall for a 500cc rider, at 5 feet 10 inches, and heavier than any of the top 250 riders, but I was also thin, and so shedding seven pounds before the season was going to be hard. In 1984, sports science and nutrition were in their infancy, so I did my own research and came across a book called *Eat to Win* by Dr Robert Haas. It promised to make readers lose fat and not muscle by limiting protein. From September to December I followed the programme and ate a lot of vegetables. I was helped by the fact my body had been trained to respond to change and being pushed to excel. I got down to 146 pounds, which was the lightest I had been. My fighting weight for the 500 was around 153. It was going to be a huge physical challenge, compounded by the fact my feet were still bothering me, as they would for most of the next three decades, burning most days with every step I took. I would be walking on eggshells for years.

It was when we went to Australia to test in December that I realised Honda were taking this as seriously as I was. I saw the commitment first-hand. Basically, we had two teams now. Jerry Burgess, later to find fame as Valentino Rossi's crew chief, came in as one of the 500 mechanics. Stuart Shenton was going to do that job for the 250 team. If the 250 felt like a hand-in-glove dream bike, we were still playing around with the 500. There were still no decisions on the design so we had to make do with testing the 1984 version.

We had our first proper meeting about what lay ahead while down under. I had a list of challenges I thought were going to be hard – the fact practice sessions would be run back to back, how could I jump from one bike to another and spend the least amount of time adjusting, the realisation that there would be no time for post-practice debriefs until after both sessions. I would have to store up the info.

I decided we should simulate a real Grand Prix scenario by running tests back to back as much as we could. It would prove brutal. Michelin were also developing their new radial tires and so when I showed up there were about 200 different varieties. As a factory rider, my job went beyond trying to win races. I had to recognise each sensation, feeling and action of the bike. My job was being the modern-day telemetry and if I failed to give the right feedback and got us going in the wrong direction with our development then it would disastrous for the team and for me. It is why I've always felt that testing is where I am the most focused and most often ride beyond what I'm comfortable with.

By the third day I woke up in my hotel room with my hands so badly blistered that I had to call on a doctor to lance and retape them. I did that for every day of the test after that. On the fifth day, the heat was searing and I was totally exhausted. I caught myself in the bathroom mirror and looked at the drawn face and tell-tale lines. 'Whose bright idea was this?' I asked my reflection. I was doing between 100 and 150 laps a day.

Just before I went to Australia I had bought my first house at 417 Landmark in a nice part of Shreveport. I also felt I should get an office. I had businesses and so I got a place on Milam Street, in a building that was a throwback to the days when the city was a trading port on the Red River. I hired two ladies, Jan and Judy, from a decorating firm in Shreveport to help. We picked out the paint, Ford blue, and made my office an homage to the Ford Dealership I had bought. Then we went to Dallas and the World Furniture Mart. Judy said she had got a discount on this bare sofa that supposedly had the best springs on the planet. 'Six hundred dollars,' she said.

'That's great,' I said. 'Six hundred dollars is not a bad price.'

'Oh no,' she said. 'That's the discount. The price is six thousand.'

I was shocked and said we had better go look elsewhere. I didn't think the springs looked that good, but it made me stop. I was in the market for $6,000 sofas after growing up in a house where Mom was forced to have an old black furniture set that never saw the light just so I could race.

Up until this point I had been certain about my racing and my direction. It had not seemed predestined as such, but you either believe in coincidence or you don't, and I had faith in the future. It was a faith that was about to be rocked.

Breeze, Louisiana, 2010

It started raining about halfway through my walk so I hustled it back to the hotel. After I took a shower I called Mr Williams to see if he could come by and pick me up. I needed to go to my storage room and pick up posters I had to send to some fans. And while out that way I wanted to get a haircut.

I had called and made an appointment with Kim at Olson's Hair. I always enjoyed seeing Kim and our conversations were usually about sport and mainly LSU football. Most everyone from Louisiana this time of the year is focused on football, especially LSU football.

After getting my hair cut and going by the storage unit, Mr Williams took me out to the Shreveport Country Club.

Mr Williams dropped me off and it had stopped raining so I played nine holes with Mary Lynn. We were becoming quite a team, playing together against another twosome in a little nine-hole scramble. It was more than just passing time.

After a good night's sleep I was looking forward to my morning walk, but first I had to check in with Mrs Ada.

I finished my writing for the morning and walked down the hall and looked in the laundry room. She wasn't there yet, which was unusual because it was about 4.45am, but she had mentioned that today was the day she was going to finalise all the arrangements at the funeral home. Failing to find her, I headed out on my walk.

Ever since I was a kid, whenever I was ready to ride I would just flip the switch to get in the zone. It was a mental process of intense focus. When I put my helmet on it was like shutting out the world. My mind was so clear I could see everything around me. So for me these walks were a similar experience. As soon as I walked out that side door going out to the back of the property, listening to my iPod, I would let my mind go still.

That morning as I walked, an image just appeared to me. It was just there, complete and perfect, right in the centre of my thoughts. At first I stopped to focus on it. My initial feeling was how visually incredible it was. It was a side angle view, almost translucent, a whitish grey outline of three different types of motorcycle. Each one was a slightly different size and you could tell they were at different angles and positions relative to the same place in a corner. Then the view changed to the front. Everything else stayed the same – colour, transparency, size and shape. It was a place in my thoughts I'd never been before.

The feeling hit me. This was how to show the bikes in the same corner in the DVD – how they would be positioned if you tried to go through the same corner on the same line. They would all react a little different and this would show it much better than camera angles or static shots. Layering them one on top of the other, like a computer-generated image, was a much better way.

Then, as I was comprehending what I was seeing, the image suddenly had lines drawn for each bike that showed exactly the differences in height, wheel base and geometry.

It was an interactive image and, as I understood more, it went into even more detail. I slowly started walking again and changed songs on my iPod. I took a long, slow breath and then refocused on the image. It was still there, complete in its detail, awe-inspiring in its beauty and clarity. It was the most amazing image I have ever had in my thoughts.

But then my thoughts turned back to Mrs Ada. I wanted to get back to her and see if she had made it in yet. This was going to be the toughest day yet for her and if I could help in any way with my presence or moral support then I would.

Chapter 10: **A GLIMPSE (1985)**

THE TOWNHOUSE was decorated. The office was done too and was featured in a local interior-design magazine. Mercedes AG in Germany had a deal where Formula One and motorcycle world champions could buy anything they wanted at a reduced price. I went to see Mr Kramer, the vice-president at Mercedes, and picked out a two-door coupé that was not even on sale in America. I had it shipped over.

Before the season started I sat down with Sarie to make plans. We'd been engaged for a while now. I broached the subject and we decided to get through this season. It seemed right. She had so much potential to do anything she wanted. She was brilliant. Marriage could wait. Anyway, there was a practical side to that too. I had plenty on my plate with my attempt to win two world titles in the same year and Sarie was also looking to compete in the Miss Louisiana USA pageant. Back in those days they did not like entrants to be married. Even being engaged was frowned upon. I encouraged her and told her I would support her as she had me.

She went to Monroe, Louisiana, in February and won the state pageant held at the local television station. Now she had her sights set on the Miss USA pageant in May. We both had our goals and trained hard together.

The Miss USA pageant was in Orlando and so she would come to Daytona with me and then miss the Grand Prix races in South Africa and Spain. This separation was the beginning of us going our own ways. Only years later would I realise we had already done that.

Daytona was changing too. The 200-mile race was now run with Superbikes rather than 500s and the track had been altered and so the 200 would be a slower, safer race with more reliable machines. The manufacturers sold the Superbike-based bikes to the public so the old adage – 'win on Sunday, sale on Monday' – really meant something.

For us it was a vital testing ground for the 500 campaign. So far we had not had any testing on the new bike and it had taken months to figure out how they were going to build it. Within HRC there had been puzzlement and butted heads because it was so different to the 1984 version. But the advantage was building a new 250 and 500 in tandem meant they ended up more similar than if they had been developed in isolation in different years.

I qualified quickest for the 200 on the VFR750 and for the Formula One race on the NSR500 V4. The latter was run on a Friday. I circled on my sighting lap when my face shield on my helmet came loose on the left-hand side. I came in and the team frantically tried to tape it closed. But then I stalled. I pushed the bike back and got back in position just in time and so avoided being sent to the back of the grid. I won that race from Mike Baldwin and so that was one race down. The bike felt good. Uncertainty gave way to confidence.

The next day was the 250cc race. I had a problem with leaking fuel and an exhaust pipe but won that race, as I should have done, given the performance level of my bike.

That left the 200 for the hat-trick. I did not feel any extra pressure from that scenario; I always felt pressure because it mattered. When you go out and prepare, when you have the right equipment, the right situation and the right speed, things either go your way or they don't. So far, I had broken a face shield, stalled my bike, suffered exhaust pipe failure and leaked fuel, but we had got through it all.

I got a great start and was leading the 200 as we went into the infield for the first time. Then, on lap two, the engine started to misfire, as if it was only running on three cylinders. I came around slowly. I pulled down off the banking and headed down the pit road. And then, all of a sudden, inexplicably, the misfire cleared up and I was running on all cylinders again. I stopped at my pit stall and Mike Velasco asked what had happened. I told him. They checked the bike over quickly and patted me on the back. I took off again to rejoin the race in last place, some 30 seconds back.

Words formed in my head. 'Okay, just one lap at a time.'

It was 57 laps and this had happened close to the beginning. Time was on my side. As I picked my way through the field, I caught the leaders around half distance. After that I settled into a conservative pace and brought it home to win my first and only Daytona 200.

That night, with three wins accomplished, I sat in my room with Sarie. I said: 'I know that I was expected to win these three races, because of the support I have and everything, but we overcame some issues. What's special, though, is this is Daytona. I come here and I play back images in my head about Dad and me, about going through the infield tunnel, rolling down the van windows so I could hear all the different sounds, the different bikes and the beautiful music of exhaust tones. I would listen and could tell the bikes from the sounds and could only dream that one day I might be out there on that track winning the Daytona 200.'

We should know and respect the past because it gives depth to what we are doing today. On any grid there are a hundred stories of riders, mechanics, families and owners, and the timeline of history multiplies that a thousand-fold. It gives colour and texture to the story of the last man standing on top of the podium. My appreciation of what I had done was formed by what others had done before, and so even though I was thrilled to be booked for *Good Morning America* on Monday morning, a huge TV show in America and an important opportunity to champion my sport, I was more humbled by my forerunners. Unfortunately, my spot was bumped for some celebrity news. Maybe next time.

That was the first race with the conventional NSR500, fuel tank on top and exhaust pipes under the V4 frame, the NS500 V4 would become the most successful Grand Prix motorcycle of them all. It was the start of a lot of amazing things, a redefining of history informed by all that had led to these raw moments.

Now we were heading into our shot at history. The first Grand Prix of the season was at Kyalami in Johannesburg. Now we were not riding under the HRC banner for the first time in the company's history. The team had a big-name sponsor for the first time and so we were Rothmans Honda with a blue-and-white tobacco livery. There was a small battalion of riders and mechanics, with Randy Mamola, Wayne Gardner, Ron Haslam and Didier de Radiguès all competing for the team, but I knew my main rival was going to be Steady Eddie Lawson.

I had tried to keep things as similar as feasibly possible, but the riding style had to be different for the two bikes because speed, performance and power were different. I had worked out how to leap from one to another and had ridden a myriad of bikes throughout my life, but this was a competition against the greatest riders in the world. Eddie was determined to defend his title and silence any lingering doubters, while Anton Mang, Carlos Lavado and Martin Wimmer were not about to let me just come in and rule the roost in the 250 class.

The 250 race was first in South Africa. It was good from the start. Anton and Carlos gave chase, as I knew they would, but I led into the first corner and pulled out a seven-second lead. After that it was never really in doubt. It was Honda's first win in the class since 1967. Carlos told journalists: 'The circuit was ideally suited to Freddie. I hope he does not think it will be so easy all the time. It will be different at the tighter, more demanding European circuits.'

After the podium celebration, it was on to the grid for the 500 race. This was different. If there was that beautiful symbiosis of man and machine in the 250 race, the 500's problems returned.

I had massive front tire chatter problems in the race, effectively constant vibration that would grow so bad that my jaw would hurt as I clamped my teeth shut. I settled for second place behind Eddie but it was a promising start in searing heat. Physically, after my training regime and weight loss, I felt I could cope. Mentally, well, that would be a different test.

There was a month between South Africa and the next race in Spain, so we went to the Rijeka circuit in Yugoslavia to test tires. My friend Butch came along and was so excited that he ignored my advice to get some rest on the plane and stayed up watching a film into the wee small hours.

We did all we could think of to solve that chattering problem. We tried different crank shafts in the engine with more and less weight, different chassis combinations, anything to rid us of this curse. It was a long process and, all the time, poor Butch was asleep with his jet lag in my motorhome.

By around 2pm on the second day it was time to go if we were going to make our flight from Zagreb. Testing is a never-ending search for solutions and Erv wanted a few more stabs at the conundrum. 'Why don't we do a little more?' he said. It became the refrain that afternoon. Time passed, more things were tried and the results remained inconclusive. Finally, we had to go, and I made it to the car with the now wide-awake and anxious Butch. We worked out the distance and how much time it would take and realised it was going to be quite a race for the plane.

It was beginning to rain. As we set off, the rain turned to sleet and started to restrict our vision. I gave my instructions to Butch as we travelled along the snaking mountain rounds. 'Listen, you look around the corner and tell me if there's a car coming or not.'

We drove like that in this small Yugo car, me pulling out and driving racing lines through the miserable conditions and tight corners.

'Freddie, I don't think we're going to make it,' Butch would say as his knuckles whitened and the colour drained from his face. I was not sure if he meant make the flight or the corner. I did that for around an hour and a half and, when we got to the airport, Butch had left permanent indentations on the door handles. But we made it. And now we were heading to the Spanish Grand Prix.

I did not often bother with the Sunday morning warm-up in those days. Our goal was to be ready by Saturday afternoon and so, in that last session, we would put in the race engine and do the minimum laps possible. If nobody went quicker I would just sit and wait. If somebody did then I was ready to go out there. Every session counted as qualifying at the time. The morning warm-up was used when things were not going right and we had to take things up a notch. That was the case in Spain.

We had added some weight to the engine crank shaft and that smoothed out the power delivery a little, but that day in Spain we were still trying to figure out what front tire to run. I tried two new ones but they were no better. Frustration mounted. I tried a third, the last of the new ones they had brought, and felt the improvement. There were five minutes left in the Sunday-morning warm-up session. The race itself was due to start in little more than half an hour. Things might just work out okay. As I began my first flying lap, I went through turns one and two and it felt better. Then I came to turn three, a right-hander by the pits. The only thing you can do to test a tire is to push it to the maximum. As I turned in and got to maximum lean angle I felt two little hops and the front tire lose grip. The bike went down so quickly that I did not have the time to get my right hand out. It was caught under the handlebar. My helmet hit the ground hard. I slid along until I finally came to a stop. That nanosecond of resetting, a mental check for pain, ripped leather and aching bones. I tried to stand up and then I knew I was in trouble because my right ankle screamed. Even worse, the bike had slid into the embankment and flipped into the fence. I finally stood up. A corner worker asked me if I was okay and I said I was. I got back to my motorhome as best I could. Mr Williams was already in there and could see I was hurt.

'Only let Erv inside,' I said.

It was a story that Mr Williams would delight in retelling. He would tell it again to Jeff when we went over to his house decades later, by the rocking-horse tree spinning in the wind, thinking about the DVD, sipping sweet tea and retracing those days on the carousel.

'Well, so Freddie's sitting there and it's about 10.30am, 20 minutes to go before he has to be on the grid for the race. And I know his right hand is broken. The X-rays would show that later. He has a hole in his right elbow. His right ankle is swelling too and is possibly broken. The X-rays would show a hairline fracture later. I am trying to keep ice on his hand and also trying to figure out how we're going to get a glove on that hand as it was swelling.

'It's just me and him sitting in the motorhome in silence. And I'm thinking, "I don't think he can race. I don't believe he should race." Freddie's just sitting there saying nothing but I know he's hurting and is dazed from hitting his helmet. But there are 120,000 people here and he's supposed to race two Grands Prix today – each a gruelling 40-plus minutes against the best racers in the world!

'Then the silence is broken as we hear the helicopter flying right in over the top of the motorhome and it lands next to us. And that's when I say, "Freddie, I've never said this before but I don't think you can race today."

'Freddie doesn't say anything. I just keep working on his hand and keep thinking how in the world am I going to get a glove on this hand and thumb, never mind his problem with his elbow and ankle?

'After a few minutes, King Juan Carlos came on the PA system and welcomed everybody to the 1985 Spanish Grand Prix. He said a few more words in Spanish and then welcomed his special guest for the day, the founder of the Honda Motor Company,

Mr Soichiro Honda, who was making his first appearance at a Spanish Grand Prix since the late sixties.

'The announcer said to Mr Honda, "As you may know Freddie crashed late in the morning warm-up. The bike was severely damaged and we believe Freddie may be hurt. Are you concerned?"

'Mr Honda said only, "He will win."

'Freddie sat up, looked me right in the eye and said, "There's your answer."

'I finished with the glove as best I could, put tape on his hand, elbow and ankle. He put on his gear about 10 minutes to 11 and he walked out of the motorhome – with a broken hand, fractured elbow and fractured ankle.

'I looked over at Freddie right before the start and he smiled and gave me a thumbs-up with his broken thumb. Nobody knew how bad he was hurt.'

I had to race. I had to race because Mr Honda had arrived in that helicopter and said I would win and because I could not slip further behind in the points table. I also had my team working so hard to get me out there and fix the bike, doing all this and worrying about nothing but me. That's trust and that's humbling.

'I guess we're racing,' Mr Williams had said. I guessed so too.

And when I got out there I raced as normal. Ron Haslam was always a good starter and he led but I got by and pulled away from the pack. Eddie made do with second place a long way back.

On the victory podium, I listened to the national anthem. It started to drizzle and I looked down and saw Mr Honda standing there. I waved for him to come up here with me and he walked on to the stage.

I immediately gave him a hug and whispered: 'That win was for you.'

Mr Honda smiled. 'Thank you,' he said.

I replied: 'Thank *you*. I am standing here because of you.'

He was a hard-edged self-made man with tears in his eyes as he came to the end of another road. I did not know it but he would never go to another of my Grand Prix races again. He, at least, had found the perfect full stop.

About two hours later, after the lunch break, I was back for the 250cc Grand Prix. I was leading and loving the bike, but then an exhaust pipe cracked and the engine lost power. Carlos Lavado, the Venezuelan maverick who could do really amazing things but lacked Anton Mang's consistency, won the race and led the championship. All I could do was circle slowly to finish ninth. That saw me slip down to fourth. Eddie and I shared the lead in the 500 series, but the double was going to be every bit as hard as we had thought.

Sarie was away in Orlando for almost three weeks getting ready for the Miss USA contest and there was not much communication as she was staying in dorms.

She had supported me in my racing for the last three years so now I was excited to be there for her. We had taken a trip to Dallas to watch the Miss Texas USA pageant and had been blown away by the scale. That was huge production with lots of support.

I flew down to support her. It was just the pilot and me. When we came into the executive terminal where the private planes go, he said: 'Look, Mr Spencer, it seems you have a welcoming committee.'

I looked out of the window and spotted two fans. I thought, 'That's pretty cool.'

The steps came out and the door opened. The younger of the two fans was in the front with a pen and piece of paper. He studied me before a huge disappointment consumed his face. He looked up at me and said: 'You're not Freddy Fender.'

The picture of Freddy Fender popped into my head. He was a hirsute country and western singer of Mexican origin, with a curly, thick, bushy head of hair and moustache best known for two hits 'Before the Next Teardrop Falls' and 'Wasted Days and Wasted Nights'. I walked down the steps.

'No, I'm not,' I said. 'Sorry, buddy.'

The young fans had been expecting someone famous. He shrugged and they walked off. The pilot laughed.

'You definitely don't look like Freddy Fender. It doesn't bother you what just happened?'

Still laughing as I thought it was hilarious I told the pilot: 'Absolutely not. My friend Butch and I will have something to laugh about for many years to come.'

I got in the car and drove to the pageant. Miss Texas became Miss USA, and Sarie was the fourth runner-up. She won the swimsuit competition and told the host, Bob Barker, that her boyfriend was the 500cc world champion. Then they made a joke about her dog which was called Whatshisname.

I was very proud of her, more than she ever knew. A lot of people just viewed the event as a beauty pageant but the dedication she put in every day was huge and she got scholarship money as a result. That paid for her further education and she went on to get degrees and work in finance for years. She was and still is very active in helping others in her community, raising money for many concerns.

We flew back on the Learjet and did not really talk that much. She was tired and disappointed. She had got so close, but her success gave her the opportunity to travel.

The schedule was hard but do-able although it cemented my reputation as a loner. That was not entirely fair. My entire life was about other people, and the highs and lows were related to my awareness of that fact. The pencil cracks in my relationship with Sarie were widening.

Breeze, Louisiana, 2010

I walked back in the side door and went straight to the laundry room. Mrs Ada was there and so was her stepfather Isaiah, who she calls Pee Wee. They were deep in conversation away in the back of the room and so I was going to turn around and walk back out the door. I didn't want to disturb them.

I had only made it to the lobby when Isaiah walked up behind me. I could tell that he was feeling the weight and sadness of the week. I had only known Mrs Ada and Isaiah for a few months now, but I felt very close to them. He confided in me that they needed some divine help because they owed the funeral home $1,100 and needed to pay it by 1pm that day. He and Mrs Ada just didn't know how they could get the money in that space of time.

I told him: 'I'm sorry about everything and for the loss of your wife. If I had $1,100 I would help you.'

I thought back to all the times I had spent that amount of money or far more on things that I thought I needed.

Isaiah had to make an airport run in the hotel shuttle, so I said I would talk to him later and went to check on Mrs Ada.

I found her working away. 'How are you?'

She said: 'Did Pee Wee tell you about what we owe the funeral home today?'

'He did and I wish I could help.'

She waved her hand and said: 'It's okay. I know you would if you could.'

Then she added: 'I've been praying. *"Momma, put in a good word up there so that we can afford to put you in the ground."*'

'I know you've talked about how strong-willed your momma was.'

As I was talking to Mrs Ada, the image I had been given earlier that morning, the translucent bikes and the corner, was still there in my thoughts, not distracting my focus, taking no mental energy at all, but totally complete in its detail and depth of clarity.

I told Mrs Ada I would be thinking about her today and would check in later.

What struck me about Mrs Ada that morning was that she seemed concerned but okay, at peace somehow about what was owed to the funeral home, secure in knowing that, with faith, it would work out.

Later in the day, when I saw her back at the hotel, she said she was doing much better. 'About ten this morning the phone just started ringing,' she said. Some calls were from concerned friends and some were from people she didn't even know. Friends of Momma's from way back had heard about her passing and were ringing and offering to help.

Mrs Ada was starting to get tears in her eyes as she continued: 'They would say, "I just had a feeling to call you today and offer my help". And Freddie, if one said that then five did. It was a miracle. It was as if Momma was up there telling them, "*Pick up the phone. My people need help.*"'

I was so happy for her and I gave her a big hug.

It was a powerful moment for Mrs Ada and her faith.

Mrs Ada smiled and said: 'Amen.' She had to go and take care of more arrangements because she had a lot of family and friends that would be coming for the weekend.

I was happy to get to bed early. It had been an emotional day with the image that had appeared to me in the morning and then watching what Mrs Ada and Isaiah were going through, from uncertainty to the grace of believing it would work out.

It hit me as I lay there. The two things I had never been able to figure out were what happened between Sarie and me – the personal side – and how to demonstrate all that I had learned – the professional. Now I had this image in my head and both were answered.

Chapter 11: **RAIN DANCE (1985)**

TWO WINS in one day. That was my goal. I was where I needed to be in the championship standings but I had not been able to do a double. I did not feel I needed to prove a point, but it would certainly quash the scepticism and the doubt and prove that physically and mentally I was up to the task.

I didn't manage it in South Africa, Spain or in Germany. The 250cc race was first in Germany and the weather was changing. I was on the grid and in my cocoon, the confines of that taped-up visor my comfort zone. Through that narrow strip I saw Erv getting madder than I had ever seen. Some others had been able to change their tires but we had left it too late and weren't allowed. I had to run an intermediate front and rain rear. I caught Erv's eye and motioned to him as if to say, 'It'll be okay.'

But it wasn't.

The weather turned against us. I needed a rain front too. Martin Wimmer won his one and only Grand Prix in front of his home fans and it was, of course, enthusiastically received.

A very brief hiatus and then it was the 500 race. It had finally stopped raining so hard but the track was still completely wet. I got out in the lead but then, about ten laps in, coming out of turn one from the stadium section and heading on to the first long straight, leading out of the trees, the rear wheel started to spin so much that I thought the clutch was slipping. I began to slow and had no response to Christian Sarron, the 250cc world champion who was stepping up and doing an incredible job in the 500 class. He caught me, passed me and then he won.

Afterwards Ron Haslam came up to me. He pointed. 'Freddie, look at your rear tire.'

The cord was visible all the way round the right side of the tire. It was worse than I'd ever seen before. I had burnt the tread off from all that excess wheel spinning and was looking at the bare carcass. It was a miracle that I had not crashed. It was another of those moments when anything could have happened.

I actually left there buoyed. The double still eluded me, but I had set a new lap record on the Saturday in the dry after Michelin finally made me a front tire that drastically reduced the chatter. After all the issues, from the chatter to the split pipe, I felt I was done with the problems, that it was a break in the clouds and the sun was peeking through. I was four points clear of Eddie Lawson in the title race and four adrift of Wimmer in the 250.

And so we came to Mugello.

The heat was brutal once more, claustrophobic, intense. I knew Eddie would be tough here, Steady Eddie, consistent and relentless. But now, with a bone-dry circuit, I had the front tire that I could trust and felt I could start putting some good races together. I knew this weekend was pivotal. Now I needed to stake my claim in the 500 title race. Winning at this level is very much about taking command of the moment. Now was the time. I had to believe.

My goal was always to get out quick and manage the race from there. I would go for those soft brake pads, trading maximum feel for brevity of life. All over the grid little head games were taking place, men locked behind visors and focusing on what they needed to do and banishing the spread of fear and weakness.

My plan worked. I got away quickly and soon opened up a lead on Eddie. By the time my tires started to fade I had enough of an advantage so that I could ease my pace and manage the remaining grip. To win at Mugello on a hot Sunday afternoon is never easy and is a battle of managing your resources and maintaining your belief in the bike and you.

On the podium I listened to the anthem and then tried to pop the champagne but my arms were just too tired. I could barely lift the bottle and handed it to Eddie. I hoped there would be a delay of some sort before the 250 race. There was usually time to grab a litre of water and change my shirt, but not that day. I heard the 250s going out and, literally, ran from the podium. 'Better you than me,' Eddie said as the anthem finished.

The pre-grid is where the bikes are held before they go out on the sighting lap. When I got to my bike only Anton Mang was waiting. There was no real reason for him to do that, but it was a professional courtesy that I appreciated. My respect for Anton as a racer had always been immense but at that moment it increased further. He kind of smiled at me, almost imperceptibly, but it was enough.

On the grid I tried to push my bike but it was as if my legs were made of jello. The others powered away. Normally I was a good starter, but by the time we came around after the first lap I was down in 19th place and, at that level, you don't normally make that up.

But on the bike, in my comfort zone, in the groove and rhythm, the energy slowly returned and I did begin to pick my way through the field. I got past Alan Carter, Fausto Ricci and then Anton. Only Carlos was ahead but I was able to run at his pace and then overtake him on the 16th lap. By the last lap, my 49th of that lung-sapping day, I was nearly three seconds clear of Carlos. That was unbridgeable if I stayed upright. And I did.

The feeling was one of overwhelming relief. Finally, I had the two wins in the same day at the most difficult weekend of the year. I went to the Rothmans tent, which they had started using for our press conferences. It was still a part of the sport that I was not completely comfortable with and I would not have been anything like as forthcoming as I am now. I would never have told them about what I felt on the start line, the burden of the pressure to deliver, the tiredness when trying to uncork the champagne. I did worry, sometimes, about how what I said might be construed so I kept my secrets.

I made my way back to the motorhome. Mr Williams was there but he left to go and take something to the tent, so I was alone. I sat down on the bed and looked down the length of the motorhome to the front and the table where the two trophies sat. They had said it couldn't be done, that I was crazy for trying to win two Grand Prix titles in one year. Now these two silver trophies were exhibits A and B in the case for the defence. This was everything I had ever wanted or could have imagined. This was the greatest day. I went up and touched those trophies, glinting in the softening Tuscan sun coming through the window, and then lifted them up. A strong feeling came over me. Now I know it was a foreshadowing of what was to come, but then it was as if a small window opened and, fleetingly, today, at the pinnacle of what I do, I wondered if this was all I was supposed to know.

Is this all there is?

At 23 years old it was an odd and unsettling sensation. Why would I feel like that staring, literally, at the culmination of a life's work? Why did I not feel an unshakeable sense of accomplishment? Almost as quickly as the feelings came, they went. Mr Williams came back and the window of opportunity, of choice, slammed shut. I slammed it. The choice in that moment was to recognise it and examine it or forget about it. I went to the debrief. There was a week until Austria. Another chance to win two in one day. That was my concern.

The way I could tell what was happening behind me at the Salzburgring was by watching the flags on the hillside at the top of the back straightaway. If they were waving German flags then I knew Anton Mang or Martin Wimmer was behind me. If they were the red, blue and yellow of Venezuela then I knew Carlos Lavado was charging. Even at speed I could see the enthusiasm in those faces. There were always some American flags too and they were moving as the race panned out. I had a great battle with Anton but pulled away towards the end. Another 250 win.

The 500 race was run over two parts because the rain started to fall during the race. The weather in Europe was always unpredictable. We decided to make a conservative tire selection for that second 10-lap segment. With dark clouds over the mountains, Erv and I decided to go for a full wet front and an intermediate rear. I reasoned this would give me an extra margin of grip on the front and I could manage the rear with my throttle control. After only a few laps I knew we had chosen poorly. I could barely stay with Eddie in that second part, but he got held up by a couple of riders we were lapping going through the esses leading to the finish line. That helped. Eddie thought he had won and he rode around acknowledging the crowd. I accepted that we had lost that one. We had made a mistake and Eddie had taken advantage. Fair enough. That was racing. And then, when I pulled into the pits, there was George smiling. 'You won!' he said excitedly. 'You won!'

I was relieved. Sure enough, when they added the times together from the two parts of the race, Eddie was actually three-thousandths of a second behind me. It was the closest race in my Grand Prix career and, needless to say, Eddie was not too happy about it.

The double adventure was taking its toll physically. That moment of doubt in Mugello was gone. Banished. In its place, my body was hurting. I had two double wins but had torn my tricep in the 500 race in Austria and was having trouble moving on the bike.

I took the week off after Austria and went on vacation with Sarie to La Coste, California, before the next Grand Prix, a time to reflect on a better-working bike and the rosy hue of the championships, but the injuries were stacking up. After that break I wanted to get back to business and get enough points on the board to avoid having the title races come down to the last rounds. In Yugoslavia, the next race, I qualified well on both bikes, but at the start of the second lap of the 500 race, I got distracted by a rider in front of me and hit my knee on a straw bale on the inside of turn one. At that speed it almost took my leg off and felt as if someone had swung an iron bar at me. I ran off the track at turn two, but I managed to stay on the bike. It took me a few laps to recover my bearings and my leg was hurt, but I finished second to Eddie and the lead was down to seven points.

The turning point came in Holland. It was wet again and grimy. The 250 race was routine enough, finally a win at the Dutch TT, but I didn't get to finish a single lap of the 500. From the age of 14 I always wore contact lenses when racing. I was minus 600 in both eyes and I would always have my eye doctor in Texas explain the advances in corrective surgery in case I could take advantage. It could be hard racing with contacts. At Daytona once, during qualifying on my 500cc Grand Prix bike, a lens popped out and stuck on the inside of my face shield.

I had to blink a lot to moisturise my eyes because of the lenses. One day a French magazine published a cover picture of me going into a corner with my eyes closed. For the French fans I became ET, like the extra-terrestrial in the movie.

Now I taped my helmet shut so I could avoid turbulence, because if you are going to race at close to 200mph then it helps to see.

Nobody could see much at Assen that day in 1985. Randy Mamola got away and as we were making it through the right hairpin corner I was hit from the inside. I didn't even see Christian Sarron coming. He hit me from behind. He later admitted he could see nothing because of the spray and he had to lay the bike down to try to not hit anyone. But he did. In the video of the crash it looks almost subtle, and it was as if his bike just slid under me. I became tangled up in his machine. We both crashed and I was angry at first because I knew the points lead was gone.

Then I became resigned. Eddie was in third place behind Randy and Ron but that was enough. I sat in my motorhome and saw the title lead evaporate into that dark-grey sky.

It was not the fall that was the turning point, though. The significant moment came just a lap from the end. Maybe Eddie lost his focus. Maybe it was just one of those things. He got past Ron, who later said there was no way he could stay with him doing that pace in the wet.

I will never forget the moment when Audri opened the motorhome door and said the Marlboro bike was down. I thought he must be talking about Raymond Roche on the other Marlboro Yamaha, but Audri said: 'No, it's Eddie!'

There was just no way that could have happened. Steady Eddie, relentless and consistent.

A week later I got another double in Belgium and then it got worse for Eddie in France when he failed to get off the line. As the entire field roared away into the distance he was left there, desperately trying to get his bike firing – dismounting, pushing, demanding.

Who knows what he thought in that moment, but even though Eddie rallied to fourth I was now 17 points clear. The advantage in the 250 championship was even bigger. There were three races left. I had been competing for 17 years, I had travelled 100,000 miles a year with my dad in our Dodge van when a teenager, raced 40 weekends a year, listened to the endless sound of the road and the echo of bikes, I had promoted races as a kid, outrun the police to Pop's house, I'd been an 'outlaw' and an outsider, and now those thousands of races and trophies and disappointments and spills crystallised into three more races.

What made that French Grand Prix even more special was that Bob Griffin, the local sports TV broadcaster from Channel 12 in Shreveport, had come over to report for my hometown station. His cameraman-cum-helper was my friend Gilbert Little. I told Gilbert that the weekend had turned out better than the one where we almost lost the boat and trailer on the Red River Bridge. We laughed together.

My fame was growing and I was nearing an incredible achievement, but there had been that warning sign in my motorhome in Mugello and something else was happening that I did not understand.

I needed fourth place at Silverstone to wrap up the 250 world title. The rain was relentless once more and the injuries were piling up. Martin Wimmer was sidelined after breaking his wrist at Le Mans; Carlos Lavado crashed and damaged his ankle in practice. I crashed too. It was wet but I'd found a dry line and I knew I could stay on a pencil trail if I had to. I knew how to be precise and was comfortable with my judgement. We put on an intermediate front and slick rear. I went out and in turn one got just a fraction off the dry line. I lost grip and went over the handlebars, but the bike stayed upright. I actually got up and ran after it, but I had reinjured my right thumb.

It was a bruising year. One glance at Martin on the sidelines was enough to show the vagaries of this sport. Strength of will cannot always compensate for the strength of bone.

That Sunday at the British Grand Prix were the worst conditions I had ever raced in. Before the start of the 250 race I told Erv that I just needed a fourth place, so for once let's forget about the win. In these conditions I just needed to survive. In hindsight it was the worst strategy I had all year and every lap was a struggle. Aiming lower meant my mind was hesitant, something I knew was a fatal flaw from watching Danny all those years ago. I was fifth with a lap to go, just short of what I needed. Freezing water was coming sideways into my helmet and I had to tilt my head coming on to Hangar Straight to keep it out.

They were brutal conditions. It was cold and the wind was howling. Alan Carter, a young British rider, was riding well and thrilling the home crowd but it was treacherous out there and he crashed. It was so difficult and I was barely hanging on, but I managed to stay upright and finish fourth. It was physically and mentally exhausting. It was also enough.

There was little time to celebrate before the 500 race, but riding in the wet in the 250 had helped me. At the start, the wind was blowing even harder but I opened up a big lead right away. I wanted to escape. And then it became a different sort of race. Where I had been hanging on in the 250, now it was a case of surviving. I saw my board. Sixteen seconds up after four laps. I was comfortably in the lead. Gone. But now the race became harder. Every lap took for ever. Eventually, after an eternity of lonely riding and elongated seconds, I won. And now we were close. So close. One title is in the bag. Two races left. Two chances to wrap up the double.

Sarie and I stayed at the Park Lane Hilton for a couple of days and then flew to Sweden. After the drama and wintry weather of recent races, it was a little brighter all round. I was fastest around that track in practice and then I took off in the race and there was no catching me. Eddie did all he could to get second place but I was 20 seconds clear. A country mile. The satisfaction and jubilation were huge. I had made good on the boldest of ambitions and repaid Honda's faith in supporting it.

There is a picture of me with the two bikes. I'm 23 years old and I am the three-time world champion. My overriding emotion is one of relief that I have done it. Relief that it is over. All I had thought about had been winning the championships, a single-minded focus with an intuitive driven will – at the unseen cost of everything else.

Now I realise the joy had been diminishing since 1979 when it became my job. Back at school, I had thought that maybe I would become a mechanical engineer if the racing didn't work out, even if I knew racing was my purpose. Since then the joy had reduced piece by piece, year by year. In all honesty, it was like that the whole of my Grand Prix career.

Sarie and I took a helicopter to Gothenburg Airport and

then a flight back to London courtesy of Rothmans. They put on a reception for me at the Tower of London and the British papers, the BBC and the radio were all there to document the occasion. The next day we went to Heathrow and the paparazzi were there for the world champion and the beauty queen. We were chased down the concourse and took refuge in the British Airways Concorde lounge. I had tasted it a little before at the British Grand Prix, when they closed down Regent Street for me so I could appear on my bike for the BBC's breakfast TV show, but this was a step up. We were getting attention from outside the sport and that was good for it.

This time we flew back on Concorde to New York and then took a private Learjet to Shreveport. It was an incredible sequence of events for a boy from the Deep South, but it was different to 1983. This time it all felt more matter of fact.

I went to the final Grand Prix in San Marino but I didn't race. My hand and thumb hurt from the fall at Silverstone and I was feeling exhausted. That didn't go down well. People felt I should have ridden and was making excuses. I was just drained, mentally, physically and emotionally, and I did not articulate my standpoint very well. Inside I felt they should know how hard this was.

I had to go to Japan for the end-of-year race and thank-you event for Nankai, my leathers sponsor, but I pushed too hard in practice and crashed. I hit the ground so hard that I burst open my left knee. As the guys working on that corner came up to me the bike burst into flames. I was hurting and the bike was blazing. It was a horrible end. They sewed my knee up but I couldn't race. No victory party with Nankai because I had to keep my leg elevated all night, just me, spending that Saturday night in my hotel room in Suzuka, locked away with a feeling I couldn't shake, a feeling that told me I shouldn't be there.

After Suzuka I had a few weeks for my knee to heal up before the State Fair. I was honoured with another Freddie Spencer Day, the mayor John Brennan Hussey handing me a certificate that stated a certain day was to bear my name again. It was like getting the keys to the city. It was kind and thoughtful. At the beginning of October I had another party to celebrate the championships, but it was smaller than the one the city had held for Hal and I in 1983. The Japanese came over for it and I negotiated a new three-year contract. It was all I could have hoped for. However, there was a distance I had noticed between Sarie and me and we just got through the party. The following week she came over to the townhouse and told me she was leaving. She was moving to Los Angeles. There were some opportunities out there, maybe some TV work, a new life. We never really spoke about it but it was inevitable and I didn't really think anything. In a minute she was gone.

I stayed in, more or less just sleeping. A few days later I went to the front room of my townhouse one evening, sat down on the sofa in the dark and looked out of the window into the night. I thought about how, when I was a kid, I had been so scared of the dark, but sitting here now I wasn't and then, a sense came over me.

A sense that it was over.

But what? My career? How could it be?

A year earlier in December 1984, I'd had a similar feeling. I had been sitting on the floor by the front window in the same room. The house was still and empty, waiting to be furnished, and the streetlight outside reflected a filtered glow through the half gloom, painting the dark corners. It was not a comforting light. Then, I'd had my first sense that maybe things were about to change. That night on the sofa in 1985, the feeling was even stronger.

In November I agreed to attend the NEC Bike Show in Birmingham, England, a big deal for the manufacturers and the fans. Rothmans had commissioned a famous artist called Nicholas Watts to paint a picture of me at the British Grand Prix. It was called *Rain Dance* and they had sent 500 prints for me to sign. Then I was to bring them to the show to sell. I was so bereft of energy that I found it hard to do that simple task.

I landed at Heathrow and drove to Birmingham by myself on Friday morning. I sat there in my hire car. I had waited until the last moment to arrive and now the last thing I wanted to do was go inside, because deep down I knew this part of my life was over. It connected with what I had felt before. In my car in a giant parking lot, 500 prints in the back, fans queueing outside the large warehouse, I wasn't sure what would happen next or even what I wanted to happen.

Breeze, Louisiana, 2010

I finished my walk about 7am and when I got back there was a message from Mr Williams. He wanted to know if I wanted to come round because Mrs Williams was going to make one of my favourite dishes at that time – Mexican chicken casserole.

Mrs Williams has been making her casserole for longer than I have known them. Her recipe came over to Europe with Mr Williams who would make it for us in my motorhome at Grand Prix races. So as usual, one time at the Italian Grand Prix at Monza, he made a casserole from the pre-packaged little bags of spices and ingredients that Mrs Williams sent with him. She knew the surest way to mess up her casserole recipe was to let us have too much to do.

I had set the fastest time in qualifying. We sat down and Mr Williams said: 'Well, Freddie, I guess you gave them something to sleep on tonight.'

'We'll see tomorrow, Mr Williams,' I said. 'Let's eat.'

We both took a bite of the casserole and looked at each other. Our mouths dropped open. I grabbed my drink. He went for his. I was afraid his eyes were going to bug out of his head. I tried to talk but I couldn't. My mouth was on fire. Heck, my whole head was on fire.

Finally, I said: 'What in the world happened, Mr Williams?'

He said: 'I know I only put one packet of spices in like normal. Freddie, I know I did.'

'You sure?'

He got up and checked and, sure enough, he had only used one packet.

Then I said: 'You know Mrs Williams made those packets up for you, right?'

'Yes.'

I started shaking my head. 'You don't think …'

Mr Williams started laughing. 'She did say after last season that she better get to come over for a race or two.'

'No! She wouldn't! Would she?'

We ended up having pasta for dinner that night.

Every once in a while, when Mrs Williams served her Mexican chicken casserole, I'd bring that up. Mr Williams and I would talk about it and laugh. Mrs Williams still didn't think it was that funny.

On the ride back to the Courtyard Marriott, we did not speak for a while. Watching the sun set, I had never felt more in the moment.

I said to Mr Williams: 'I miss Dad.'

I had never said that before.

He said: 'I know you do.'

'It was 11 years ago on 26 October that he died, and what I'm thankful for is that he knew how much I loved him. The last three years I only saw him a couple of times a year. We talked on the phone, but it wasn't like when I lived in Shreveport.

'And you know what I remember about the last couple of times we talked? It wasn't about my world titles or the race wins. We talked about the time spent on the road together, sharing a ham sandwich, a cold drink out of the ice chest we carried in the van, all the moments that are now funny but at the time seemed hard and small. But they were the moments that were the most priceless. Like now with you and me Mr Williams.'

Part 2
MIDDLE
(1986–2007)

Chapter 12: **NUMB (1986)**

IT STARTED in my fingers. It was a numbness that over the next year would spread up my arm and into my neck and back. My success, my very existence on a motorcycle, had been based on feel. And now that inability to feel was symptomatic of how things were going. I was becoming desensitised in every way. From the top of the podium to the tips of my fingers, there was a sense that all was not right.

The HRC team for 1986 was going to be Wayne Gardner and me. It was the template for the two-man HRC team that would be the norm for decades to come. It would be Wayne and me, then Wayne and Mick Doohan, and then then Mick and Alex Criville all the way to the modern day with Marc Márquez and Dani Pedrosa. We were to be the tandem that would start that Honda dynasty.

There was something not right with my right wrist and hand. I contacted Erv the night after I got back from Birmingham and told him I didn't think I'd be ready to test the 1986 bike in December as planned. I told him I was struggling to get prepared. That was hard to say, because since I was four years old I'd always been prepared. Erv said we would have to let HRC know. That set off a panic in me.

When Erv came to see me in Shreveport he could feel something had changed.

'You have to do what's best for you,' he said. 'What do you want to do?'

This was my friend who had taken over from my dad all those years ago. We had climbed the mountain together and now? We fired off a fax and Honda's reaction shocked me. I felt I was not getting the support I needed, or even deserved, from them. Through two world titles in a year, three in total, we had been a winning team, but now I felt they treated me like an automaton that could just repeat and repeat. They didn't know how to react when I wasn't performing like they thought I should, and I didn't know how to explain.

I was burnt out. What I didn't see at the time were all the signs that it was time for me to move on. It was me, alone, who was unwilling to see it. I was not blameless and I would become increasingly isolated and, to a degree, misunderstood.

But beneath all of this a more worrying feeling lingered and festered: racing did not seem like the most important thing any more.

I was never in it for the adrenalin rush. I was never in it for the speed. My reasons for racing were very intimate and personal: I was purpose-driven. Now Honda were questioning me, and I felt targeted and vulnerable. I wasn't so much depressed as confused. A change had happened since that night on my sofa and I couldn't shake it off, but I would get through this.

From the outside my life continued to look like the stuff of dreams. I had my second letter from President Reagan – this time it was just for me whereas before it had been jointly addressed to Hal Sutton. Yet beneath the surface I was feeling so uncertain as I waited for my hand to heal. The pain and numbness was not going away. Even my feet were getting worse. In December, Butch suggested we take a trip to get me out of my townhouse. I could afford for us to go anywhere in the world and the options were whittled down to skiing or the beach. I was so crippled by indecision that I could not decide and so we went nowhere. Sitting on my sofa in the townhouse, all alone, numb in thought, a 23-year-old world champion looked to the future with a deep-set frown.

The oddity of that time was that I was having no problem attaining success. That is the goal for most people, but we sometimes become inured to our goals and do not re-examine them for faults. They become part of us and so it is hard to change them because it involves upsetting our long-held intrinsic beliefs.

Now I look back and think something was telling me to move on and evolve, but to what? I had trusted my instinct my whole life – turning down Kawasaki for a team not yet made, feeling a sixth-sense connection with photographs of people I didn't even know – but how could I give up all this for that same sense? How could I give up what I felt I was supposed to achieve?

I'll get over it.
Shake it off.
Tomorrow will be better.

That was my thought at the time.

It was just a tough period. Sarie had gone west.

Everyone was speculating, even those closest to me.

Maybe he doesn't want it any more? Honda didn't ask what they could do to help. I was their automaton and they were annoyed. Just do your job, was the message. I told them I'd start preparing in January and could test in February.

Two decades later I was invited to the 2006 Honda Thanks Day Celebration at the Motegi circuit in Japan. All my original engineers, except the now retired Mr Oguma, were brought together for a private dinner. I sat down next to Suguru Kanazawa, then the president of HRC but once my engineer. He had seen me push the bike to the limit and beyond. He looked over now and said words that meant more than he could ever have imagined.

'Freddie-san, I am sorry about what happened between us at the end of 1985. Shy as you are, we didn't recognise that in you.' It wasn't just the words that meant so much but the meaning behind them. Then he added. 'I am shy too.'

The response of Honda all those years before had been devastating. My initial reaction then was to blame myself and believe that I should have explained myself better. I thought it would sound selfish and that it would seem that this was all about me, but it was deeper than that. I felt it was unfair. I felt betrayed.

In some ways I could understand their frustration. I was not good at expressing myself and, even if I had been, there would have been much I would have kept to myself. But I knew I should stay with Honda in the deepest of places within me and you either trust that or you don't. In return their basic message was, 'What's wrong with you?'

In those troubled days I sought refuge in the things that were constant so I drove out to see Mr Williams at Christmas. He could see my struggle. I had lost more weight. We took a walk to get some fresh air and I told him I really needed to start training. Across the street from his house was a large, metal barn next to Keithville Baptist Church. He pointed to it.

'That's your building isn't it?' I said.

'Yes it is,' he replied.

'Do you think the pastor would mind if I put some equipment in there to train? I want to get out of the house and gym. It's inspiring out here.'

He said: 'I will get in there later and clear it out.'

'Thank you, Mr Williams.'

My nephew Carey and I began to work out. We trained to the music from *Rocky*. Every day, Carey would come by and pick me up at 6am and we'd drive south down Mansfield Road and then turn and head to Keithville, where railroad tracks dissected a feed store and the post office where Mr Williams' Jeep would be parked out front as he collected the mail.

For around two hours a day we would work out. I punched a bag like in *Rocky* and, later, I would look back and wonder if that was the best thing to have done with a damaged hand; at the time I didn't understand the issue.

There was not much from Honda but I was determined. For almost three months we locked ourselves away in that barn by the Baptist church and toiled. The Robert Haas book *Eat to Win* became my guide again, although this time I was trying to add about eight pounds. I hit the bag with my taped-up wrist and missed Daytona, which did not go down well with the organisers, the media and the fans. I wanted to be 100 per cent ready for the first Grand Prix. I was hoping every day and, little by little, it seemed to be getting better.

It was not all bleak. I had a new girlfriend, Sharon Townson, who I met through Butch. She was a sweet, hometown girl who ended up creating her own swimsuit company. I also bought a new deluxe Newell motorcoach. Custom built in Miami, Oklahoma, it had a whirlpool. It was the start of racers having these huge, movable homes. Ron Dennis, the McLaren Formula One boss, actually came to have a look at it and bought one for his team. Nowadays it would cost around $1.8 million.

I never felt comfortable about my focus turning to money or the material, but I tried to make thinking that way a priority. It was what I saw around me, that being a grown-up and, more specifically, a responsible man, was most important. I never viewed it as a measuring stick of success, but I felt I should.

I would arrive in a room full of older gentlemen, all very successful at what they do, and all I sensed was an innate battle of ego and pride. It was uncomfortable for me because it didn't seem right.

Even then I would ask myself why. What was wrong with this picture? Was it because it was their choice – our choice? Was it because the self-interest would limit the enlightenment that can come from being together?

I saw that enlightenment in Levy C's life. He wouldn't have been accepted in that room because he had nothing they would consider respectable and valuable – no education, no material possessions. But for me I saw the most precious of possessions in him: the person he was in his mind, heart and spirit.

My first time back on the bike was a week before the season began, when we finally went to test at Jarama, venue for the first

Grand Prix. It was incredibly late because of all the issues and it meant a few reporters turned up to see if all the rumours of my demise were true. The Japanese crew was there. So was Erv. Jerry Burgess had moved from our team and would be working with Wayne as his crew chief.

I had not tested my hand much in the interim. I had thrown punches and hoped it was okay. At the end of the previous season my hand had been pumped full of cortisone injections so I figured it was part and parcel of racing. Nothing came easily.

Back on the bike for the first time since I had got off in Sweden after wrapping up the double, I was back in my comfort zone. I assumed it would be fine. Months of training and reflection would get me through this passing phase and I was in the best physical shape of my career.

There were a lot of rumours that I was even going to retire, but they disappeared after I qualified for the Spanish Grand Prix.

I felt great. The uncertainty disappeared. My disappointment about my relationship with HRC was pushed aside. Now I was focused again. One corner, one lap at a time, just the bike and me, like it had always been.

Once in the lead, I open up an advantage with every lap. I can feel each moment of improvement. The first five laps are great and then, gradually, the numbness gets worse and worse. I have worked around it in the past. I always look forward to seeing '10 laps to go', so I keep trying to block the uneasiness. My pit board reads + 11 with 10 laps left. It will be the last time I ever see a lead like that. On the back of the circuit, through the right and then after the fast downhill left I begin to brake for the left-hand hairpin. But as I squeeze the front brake lever nothing happens.

For as long as I live I will never forget that moment of raw panic. In racing you leave a margin for error, but it is a matter of feet or yards and it was gone in the blink of an eye. I was in first gear so the speed was low and I saved myself by running wide but I didn't crash. I got back on the track but I couldn't fathom what had happened. Thirty-one years later, I still can't completely explain it.

And now you can really talk about feeling isolated. As Wayne goes by I am trying to absorb what has happened and what might be next. I try to squeeze the brake again but my hand is not responding. When it does it is barely moving. I crawl around that circuit and pull in because I cannot race a Grand Prix bike without being able to use the front brakes. As I come into the pits the Japanese mechanics are there and – this is heartbreaking to me – they have tears in their eyes. They sense the gravity of the situation.

I tried to make sense of it.

Erv asked: 'What do you mean? The brake's not working?' The confused look on his face said it all.

'No, no,' I stuttered, as if not wanting to say it out loud and confirm it. 'The brake's working fine but ... ah, it just didn't work.' I can hear my own lack of logic. I was traumatised and absolutely in shock.

To the naked eye my wrist is a little swollen, but it is weak. Now I have to go to face the press. Iain McKay takes me into the bigger Rothmans tent – we are stepping up this year – and the journalists are all here. I know what they are thinking. I go in and sit down. I start off explaining how good it was to be back and how the race had been going really well. I know nobody has any interest in this and they just want me to fast-forward to the end. I also do it with a smile that is probably misinterpreted – arrogance, complacency, maybe even contempt, all things that are alien to me. The faces of the journalists are as one and I read the crooked smiles and cocked eyebrows. The face that says, 'What's wrong with him?' Some are concerned and avoid eye contact. I can't put it off any longer. I describe coming down the hill and say I went to

squeeze the brake and it didn't work. I begin talking about how
bad it had been at the end of 1985, when they had all pilloried
me for not racing that final Grand Prix at San Marino. I should
go further and explain just how bad it was – the injections, the
numbness, the lack of support from Honda. I should say more.

Instead the first question cuts through any explanation like
a wrecking ball. 'Freddie, there's speculation you wanted more
money and that's why you didn't go winter testing.'

'That is not the case,' I say, but how can I explain what I felt
in my motorhome that day at Mugello in 1985 or then on my
sofa at the end of the year? I wouldn't know how to begin to
explain something so painful. It goes beyond the normal sporting
interviews.

I'm shaking my head but the questioning gets worse. 'Did you
pull in because you wanted more money?' Other journalists nod
their heads and now we are adversaries. I've never mentioned not
being happy with my contract.

I think, 'You don't have any idea what I've been through.' I feel
frustration and some anger. I figure they are going to write what
they want anyway so I close up.

My reaction is no better than theirs. 'Absolutely not,' I say
curtly and it goes downhill from there.

I went home and Dr Bundrick gave me another injection. It was
normal in those days. It was routine for athletes to get cortisone
shots to get them ready to play.

The good news was I knew I had been fast before the problem
set in at the Salzburgring. In first practice, I quickly got back up
to speed. By the time Sunday came around the wrist was not good
and the numbness and pain were there. That wasn't the issue
because the Salzburgring was not that demanding, with only two
hard-braking zones, and I was running with Eddie and Wayne.
Then I came out of the chicane at the end of the front straight and
the handlebar was shaken from my hands. I managed to save it but

then I went into turn two. At the beginning of the climb up the hill I got another more violent headshake. I looked down at the front end and saw the steering damper was only connected to the frame and had broken away from the bracket connecting it to the front forks. My heart sunk. I knew the race was over. You can't race without brakes and you can't ride without a steering damper. I pulled in and was smothered by a sense of dread. Two races gone, two races unfinished, and now I would have to face the press again and the speculation and questioning would go up a notch.

I questioned myself too. There were reasons for what had happened but did I want to do this? There was a lot of talking behind the scenes and my relationship with HRC was becoming even more strained.

Around this time I started to feel bitter and angry.

How could this be? Everyone was looking for a quick, simple explanation so blame could easily be apportioned. I could not accept there was a real problem. I asked Dr Bundrick what was going on in there and whether I was doing lasting damage, but there was an element of denial too. My relationships began to change. Friends would ask what was wrong and, although they were trying to help, they didn't realise they were the 30th person to ask the same question. They say it's tough at the top and I was finding that the air is really thin up there.

Mom would always try to wash away the pain with her kindness. 'It will be okay,' she said, but even Mom, my rock, was struggling.

Dad's left arm was paralysed and he could not work at the store in the same way, so they sold Hotchkiss Street Grocery and Mom got a job at a local drugstore on the corner of Mansfield Road and 70th Street. One day that spring I got a call from my sister, saying Mom had had a fainting spell at the store and had passed out briefly.

Not long after, I drove over to their house to find Mom packing up and intent on leaving Dad. I had never seen my Mom so upset. She said she knew. She didn't have to say more.

We had known Dad had been having an affair. At Daytona in 1984, Sarie heard that my mom was also attending, as someone had seen my dad with a lady. But when Sarie knocked on the door of dad's motorhome, it opened and the lady wasn't mom. She was really upset and shocked at what she saw.

Sarie's first thought was to protect me, because she knew how I would feel. Later when I found out, I told Dad to never bring that woman to a race or anywhere near me again.

I felt anger and guilt at the same time. I told Mom not to leave and she didn't, but I think she sensed the change in their relationship and her health deteriorated.

The affair led to me saying something to my dad that jarred with all that had gone before. I found him and said: 'I will always love you but I will never respect you again.' It was a harsh statement, I felt I had to say it as I was seeing my mom suffering and feeling humiliated.

It was not that I looked at my dad as being perfect and he had never done anything to me as a kid except support me and do the best he could.

I'd never even raised my voice to him, never been disrespectful, and I thought he would be upset when I said that but he wasn't. We had been such a great team. 'I build them and Freddie races them.' That was the slogan he proudly repeated. Now the innocence and respect of those days was diminished.

Back in the spring of 1986 I was dealing with these things in my personal life as well as professional trouble. Honda were getting increasingly impatient and the racing community increasingly sceptical. I knew I wasn't riding badly. The speed was there. And I was the only one on the bike, feeling what was really happening.

I went to Germany where Honda wanted me to get my wrist checked out and see what was going on. They were questioning my commitment and did not know what to believe. The trouble was it was internal. It was not like a break or a sewn-up wound with a tell-tale scar. There was no tangible proof other than my word. Within me I was also still wrestling with the lingering question of what I should do. Where was this all going?

There were still things I wanted to accomplish in the sport. There were World Championships to win. I wanted another Daytona 200 because I'd led so many and only won one.

I had already started to think about cars. There was talk of a Formula One test with the Williams Honda Formula One team and so it seemed natural that I might step into that arena at some point. It appealed to me for many reasons, one of which was the respect I had for John Surtees. He had made the switch and won, and maybe I could too. Yet these were flights of fancy because I was unable to tell anybody why my wrist was not working and why I could not even finish a 500cc race any more.

Erv and I talked about it and we decided we had to act. I just wanted to get it fixed and then maybe those moments of change and uncertainty I felt would recede into the past and I could get back to winning. I had a nerve conduction test and clearly there was a problem. We decided we could continue struggling on or we could figure out what was wrong and get it fixed. The latter was the rational and logical decision.

Nobody knew much about carpal tunnel syndrome back then, but Dr Bundrick cut my wrist open and took pictures of frayed tendons and a nerve so over-developed that it was ten times larger than normal. The surgery involves cutting the transverse carpal ligament. Dr Bundrick stitched me back together and we started therapy.

My season was over. It was June 1986 and the Grand Prix season ended in September. I could not even bend the wrist for six weeks. All I had as a goal on the horizon was the thought of going to the Japanese Grand Prix at the end of the year, which was a tradition for me but not part of the 500cc championship. A press release was issued. Honda continued to question me. My anger and bitterness simmered alongside my boredom. For an athlete, therapy is the most excruciating part of our existence – you have to learn to be patient and disciplined – but I went to Dr Bundrick's each day where Terry Eberhardt, my physical therapist, worked away.

My attempted recovery was made worse by the fact I knew people were looking at me with sympathy. I appreciated that, but the last thing in the world I wanted was pity. I felt like I was letting everyone down. It was not a bad life all told. I had Sharon; I'd go out with Tony Trailor and Butch to our favourite restaurants in Dallas and Bernard the doorman would put a cone outside for us at Fast & Cool; there was always a glimmer of hope too, but it was the beginning of an emotional downward spiral.

Eddie won the world title from Wayne. Three years after becoming the youngest ever champion, and a year after winning two titles in the same season, I did not score a single point. I packed for Japan and Terry came with me. He had worked with professional athletes before and he would help explain to people what was going on. Pipe dreams of racing in Japan soon faded. There was no way I could ride, but we flew into Narita and then took the bullet train to Nagoya and then the ride to the Suzuka circuit.

Japan is always an assault on the senses and my abiding memory of that trip is the look on Terry's face as he experienced it. I was watching him looking at my world. We got to the circuit late, because there was no need to make it for practice, and then we opened a door to a sea of flashbulbs, frantic shouts, microphones and TV cameras. Terry's face went completely white and he was lost. He did not know whether to go left or right so I guided him to a table where we sat down. Somehow, watching Terry made it a little easier for me at that press conference. It was as if I could hover above the chaos and be on the outside looking in. Behind Terry was the dramatic vista of the Suzuka circuit, in front of him 50 or 60 eager faces. Sitting there, listening to Terry explain the bare, practical side of what I was going through, I drifted away and felt only numbness in every finger and fibre.

Breeze, Louisiana, 2010

Martin arrived at 6.30am as usual and took me from the hotel to the club. There was a golf tournament at the weekend and he had a lot of work to do. I was happy to see how the club was beginning to stage some good events. I hit some balls on the range.

As I was getting ready to leave, I noticed all the golf carts were lying out. I saw Adler, a young man who helps out around the pro shop, and asked him if he needed to wash all 70 carts for the tournament. He said he did.

I put my bag down and said: 'Adler, you go into the barn and get the hose ready. I will bring them in and you can clean them.'

He said: 'Mr Spencer, you don't need to do that.'

I said: 'Yes I do.'

Before I knew it, it was dark. I was running back to get another cart when I heard a voice.

'Hey, what are you doing?'

It was Pastor Duron.

I said: 'Helping Adler get the carts ready for tomorrow. He's a good kid and needs the help.'

Denny stopped. 'What can I do?'

'Help me take them into the barn for Adler.'

'Okay.'

We had a blast and, when we were finished, we could tell that Adler was grateful for the support.

A few days later, for the first time since I had arrived at the hotel, I had a feeling that I would be moving on soon. I had trusted that when I left Las Vegas and then when I had left my sister's. It wasn't that anything had changed here, but this was not permanent. When I walked in here two-and-a-half months ago I didn't know how long I would stay. I had a few shows and events scheduled, but that was it.

I missed my kids terribly. Keeping their pictures helped, but it wasn't enough. I didn't know how much longer I would be here or where I would go next, but I had trust and faith that I would know where when it was time.

I sat at my desk and wrote down my feelings and thoughts. I took my walk. I am very thankful to be able to walk now without any pain.

I enjoyed my morning time with Mrs Ada and I knew that it would be tough to not have that any more; the same with my chit-chats with Teresa, hearing all about her daughter who she calls 'The Queen' because she thinks she runs the house.

I'd miss Kim too. She had been cutting my hair since May when I had walked into Olson's by chance and she was the only hair stylist who had an open appointment. She had been working there for twenty years.

That Thursday, before I started feeling that I would be leaving soon, I had walked in again. Normally I would call to make an appointment with Kim but this time Mr Williams took me up there and she had a vacancy at 12. We started chatting about the usual. I told her I was going to England next month to do a special event at the London Motorcycle Show in January. Then we talked about the usual, LSU football and the like.

Then Kim said: 'How long has it been since I cut your hair.'

I said: 'About two weeks.'

'Really? Your hair is really growing fast – like really fast.'

'I noticed that too. It's one reason why I came in today. I hadn't planned to.'

She said: 'Mine does that.'

And at that very moment, I can't really explain why, I just had the feeling to say: 'Kim, do you think everything happens for a reason?'

Without hesitation, looking directly into my eyes, she said: 'Absolutely it does.' And I just knew I had to share with her what happened to me on 30 August 1987.

'Kim,' I said. 'I want to tell you a story that I have never told anyone.'

She stopped cutting my hair and sat down in the chair next to me. She leaned in with complete focus and attention and said: 'I'm listening.'

Chapter 13: **GUN-SHY (1987–88)**

DOWN ON the 673 acres I bought from some of Mr Williams' relatives, west of Shreveport in Greenwood, there were five graves of the original owners. There was a beautiful old oak with branches that reached out and gave protection from the elements. I wanted to do my best to honour these old settlers and could feel the care that had been passed on from them and down to the Williams family and now me. I planned to put a white fence around the graves and make a little walkway down there from the home I planned to build on the hill. It would literally be a path to the past and thinking about that was a brief release from the present where I was tangled up in stress and bitterness.

Everything was uncertain going into 1987. I had always been strong, but the last years had taken an emotional toll and now Honda pulled the Rothmans sponsorship deal from my team. Now I can view that as a small act of taking the pressure off me, but it was also a way of distancing themselves. I did not tell them what I felt about that decision because it was raw and real and the last thing I wanted to do was talk about it. Apart from that, I wasn't sure how to explain it anyway. I could see the sympathy snaking down that overgrown pathway to the headstones and my own name being slowly washed away by the passage of time.

The first race of 1987 was Daytona. I was hopeful and determined, ready to get the season started off right. There was still some residual friction about not being there the year before. That meant I was happy to get out on the bike and forget about everything.

I was aware how my performances would be judged and I never wanted to be accused of holding on too long, inspiring nostalgia and sympathy but not the awe of old. I could see the doubts in everyone's eyes and it hurt, but I was determined to show I could still cut it.

Kevin Schwantz was one of the newcomers. He was young and I could tell instantly that he was going to be tough. It had been two years since I had last ridden the Interceptor but we were like two old friends and I got the pole position, with a time that was almost two seconds faster than Eddie Lawson's record from 1986. I came back into the garage and the team was jubilant. All the struggles meant every little victory was appreciated and magnified. Mike Velasco, my tuner through all the Superbike years, smiled broadly. He was my 'Erv of four-strokes' and he was relieved and pleased for both of us.

'Listen, Freddie, we could do with breaking in some new pads. All we need is one lap.'

I just needed to take the bike around the track at a slow pace and lightly use the front brake to scrub in the pads on the rotors.

There were only five minutes to go in the session, so I said: 'Okay.'

No big deal. One lap. At Daytona the pit lane runs along the inside of turn one and you join the track on the outside of turn two. I saw a rider on my right coming into turn two. I did not know if he was on a fast lap or not, so I did the respectful thing and waited. Then I blended in behind him and entered the corner.

In just a few yards I was going to accelerate past him on the exit of the corner. As I moved to go by him, he crashed directly in front of me. It was a slow fall but I had only thousandths of a second to react and I have thought about my choice a thousand times since. The first option was to try to go between him and the bike, but he was still attached because of the slow speed and so that was not an option. I was not going to run over him so I decided to try to go around the bike. But I hit it and in an instant was flying in the

Eddie Lawson, Randy Mamola and me in August 1983, at the British Grand Prix at Silverstone.

Behind the fence: Mr Kanazawa, Erv, me and Sarie in August 1982, watching the air show in Sweden.

My favourite circuit: SPA Francorchamps. I'm bike #3 in the front row. Belgian Grand Prix 1983.

I'm very proud to be part of this group; this was a very special year for the Americans in Grand Prix. Kenny Roberts, Randy Mamola, Eddie Lawson (in the background) and me.

The finish line at that controversial race at the Swedish Grand Prix. Me winning against Kenny Roberts in Anderstorp in 1983.

Barry Sheene, Franco Uncini and me.

Push starting my Honda NS500 for the 1983 German Grand Prix in Hockenheim.

Sunday night in Imola after winning my first 500cc World Championship. Me, Sarie, Ronnie Hampton and all the people who made it possible.

Celebrating my victory in the 1983 Yugoslavian Grand Prix in Rijeka.

Erv and me deciding what to do next. This was taken at the Austrian Grand Prix in Salzburgring in 1984.

Randy Mamola and me in 1984 on the NS500. I loved this bike!

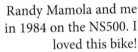

My 1985 250cc and 500cc crew. Jerry Burgess is holding the pit board. In my opinion the greatest team ever assembled – I couldn't have done it without them.

Sarie, Mr Williams and me
in 1985.

Erv and me waiting for
the right time to go out
and do a fast lap in 1985.

Celebrating with the
team after winning the
500cc race in Sweden
in 1985. I was double
world champion.

Sharon and Mr
Williams watching me
struggle in 1987.

Chelee' and me at the
Australian Grand Prix in
Eastern Creek in March 1993
with a Yamaha YZR500.

Eraldo Ferracci and me at Daytona
in March 1995 with the Ducati 916.
Eraldo gave me the chance to end
my career with a win.

Nick Ienatsch, Didier Constand (a French Canadian journalist), me and Jeff Haney at my school in Las Vegas. Along with Dale Kieffer, Ken Hill, Andre Castanos, Gregg Kearns, Yvonne and Rick, they made the school so special. We shared the joy of motorcycling with so many students.

Jordyn, Connor and me at Mom and Dad's gravesite in March 2007.

Connor doing some racing aged seven like me. Now he is making his own footsteps in track and field and I'm so happy for him and proud of him.

Jordyn and her broken arm with Grandma Spencer at her 100th birthday party in 2002.

Kenny and me on stage at the Suzuka 50th anniversary in September 2012.

Mrs Lorraine, Mrs Ada, Mrs Reine and Teresa at the Courtyard Marriott in 2017.

Alexandra and me in Sydney in March 2016.

Alexandra and me in London in 2016 on the way to a charity auction for the Distinguished Gentleman's Riders and the Movember Foundation.

air and then crashing hard into the unforgiving asphalt. My right shoulder was slammed into the track at great force. I instantly knew it was bad and I lay there with that knowledge.

The comeback of Daytona was over before it had begun. In the back of the ambulance I thought back to my first race here when I was 12 and had ended up riding in an ambulance after crashing at this same corner.

I had broken three ribs, my collarbone and separated my shoulder. Worst of all, I broke my scapula, the bone connecting the arm to the collarbone, some achievement because it is surrounded by muscle and you can take a baseball bat to it and struggle to damage it. There were two weeks before I was due in Japan for the first round of the Grand Prix season. I thought I was going to race but I was fooling myself.

I couldn't even do two laps. Everyone knew how badly I was hurt. It was blindingly obvious I could not ride, but I tried anyway. Then I accepted defeat. I stayed in Japan for the race, which Randy won, and did not wonder about fate and chance, how I got back on pole and then crashed through no fault of my own, and how I have walked away unscathed from far worse falls.

It got worse in Germany in the third round of the championship. During practice I hit my right knee on a concrete ball near the kerb on the big sweeper on the back part of the Hockenheim circuit. It was one of my favourite corners up until that moment. That weekend was notable because I was using added knee protection for the first time. When I started out leathers were almost paper thin with some basic foam padding, offering scant comfort in the event of a crash. Now things were moving. The top manufacturers realised that if they put a new substance called Kevlar into their suits then it could help. Sidi started to use it in their boots, which was a help because my feet were still burning every single day. Now Nankai put Kevlar in their suits and the first place they put it was in the knees. I had hit that concrete ball so hard that the Kevlar plate broke and splintered into my knee. When I got back to the pits I had to have it stitched up.

That was painful enough but it did not stop. In Yugoslavia, I came off my bike again, flying over the No 19 plate and then down into brutal, hard reality, and fracturing my collarbone once more. Was it mindset? Was it bad luck? And if it was bad luck, did that mean all the high points had been good luck? It was hard to fathom.

At Daytona I had been as fast as ever and then someone else had wrecked my hopes with their own misfortune. In Yugoslavia, I had barely gone down and yet broken my collarbone. In Germany, I had suffered at one of my favourite corners in all of racing.

The Grand Prix season carried on regardless. Wayne Gardner won his third consecutive Grand Prix in Yugoslavia and was on his way to the world title. Anton Mang was on the way to his third world title in the 250 class. He was 12 years older than me and would become the oldest champion of all. The vagaries of racing meant a crash in Yugoslavia the following year would end his career at the age of 38.

Time had always been more accelerated in my life. I felt responsible for the team and the mechanics and I could not let them and myself down. But the horrible truth gradually dawning on me was that I was getting a little gun-shy. Yet, after all the problems, I was still leading the British Grand Prix at Donington Park on my return.

'Absolutely sensational!' cried Murray Walker, the well-known British TV commentator, at my pace. Barry Sheene, working as his co-commentator, added: 'It's taken everyone by surprise.' Barry questioned whether I could keep it up, but in those early laps I was riding as of old.

'Racing is like riding a bicycle,' Walker enthused. 'Once you know how to do it you never forget.'

The crowd loved those laps and I rolled back the years and eked out a lead from Wayne and Eddie and the rest. But then the bike started to miss a little. A phalanx of riders went by as I slowed. I felt the chatter at the front.

'He's got a mechanical problem,' Barry said on the commentary, but it went deeper.

I pulled in and told Erv there was something wrong with the bike, but it was also my head. Gun-shy. The last place I should have been was on the track. Doubt had grown and polluted my belief. I was driven by the desire to prove I could overcome this, but I couldn't. I was back in the next round in Sweden and got seventh. I was 11th in the Czech Grand Prix.

And now I am at the 1987 San Marino Grand Prix and it is a beautiful, clear, bright, hot day on the Adriatic coast of Italy. We are racing in front of 100,000 people.

I had won here in 1984 and feel good as I move up the field. After six laps a young Italian rider, Pierfrancesco Chili, racing in his first Grand Prix in his home country, is on my tail. As we come to the end of the back straight, with a top speed of about 165mph, I sit up to brake. Pierfrancesco is changing lines. The two things happen together and he hits my back tire hard. I go from the bike weaving to a place where I am surrounded by the brightest illumination. I have the most comfortable and 'at peace' feeling I have ever experienced. In fact, it's not a feeling. It's better. There is a powerful sense of awareness and serenity all around me.

I didn't race again that season after that. Nobody knew how to help. People just told me it was bad luck and that I needed to hang in there. The air really is rarefied at that level and I was gasping for breath. I went to see the Honda officials in Japan and felt the pressure to quit. They didn't want to pay me. My relationship with those who had been deeply and personally invested in me, like Mr Fukui and Mr Oguma, remained friendly, but the money men were less understanding.

Erv did try to help. He said I should come out to California and train there for the 1988 season. The plan was to ride out at Jerry Griffiths' place in Modesto, on a small dirt oval. I would also work with Dean Miller, a physical therapist who had worked with Eddie and Wayne. Two years before I had done it all from a book I picked up and worked out in that barn with my nephew to the backbeat of *Rocky* music; now I had a professional trainer and was working to get in shape. I was seeking the right place and programme to get me back on track. I was trying anything. I booked into a suite at a Residence Inn in San Jose, rented a car and drove to Dean's place every morning. My back and feet were hurting every single day but I had a goal.

This was serious and Dean would work me so hard in those first days of training that I would feel nauseous afterwards. Maybe it helped me that I was at Jerry's, the man who had worked with Kenny all those years. It certainly helped to have Doug Chandler riding with me. He was hugely supportive. We rode hard every day.

I was fooling myself. The one thing they tell you in Vegas is that if you keep losing hand after hand you don't double down. You walk away from the table. And now I was doubling down. The more trouble I was having the more entrenched I became in my stubborn desire to believe it would get better. I didn't want to think that maybe the house always wins in this world too. I had lost my objectivity.

Testing was in Australia and because of the issues over the last year there was a second rider, Niall Mackenzie, in the team with Erv and me. Speed was not an issue. Niall still tells the story of that test in January 1988 when we met. He says: 'I thought Freddie's back. No problem.' I was quickest but there was a problem. At the end of the main straightaway, under heavy braking, my right arm was collapsing. I had no strength. I had trained hard and felt good, but as soon as you get on a 500cc bike with any witnesses, it will show up. I started losing feeling and strength in my right arm. During this time, I had an overriding sense that there must be something I was supposed to learn from each of these struggles. There had to be. Otherwise what was the purpose?

My strength has always been my mind. It was how I was able to recognise the changes in fortune, how injuries that had been avoided were now happening much more often, how things were not falling into place as they used to. But why was it happening now? The harder I tried, the stronger the current seemed to be against me. I got tired of fighting it. I got home and said: 'That's it.'

It was only my ability to work around the weakness that got me through that test. I just kind of knew. When you get to the top of the pyramid, ability and work ethic combine with determination and destiny to enable you to work around issues. I could adapt. I'd see something and make an adjustment. I did not want to acknowledge what was obvious, that even when I had been in the gym I had felt a slight weakness in my right arm and shoulder. It was not that I was getting tired on the bike from a lack of conditioning; a week earlier I had been riding dirt bikes, which requires good endurance, but fitness could not compensate for a physical ailment.

Finally, I called Erv and told him I was retiring.

'I'm exhausted,' I said. I meant mentally and emotionally from taking one step forwards and two steps back.

'It's probably for the best,' he replied. His voice was tinged with relief as much as disappointment.

If there was one person who knew the difference between me being reluctant and certain, then it was Erv. He did not try to talk me out of it. He had seen that certainty in me when he first met me in 1977.

I told Sharon and then I told Mom and Dad.

'If that's what you feel you should do then that's what you need to do, Freddie,' Mom said. She said if my heart was not in it then I should stop. She would always use that word – 'heart'. I had always told her that the worst thing for Danny was him racing for the wrong reasons and that made him hesitant; that's what got him hurt that day at the Devil's Bowl.

'Is your heart in it?'

Mom had a way of finding the right question. Dad accepted it too. His accident had changed him. He was dealing with pain in his neck, arm and hand. For years, doctors suggested amputating the arm, but he didn't want to. I imagine he felt that if he resigned himself to that then he was accepting the inevitable. As long as it was there he had hope. I understood why he felt that way and I respected his choice. He had stepped aside and allowed me to become a three-time world champion. I never forgot that, even when saying I would never respect him. In the aftermath I thought, 'Who am I to say something like that to Dad? After all he did for me?' I just couldn't accept he would do something that would hurt Mom so deeply. That night when I saw her cry is for ever etched in my memory. But ultimately that was between Mom and him. It was not my place to interfere. She forgave him and she stayed with him, taking care of him until the end.

It was hard to think how long it had taken to get here and how quickly it had gone. Kenny and Barry had said immensely kind things about my talent when they had raced against me at the start. A few years on and it was gone.

Now I had to tell Honda my decision which I was dreading, because I had so wanted to be back at the top. I went over to the office of my lawyer, Perry. Steve, my accountant, was there too. So was Ronnie, my friend and advisor. I felt a relief I find hard to describe when the fax was worded and sent. I honestly cannot remember Honda's response but I imagine it was relief too. Some of the people there wanted to see me come back and triumph but they balanced that with the repercussions if I didn't. I did not like to lose and I had always felt riding was what I should be doing, but that was a different me.

I went to Japan for the first race of 1988 and did a little press conference, attended a thank-you party and then watched as Kevin

Schwantz won on his Pepsi-sponsored Suzuki for the first time. It inevitably made me think about how we had got close to having a Coca-Cola-sponsored bike in 1986. The budget for the one-rider programme was going to be big and we got to a meeting with Frank Bean, their international marketing chief. It was going well and the designs for the bike looked beautiful with the white wave down the side, right up until the moment one of the HRC accountants told them just how lucky they would be to be involved with us. I was only 24 but I realised that was not the best negotiating technique. The deal never happened, which was probably for the best considering all the issues with my wrist and results.

On the way home from Japan, Sharon and I went to the island of Maui in Hawaii for a few days. While there we bumped into Giacomo Agostini, the great Grand Prix racer and now Marlboro Yamaha team manager. I had always got on with Agostini, who had 15 world titles and 122 Grand Prix wins, both records, but still had to deal with people tempering praise by saying he only won so many times because he was on the all-conquering MV Agusta in the late sixties and early seventies. Agostini had shown them by switching to Yamaha and winning again, beating Kenny and all those guys. I respected him greatly for doing that and so late in his career.

We talked about things and my situation came up. I told him I was looking forward to having a year off and then maybe I would look at cars. Who knew? He listened intently as we had a nice dinner and watched the sun set over Molokai and listened to the sound of the sea.

I had no clear idea of where I was going next, but cars were one option. I got an invitation from IndyCar and Formula One champion Mario Andretti to go to the Indianapolis 500. I will never forget looking down that straightaway – it seemed very narrow because of the huge grandstands that rise to the sky around the track that hold 300,000 spectators. I asked Mario the secret of the circuit.

'Not overheating the right front,' he said. He was encouraging me to go into car racing. I met many great champions that day I spent at the Indy 500.

Around that time I went to Mario's estate in the Pocono Mountains, with its own lake and wood cabins. Sharon and my nephew Carey came with me. He was looking out of the window on the first evening there and he said: 'That's Paul Newman!'

Sure enough, Paul Newman and his wife Joanne Woodward, Hollywood's golden couple, were walking past. They were friends of Mario's and were also staying on the estate. Paul was part-owner of the Newman Hass IndyCar team that Mario drove for. I told Carey he should go outside and say hello. It would be okay. Through the window, I watched as Carey approached the actor. Then Paul Newman shook his hand and Carey turned to me with a huge smile of satisfied disbelief. Paul then went back into his cabin and came back with two beers and they had a drink together. It was a priceless moment.

Every day, Carey, Sharon and me would drive behind Mario and his grandmother as we made our way the 20 miles to the track, and every day was a lesson in car control. Whenever we were growing up and you drove too fast, the voices of wisdom would use our host as the benchmark for illicit speed. And so, as Mario sped along and a local sheriff just waved at him, Carey turned to me and said: 'Who does that guy think he is – Mario Andretti?'

My friend Gilbert Little started to sound a few people out about possible ventures. Gilbert rang up the folks at Skip Barber's race school. He ran the first of the big driving academies teaching car racers. Before long, Sharon, Mr Williams and I piled into my motorhome and we were heading to Palm Beach International Raceway to test on Monday because Skip Barber had agreed to enter me in a race on Sunday in Del Mar and I needed a licence.

Skip had arranged a sponsor to cover the cost of around $10,000 for renting a car and crew. I was told to follow a racer-cum-instructor called Jeremy Dale.

The cars were basic open-wheel things with four-cylinder, twin-turbo Saab engines. I managed to keep pace with Jeremy the faster he went. Mr Williams was clearly impressed and reminisced about his old racing days with characters like Slick Swain. He looked at my times and said: 'Well, Slick would have been very proud of you.' We laughed.

After two days in that Barber Saab open-wheel race car I had my licence. I drove the motorhome back to Louisiana, got on a plane on the Thursday and flew to San Diego for my first car race. Other than the old drag car that my dad had hidden me in and a go-kart Erv had built for me, I had virtually no experience racing on four wheels. However, something felt good about the whole project and Mr Williams was very excited. I had watched him race cars when Christi and I were still in school. I asked him if he thought I could do it. He said: 'Absolutely.'

So there I was, on the grid for my first race at Del Mar. Chris Economaki, one of the most famous voices of motorsport, interviewed me on the grid. I was in the support race but it felt natural. The problems with my arm did not cross my mind. Before practice on Friday, Dorsey Schroeder, a well-known car racer at the time, had offered to take me round for a lap and had explained that on street circuits, with all the barriers and walls, you cannot see around most corners from within the car and so you had to pick up reference points that were elevated. 'As soon as you see that lighting pole, that's your reference for turn one,' he said. That was very helpful. There was a lot to learn.

Jeremy, my instructor from Palm Beach, was the fastest driver after qualifying, but the race started and I got out into the lead. Then there was an accident and the pace car came out. They had explained this to me briefly beforehand and I had seen it on TV, so I just followed it knowing that when the lights went out he would pull off and the green flag would get us racing again. As the leader, I controlled the pace. Behind me I could see Jeremy and others dropping way back and then accelerating. It seemed a curious thing to do. They did it time after time. I restricted myself to weaving from side to side to keep some heat in the tires.

Finally, with two laps left, the green flag was waved. I hit the gas but the car barely accelerated. Jeremy shot past me followed by two more cars. After four corners and what seemed like an eternity, the power returned and I accelerated. I came in after the chequered flag and was mystified. Jeremy walked back with his trophy and garland.

'What happened?' he said.

'I don't know. It just didn't accelerate.'

Jeremy frowned and with a slight smile said: 'Oh yes, didn't I tell you? The turbos will get hot if you stay at a constant speed.'

I paused.

'No, Jeremy – you didn't tell me that.'

He smiled. 'Well this might be the only time I beat you anyway.'

It was a nice, funny moment. I got back to the hotel and felt great about the day. There was a message waiting for me from Chip Ganassi, the IndyCar boss who would achieve great success with drivers such as Emerson Fittipaldi and Juan Pablo Montoya. I rang him. He said if I wanted to test his Indy Lights Car I should get to Memphis Raceway on Wednesday. I was a little shocked. I had been in a car a total of four days and now Chip Ganassi was calling me.

'I guess we're going to Memphis,' I said to Sharon.

It was exciting for a few reasons. I was intrigued at how fast this foray on to four wheels was moving, but I also wanted to go to Graceland. Mom had often spoken about seeing Elvis when he was just beginning and it is an oft-forgotten slice of history that he got his big break in Shreveport. He was contracted to perform at the Shreveport Municipal Auditorium for $18 a show as part of the *Louisiana Hayride* radio show. A year later, Colonel Tom Parker bought his contract for $10,000 and the rest is history. As I looked around Graceland, with its opulence and grandeur, it was nice to think of my mom watching the unknown Elvis, on the edge of a cultural and personal explosion. If his story told me anything, it was that all the success in the world is no guarantee of happiness, and he was probably most content in those early days, long before Graceland was built or the statue was erected in Shreveport marking the time his path crossed Mom's.

Emerson Fittipaldi, twice the Formula One champion in the 1970s, was at the Memphis Raceway testing the Marlboro IndyCar. He came over and shook my hand and said he had a story for me. It transpired that he used to tell his mother that he was going to church but instead would go racing motorcycles. One day he came home and his mother was waiting for him.

'How was church?' she asked.

'Fine,' Emerson said.

'She said I could race but never on a motorcycle. So that's why I race cars.'

The Indy Lights Car was a big step up from what I had been driving at Del Mar on Sunday and one step down from a full-blown IndyCar. Chip was brusque and did not suffer fools. At one point, his regular Indy Lights driver spun the car for a second time and Chip called him in. 'If you can't handle the pressure you shouldn't be in the car,' he said. 'Get out. Freddie, get in.' He did not have to ask twice. Overall, I did okay, reaching about the same pace as his regular driver.

The car world seemed easy and trouble-free after the last few years. Where I had felt Honda did not understand what I was going through, now people were queuing up to help. Chip began trying to put together an Indy Lights team with Jeremy and me as the drivers. I got on well with Jeremy and I thought he would be the perfect teammate. Chip went looking for sponsors. A possible deal was in the works. I was hopeful.

The contrast between this summer and the last was huge. Another famous entrepreneur and CART race-team owner, Roger Penske, said I should call if I ever wanted a test drive. I wanted to delve deeper. I was almost oblivious to Eddie regaining the world title on two wheels.

As August slowly passed it seemed this was the direction I would take, but financially things were difficult. I was still waiting for word on the Indy Lights team when I got a fax from Giacomo Agostini and was pulled back into the maelstrom.

Breeze, Louisiana, 2010

'I'm listening,' Kim said in the hair salon.

I just smiled and began to tell her about my experience from 30 August 1987. It was not easy. I took a deep breath and just knew I was supposed to share this with Kim.

To begin with I went through the pre-crash scenario.

'I was at the 1987 San Marino Grand Prix and it was a beautiful, clear and bright hot day on the Adriatic coast of Italy. We were racing in front of a crowd of 60,000 spectators.

'I had been struggling with injuries that season, but I was on the pace that day and after a decent start I was holding my own early in the race. The rider right behind me, a young Italian named Pierfrancesco Chili, was racing in his first Grand Prix, in his home country. Pierfrancesco will tell you to this day that he couldn't believe he was right behind me, except there I was and he could read 'SPENCER' on the back of my leathers.

'Anyway, six or seven laps in, we are moving along and Pierfrancesco is right behind me, closer than he had been, and at the end of the fastest straightaway on the track, he's at his closest to my back tire. I was only focusing on the riders in front of me so I didn't know he was there.

'I braked a little earlier than normal at 165mph. But at that very moment he was drafting me and was going to try to pass on the inside.

'His front tire hit my back tire and became wedged between the tire and swing arm. All I remember from that moment of impact was the bike beginning to weave as if I had a flat and then ...'

I paused because I was going to share a very intimate experience and didn't know how Kim would respond. I just didn't go around telling this story. In fact, it had been quite a few years since I had even thought about it. When I did it was in a quiet moment of reflection as I considered different experiences and wondered what they meant. The experience and what I sensed had never left me.

I continued: 'I went from the bike weaving to a place where I was surrounded by the brightest illumination. I had the most comfortable and "at peace" feeling that I had ever experienced.'

I was looking at Kim and didn't know what to expect, but her face just lit up. With a light in her eyes and an openness that was immediately inspiring she said: 'I know what you mean. I have a story to share with you.'

I knew then why I felt I should tell all this to Kim and continued: 'So after a few minutes, I am not sure how long, that bright illumination and what I sensed as peace and comfort remained. Then, just faintly, I started hearing my name being called. *"Freddie, Freddie."* Not loud, just a distant murmur.'

Kim was just smiling now and shaking her head as if to say, 'Yes, I understand.'

'Then a few more moments went by and the voice saying *"Freddie"* started getting a little louder.

'I came around from the bright illumination to the Clinica Mobile, staring into the face of Dr Costa who takes care of us. His face was about five inches away from mine. I opened my eyes and he said, "Freddie, do you know who I am?"

'"Yes, Dr Costa."

'"Do you know where we are?"

'"Yugoslavia," I answered because the last time I had seen him was Yugoslavia. Then he asked me, "Do you hurt anywhere?"

'I didn't answer for a moment.'

Kim asked why.

'Because I had just woken up from that experience, so I looked around and then slowly I moved my feet, hands, arms, legs, slowly moved my head around and said, "No I don't hurt anywhere."

'Dr Costa said, "Good, now can you move or sit up?" I said I thought I could and so I did.'

Kim asked: 'Then what?' There was slight inflection in her voice that implied, 'Hurry up so I can tell you my story!'

'I felt a little woozy as they explained what had happened. I had just sat there waiting for the pain from the impact. But it never came. They took me to a hospital in Bologna about two hours away just to make sure.'

Kim said: 'And you were fine?'

I said: 'Yes. I had a big headache for about a day but no physical pain.'

'A miracle,' Kim said.

'I waited for what I experienced to fade away, but it never did. In fact, while telling you this, it's as vivid as it was that Sunday afternoon 23 years ago.'

Kim shook her head again and then began to tell me about her experience.

'I was about 21. I was driving my daddy's pick-up and it was raining. As the accident was happening I could sense what was like a hand coming from all directions. I could sense the truck flipping in all different directions. I could hear the metal twisting and breaking all around me, the loud crunching of steel and glass. But I felt nothing. I was aware of the terrible jarring but nothing violent and the protection just surrounded me.'

She had her eyes closed as her arms showed how she felt protected. 'Then as quickly as the violence began, it stopped. And I was totally surrounded by twisted metal. The truck was completely destroyed. The only tiny space that was undamaged was the place where I was. It still took them more than two hours to get me out using the "jaws of life" because I was completely surrounded.'

Then she stopped, took a deep breath and said: 'And I wasn't hurt anywhere either. There wasn't a scratch on me.'

There was a pause as we both sat there smiling.

Then I said: 'There's no way you could go through that and not know, right?'

She just smiled and said: 'Right.'

'I just knew I had to share my story with you.'

We walked to the front. When I turned to say goodbye to Kim, she had tears in her eyes. I started to speak, but she just put her hands on my face and smiled.

Then she kissed me on both cheeks and said: 'Thank you.'

'Thank you, Kim,' I said.

When I got back into the car I was still smiling. Mr Williams said: 'Good?'

'Great!'

'Where to next?'

'Starbucks. I want to buy you a coffee, Mr Williams, and I won't take no for an answer today.'

Mr Williams smiled and said: 'Okay then, sounds good.'

Chapter 14: **BACK TO THE BEGINNING (1989–96)**

I WAS spun around by the impact of the other car on my second lap of the first practice session at Tamiami Park in Miami. I was hit from behind and it was like being a pinball. As I slid towards the wall I thought, 'This is going to hurt.' But I was in a car and had more protection and was unscathed. It was not my fault but maybe that four-wheel finale was symptomatic of the troubles that lay ahead.

But car racing had seemed easy, a new world full of helping hands and bereft of any baggage. I seemed to have some ability and was able to transfer my skills to four wheels. I knew John Surtees had done it. So had Mike Hailwood.

I could be a multitasking racer too, but I flew to Geneva with Carey to meet the Yamaha people. The next morning at Philip Morris, headquarters of Yamaha's sponsor, I was offered an initial $950,000 to ride bikes again. I stalled. I asked for more money but what I really wanted was clarity. I never got it and, ignoring instinct, gut and even my subconscious, I eventually accepted. It was one of the biggest mistakes of my life.

On the plane back to Shreveport, I was already struggling with the choice. From the outside it looked like the obvious, easy option – stick with what you know – but inside I was a melting pot of conflicting emotions.

Things were changing elsewhere. I was engaged to Sharon and I began reducing my overheads. The struggles and uncertainty

240

of the previous years were like having a 1,000-pound weight on my shoulders. I needed to change. The new Highway 49 was coming through Mrs Gorman's Honda dealership – Mr Gorman had passed away many years before – so she needed the location she had sold me in 1982. I sold it back to her. I sold off other businesses too.

Eddie had moved to Honda in a move that shocked Giacomo Agostini. That meant Erv was working with Eddie in the Rothmans Honda team. It felt strange. In addition, my crew chief was Kel Carruthers, the Australian ex-racer who had been the team manager when Kenny won his hat-trick of titles, the man who had then led Eddie to the title. I respected Agostini and Kel tremendously but it felt like the bike world had shifted off its axis.

My Yamaha career started in modest fashion. I qualified in 14th and finished 9th in Japan and then we went to Australia. The Grand Prix was held at Phillip Island, south of Melbourne and famed for the penguin parade on the southern tip of the island. Something clicked there and I qualified in eighth. That was not spectacular by the standards of 1985, but it showed I was not washed-up and desperately clinging to what I used to be.

The race was going well too. Wayne Gardner was leading, with Mick Doohan, Kevin Schwantz and Wayne Rainey completing the leading pack. I was getting closer to them, though, and closed the gap to about a tenth of a second. I hadn't been in this position for a long time so kept telling myself to be patient. I felt sure I would have caught them by the end had the bike not started to lose grip. That meant I was having to hold it up with my knee, catching and saving a crash every lap. Eventually, with three laps to go, down I went.

I was disappointed but the team was thrilled at the promise. Kel wore the biggest smile and that meant the world to me. My wrist felt good, a little weak but it was holding up okay, and everyone agreed this was the best I had ridden for years.

The hope quickly evaporated. I rode in another eight Grand Prix races that year and there were reminders of my old self – a fifth place in the Spanish Grand Prix – but it was not right. The press had often talked about my absenteeism and turning up late for things, but they did not know about my physical problems. In fairness, how could they? I kept it to myself and shrunk away from any degree of openness.

The next time out on my bike my arm collapsed again. For the first time I had tests checking the nerves in my neck. They stuck pins and needles in me to gauge the reaction under stress. Eventually, I had surgery on it. Dr Goodman opened up the canal and found large bone chips. The nerve was badly pinched. It would take a long time to recover. That was the season. It was a struggle every day. I know that feeling of sitting there thinking, 'Why me?'

I felt bad for Agostini. It was a transition time for him as Eddie had gone. Marlboro would soon turn their favours to Kenny Roberts' own team after that. Eddie won the title with Erv and Honda. It was not an easy time for Agostini. He was a flamboyant, hugely popular star with 15 world titles behind him, but you live and die on results. It is a sport of short memories.

I had thought I could help him. Yamaha also appealed to me on some level because my first road race was on a RD100; my mini-enduro 60 had been a Yamaha; my first two road-racing championships were on TZ250s. I could ride anything, so why not? What I had not factored in was the fact that I could not overcome my restricted movement. I had the neck surgery during the season and then foot surgery. I had got to the point where I didn't want to go through this any more.

When would I listen? I bought a convenience store in Logansport, population 1,500, for Carey to run. My mind was made up. I wasn't going to race any more.

My plan to tend the graves of the original owners of my vast 693-acre property was also shelved. I had two choices – sell it to strangers or give it back. I thought about what Mr Williams had done, going to each of his relatives to get their agreement for me to buy it. That had taken him a year. There were more than 50 people to convince. Mr Williams never gave up until he got that last signature. It's maybe hard to understand why I gave it back to Mr Williams' family then, but I just felt that it was the right thing to do.

I sold the townhouse too and rented a property on Creswell Avenue. Slowly, I was realising that it was a burden to maintain all these possessions. So I sold off things, drove a Ford F150 pick-up that the store bought and wondered what on earth I was supposed to do with the next half a century.

When I was a kid I'd had such purpose. Not any more. Decades later I would be shown a quote from Steven Spielberg who said he tells his children that the most subtle whispers are the true inspiration and your heart confirms that. That is the absolute truth but it was lost in the confusion of that ill-fated comeback of 1989 and so now I would try to live a more conventional, day-to-day existence. Maybe that would be the answer.

Sharon had a friend whose dad was an executive in a local insurance company and so at the end of 1989 I actually studied to take the State of Louisiana insurance exams. The vague plan was to become an insurance broker. I was trying to normalise my life and get some stability. I had been on an incredible adventure, racing at white-knuckle speed, winning world titles, getting two letters from President Reagan, rising, falling, remounting the bike in the public glare. Now I was doing everything I could to become like anyone else. I had tasted enough of the rarefied air and insurance seemed about as ordinary as anyone could get. I don't mean that as a criticism – a lot of retired athletes move into that field – but I kept stalling.

In the end I didn't become an insurance broker because of Ralph Sanchez, who was anything but ordinary. Born in Cuba, he was still a boy when Fidel Castro seized power. He would deliver subversive leaflets for the Catholic brothers who taught him in school, and then left his parents when he got a place on one of the airlifts to Miami. He went on to become a self-made man, whose real love was motorsport. Eventually he would build his own track from the aftermath of a hurricane, enlisting old friends like Emerson Fittipaldi to help, and he contacted me to say he was promoting an AMA National Race in Miami in July. CBS Sports would televise the event if he could get a name rider to sweeten the pot and help promote the race.

I contacted my good friend and tuner Mike Velasco, who was now with a race team called Two Brothers owned by Craig and Kevin Erion. Despite what I had felt the previous year, I thought I should do it. It was just a one-off and I had always been impressed by the way Mario Andretti had gone to Formula One but returned to the US and IndyCars, helping others to get that leg up. I thought if it will help people see the championship, then okay.

Sharon and I had decided to call off the engagement, with all the uncertainty over my racing life and my obvious reluctance to become a full-time insurance broker and settle into a nine-to-five daily routine. Mostly it was me, because I knew I was a long way from where I could give her the stability she deserved.

Maybe this race was the right thing, the thing I needed to change? I took Dad and my two nephews to the race in Miami and it was great to be in that environment again, my home series. The bike was an almost stock Honda RC30 and the race did not go that well, but I was looking for a connection rather than another title. That race started the ball rolling and I would start to do more Superbike races for Two Brothers in the coming years. I was just going along with it. This was my job and I could not give it up.

Sharon and I broke up in the fall of 1989 and I did not see anyone for a time after that. Then, in January 1991, I met Druchele-Ann Nicholson, who everybody called Chelee', when Butch invited me to a supercross race in the Houston Astrodome. I walked into the hotel lounge and she was sitting on the left side of the sofa, wearing a red-and-white plaid shirt and black jeans.

As 1991 progressed, I was riding okay and had some decent results leading to the final race of the season at the event that had started this comeback: the Miami Grand Prix.

This time I was prepared and the Two Brothers bike was better too. The tight and slippery street course was difficult but that was fine for me and, besides the three restarts, it worked out well. I won and it was great, the first time I had won a race in six years, since August 1985, and I could see the joy in the team. Whether it is sentimental or nostalgia, people like to see a comeback. It makes you realise how fans are invested emotionally in what you do and the responsibility you have. People felt happy for me and the look of delight on their faces was priceless.

Yet as I went back to Daytona in 1992 it still felt like I was just going through the motions. The spark had long gone.

I was having some moderate success in the AMA Superbike series so I got an offer to race in the Suzuka 8 Hours race for the Mister Donut-backed Team Okumura. The team was getting some support from HRC and I was hoping to repair our relationship and was looking for their approval in some way.

I had not put my arm under anything like the stress needed for such a gruelling endurance event. I was in good shape but I had not done the race in 12 years. In summer at Suzuka, the temperature feels like 100 degrees Fahrenheit (38 degrees Celsius) with the oppressive humidity. I showed up and felt like I was back in my element again. Grand Prix riders like Wayne Gardner were entered. I still felt comfortable at the top. Our team was not technically a factory HRC team but it was close with the 1991 version of the Honda RVF750 that Wayne and Mick had ridden to victory the year before.

At a two-day test a few weeks beforehand I set a new track record. It seemed so easy, but I was cautious in my optimism.

For years Chelee' kept a video that contained some poignant moments from that weekend.

During qualifying I am on another fast lap and am coming up to a Kawasaki. The video cuts to one of the big screens at Suzuka and Erv's face fills it. He is watching me riding at the exact moment the screen shows my potential pole position lap. Then the screen shows a slight bobble from me and I am held up by a rider. I lose a fraction of a second. It costs me another record. On the video you can see the disappointment on Erv's face. He is working for Wayne now but he is looking out for me and wanting me to do well.

Before the race I sat down with Ryuji Tusruta, my young Japanese teammate. At the 8 Hours you take alternate hours on the bike. We were second quickest so I told him the two keys were to get a good start to capitalise on our grid spot and then to settle down. Most importantly, don't crash.

After all my problems with HRC it was good to be here. I felt good. I was not in the best shape I'd ever been by any stretch, but I knew I could get through it. With Grand Prix racers in the field, Erv there and all the attention I felt like this is where I belonged. I rewound and was Fast Freddie again but ...

When the flag drops you run across the circuit, jump on the bike and push the starter. Mine just keeps turning over. There are 60 bikes on the grid and, by the time I get it off, I am in the middle of the pack. Halfway through my hour I catch Aaron Slight. I try to pass when I shouldn't. I am committed to going around his inside but suddenly realise he has not seen me. He turns into the corner. I have no choice. To avoid hitting him I go straight on. It does not affect him but I head straight off the track at well over 100mph. I am going so fast that I bounce over the gravel trap instead of sinking. The barrier is getting closer all the time and so I lay the bike down. I have done the two things I warned my young teammate not to – I've had a bad start and crashed. I get back on the track and toil away for the remainder of my hour with a bent back brake lever. When I come in, I am so embarrassed I forget to tell Ryuji about the lever but he copes brilliantly anyway.

After each hour I have about 40 minutes to recover before my next segment. I strip to my underwear and lie down. Chelee' places towels on me from head to toe. They have been soaking in iced water. My body temperature is so high that the first is bone dry by the time she places the third one on me. I hear a voice saying 'Five minutes to go'. I could have sworn I laid down only five minutes ago. I get up and get dressed and leave for my next run. Chelee' is videoing from a perch above. She looks down at me. I say, 'It's just hell.' We keep going through those hours and we end up fourth after completing 204 laps. Erv has won with Wayne and Daryl Beattie. There are 135,000 people there. Like the old days. The good ones. There is a huge satisfaction from surviving the day. Mr Oguma comes to the garage and celebrates with us. I appreciate that so much.

I could barely walk the next day and, standing at the train station, every muscle hurt. It was not the crash but the pushing beyond exhaustion. Yet I would reflect that this was one of the greatest rides because of my pride in my teammate. With a bent brake lever, after two crashes and with bleeding hands, we had ridden to hell and back. The next week I went to Mid-Ohio and had a good race with Scott Russell and Doug Polen, who would both end up World Superbike champions. I was holding my own. I was still only 30 years old. And so the seeds of another comeback on a Superbike were sown.

There was an emotional aspect to our eight hours in Suzuka and there was a buzz that people might want more. Mr Okumura was talking to Mister Donuts about sponsorship and potential support from HRC would be even more important. I spoke with Erv. Wayne was retiring. We put a proposal together. Things seemed to be moving. I had forgotten what I had felt a few years earlier. Instead, I jumped when I was invited to South Africa at the end of 1992 to test the Honda Grand Prix bike with Erv.

The Grand Prix season had finished the day before at the Kyalami circuit. Wayne Rainey had wrapped up his third successive title but Mick Doohan, the Honda rider from Australia, was the coming force. Erv gave me a heads-up that the new 'big bang' engine gave the bike a radically different power delivery to the engines I was used to. The only thing he said was: 'You can get on the throttle sooner than you think.'

There was also the new Kyalami circuit to consider. I had been there years before but there was only one corner that remained the same and that was now run in the opposite direction. Erv told me to take my time, but by late morning I was clocking times that would have put me second on the grid for the previous day's Grand Prix. It would have been easy to believe I was back after that. Inevitably, the talk continued.

The Honda package never came together and Erv could not wait. It was not meant to be. I got a fax from Christian Sarron, my old rival from 1985, and he offered me a chance to ride for Yamaha Motor France. I accepted. Hindsight would look at the signs – the demise of the Honda deal, the retirement of other riders. But I liked Christian and so, nearly a decade after winning the world title, I was back again.

In November 1992 Chelee' and I were married by a justice of the peace in Longview, Texas, but if that side of my life was settled, the professional side remained in a state of flux.

The first race was the Australian Grand Prix at the new Eastern Creek circuit near Sydney. I preferred Phillip Island but could understand the economics of the change.

Eastern Creek had an incredibly fast turn one, around 100mph at its slowest point. It ended badly when the water pump seized and I was flung over the handlebars as I battled with Luca Cadalora, the reigning 250cc champion. Christian was so upset, not at me but just at how dangerous a crash it had been. I was dazed and could not race at the next round in Malaysia, but I returned for the third round in Japan.

On the Saturday morning, the team asked me if I wanted to test a new rear-shock suspension system. It was a completely new system that was part-computer controlled and a variant that was being used in Formula One. Wayne Rainey had been testing it and discarded it. I said okay, but as we were walking away from the garage to the little office that was my changing room, Chelee' said, *'Don't try it.'*

I assured her it would be fine, just a few laps to give some feedback. I should have listened to her.

I came in after a few laps to make some minor adjustments. I thought the system was way too sensitive to any track changes. Its active capabilities made it reactive accelerating out of the hairpin and I went through the gears – second, third, fourth – when I felt the rear of the bike collapse. The next thing I knew I was going towards the guard rail at 110mph and, for the first time in my life, I thought: *'I am not going to survive this.'*

I was still drifting and there seemed no way I could escape. Yet I did wake up and was completely alert. My eyes focused and I knew I was in the back of an ambulance. My finger in my right hand was badly damaged.

'Don't let Chelee' see this,' I said.

She was already there. They were taking me to a nearby hospital. I lay on a gurney as a Japanese doctor turned my arm and hand. The pain was excruciating. I complained and he kept saying he had trained at Columbia University as if that would make a difference. After the tenth time he had told me that I grabbed him by the shirt.

'I don't care where you trained! My wrist is broken!'

'I know,' he said. 'But we're trying to save your finger.'

It went on for a while. I looked around to take my mind off Dr Columbia working on my finger. People were milling about. Then someone posed next to me and had a picture taken. Someone else asked me if I could sign something. I thought, 'Are you joking?' My finger was completely disfigured and caked in coagulating black blood. Fresh ripples added a new layer. Finally, a man who had been standing in the corner came over. He was the president of Yamaha and said he was going to get Dr Ting.

I knew of Arthur Ting. He was well known for working in sport in the San Francisco area and had been mending Yamaha racers for some time. It turned out he had flown in from Korea that morning for the race on his way home. As people crowded into the room and took more pictures, it was a huge relief when he arrived and said: 'I'm going to get you out of here.'

He went off to make arrangements, leaving Dr Columbia to work on my finger. I could hear murmurs to one side and the occasional snippet of a sentence. It emerged that they were going to take off my finger, which is when Chelee' intervened.

'No way!' she said.

They patched me up to travel. I got up to walk and only then did I realise the damage I had also done to my ACL joint in my knee. In those times, you survive the discomfort minute to minute. The only focus is on the next stepping stone over the troubled water. I have never enjoyed that way of living and had no desire to put myself through it once more, but it is still amazing the strength you can conjure in those moments.

They put me in a car to Nagoya Airport and Delta held up the flight. Dr Ting and Yamaha were wonderful and I was in first class within an hour. Delta allowed me to have two seats and we were overwhelmed by the kindness of strangers, as people in the cabin helped me to the rest room and then two men switched seats with Chelee' so she could get a break; she was exhausted.

An ambulance was waiting for me on the runway in San Francisco and they put an IV drip in me and took me to Stanford Medical Center. We arrived at 10am on Saturday morning, an hour before I had crashed in Japan! I wished I could have literally gone back in time and listened to Chelee'. I underwent two operations, one to save my finger and the other to fix my knee. The screws from the latter remain the only ones I have in me.

I was saddling up again by the end of the season with my final race for Christian being the San Marino Grand Prix. It was a race best remembered for the crash that paralysed Wayne Rainey. It was a tough year that summed up the brutal but pure nature of our sport. If we are given lessons by the universe then I believe in every part of my soul that learning comes from awareness.

I had enjoyed and suffered incredible times and I had no intention of ever racing a motorcycle again. Yet there was a caveat to that. My last real memory of racing was heading towards that guard rail in Japan and believing my life was over. In 1994, I began doing more TV broadcasts and was at Laguna Seca for the World Superbikes. I got talking to Eraldo Ferracci, who was running the Ducati Superbike team in the USA. I told him the same thing. He said: 'Maybe you would like to have a different memory.' He asked me to the December tire test at Daytona and I have to admit that I thought the new Ducati 916 was one of the most beautiful motorcycles I had ever seen. I raced the season for Eraldo and I got my memory in April 1995 when I won the AMA National race at Laguna Seca.

It was not an easy race. I was going to end up second or third when, literally out of the blue on that Sunday, the fog rolled in over turn five leading up to the Corkscrew. They had to stop the race and reschedule it for Monday. It was raining by then and only around 100 fans showed up. I was not the quickest in the dry but I was good in the wet and I ended up carving out a huge lead of more than 20 seconds. I eased off to protect my lead and won.

'That fog rolled in for a reason,' Eraldo said. He would repeat it every time we met afterwards. All my memories of struggles over the past ten years flashed through my thoughts. This was it for me.

Druchele was relieved that I was done and it was difficult seeing the toll my racing took on her. The fear and doubt are exacerbated by helplessness. I had chosen to do this; she hadn't. It was tough on her and it put stress on our relationship. This time it really was over, without question.

Now what?

I had been doing some broadcast work for ESPN, who would help to start Speedvision, voicing over Grand Prix races for taped delayed broadcasts. It did not come naturally. I had barely passed speech class in 1979 because of my shyness and it took years for me to get comfortable talking to people, but I grew to like it and it is how I met Bob Scanlon, the executive producer at ESPN. Other than that, I wasn't sure what I was going to do except never race a motorcycle again.

Chelee' and I were renting a house in Ockley Drive in Shreveport, just down the road from my long-time friend Gilbert Little. I went to see him and we discussed what I was going to do.

'What about car racing?' he said. 'We tried to get you going in 1988 but you went back to bikes.'

He was shaking his head as if to say, 'You should have listened to me'.

I said: 'Okay. You're probably right but today is now.'

With a smile, he said: 'Let's see what we can make happen.'

Gilbert did some research and saw there was a new series just starting called the Indy Racing League, which was a breakaway championship from CART. The first race was going to be on a Disney-built track in Orlando. They had a support race for Formula Ford 2000 cars. I had tested one a few years before and Gilbert contacted a few teams. One based in Houston was willing to give me a try. I paid my way down there but we had some mechanical problems and dropped out of the race. I got an offer to do some more, but I said no. It didn't feel like it had when I was looking at four wheels in 1988. I knew about certainty because I had felt uncertain for so long. And now I had a direction that I felt would work. It was not a gamble. I was not double downing to make it all better. But I *was* heading to Las Vegas.

Vegas

In 1988, as part of my sponsorship deal with Nankai, I did a small one-day race school in Japan. It was my suggestion, even though I had no idea what I would teach or how. To my shock around 1,000 riders turned up. Someone asked what I wanted them to do, so I said line them up and let them come up to me one at a time and then get on the brakes. I would critique their technique. Should be easy I thought. The first rider was around 100 feet away and so he stepped on the accelerator and, right in front of me, abruptly applied the brakes and crashed. He was okay but I was shocked. I decided to do a talk instead. It was not an auspicious beginning. If I ever did it again, I decided I would need to know exactly what I was going to teach.

Gilbert and I had started talking about me doing a school of some kind. One day, a few weeks later, I got a call from a guy named Richie Klein.

'I hear you want to do a school,' he began. 'I'm building a track here in Vegas and think you should run a school here. Come out and see me.' Then he hung up.

It felt entirely right and I had not had that feeling for a long time. Chelee' and I flew out to meet Richie and see the track that was still getting the finishing touches. It was a simple layout but I could see that it would work for teaching. I met the designer and it seemed fitting that he was the same man who had handed me the trophy all those years ago when I had burst on to the scene at Brands Hatch in 1980. His name was Alan Wilson and he had been the track manager for Brands Hatch, Mallory Park and Oulton Park.

On the plane back to Shreveport, I began to think about how I was going to do this and it slowly came to me. I would provide the bikes and run schools in one location over two days. The first problem was getting bikes. I called my old friend, Ken Vreeke, the journalist who had saved me before at Hockenheim in 1982. He now had his own PR firm and worked with American Honda. I told him my ideas.

'You should come out here and meet the guys at American Honda,' he said.

I was a little hesitant. 'Oh, okay. Sounds good.' But I was not sure how receptive they would be.

I had got back into the fold on a low-key level with Two Brothers, but I was unnerved and anxious about all that had happened in the past. When I got there, the vice-president of motorcycling, Ray Blank, said that of course they would help. 'Where else would you go?'

Money was tight. I had retired in 1993. I was doing a few broadcasts, but I had no regular income and was now starting a business on the other side of the country.

And then, in that curious way which is hard to explain, things began to fall into place.

Twelve years earlier, I had lent a friend some money and now, just as we were about to leave Shreveport for Vegas, she was able to repay me. That got us through the winter.

I am basically a homebody. I was born and raised in Shreveport and I had always gone back. It was the land and people that had made me. It was my comfort zone and the place where I lived and loved, but now I was leaving. Chelee' and I put most everything in storage and all we had was each other, our Ford Explorer truck and trailer, a medium-sized U-Haul loaded to the top, our cat Muffin and dog Super. We had 1,400 miles to go. We were heading west. There was something nostalgic and freeing about it.

We said our goodbyes in Shreveport and then stopped in Dallas to bid farewell to our friends. Butch was there, along with Tony Trailer and Ronnie Hampton's daughter Mary-Ann.

It is 29 July 1996 and I am 34 years old, driving a U-Haul through the desert with Muffin. Chelee' is driving the Explorer with Super. We get to Flagstaff, near the Grand Canyon, and even though it is the middle of summer, snow begins falling in the middle of this beautiful oasis. We stop for gas and I am smiling at how amazing this is. Chelee' says I seem happier and I say it feels we are doing the right thing. We arrive on 1 August 1996. When we drive across the Hoover Dam I see the sign:

LAS VEGAS 2165 FEET

This is the right sort of rarefied air.

The first event at the Las Vegas Motor Speedway was a month later, the AMA National race. I announced a small press conference to coincide with it. Most of the main magazines were there, *Cycle World* and the rest.

'People want to learn on their own bikes.'

'It's not about the bike,' I said. 'I want to teach people how to ride any bike.'

There was some communal chuntering.

'You believe enough people will want to come all the way to Vegas?'

'Well, if the programme is good enough they'll come.'

I was just responding to their questions as I went along. They were looking at me with puzzlement. Then I told them the price – $995 for two days. It was a lot but Dad had always said go just under the round amount.

So far it was just Chelee' and me. I needed a staff and the only résumé that got my attention was from an ex-racer named Nick Ienatsch. He was the only person I considered. Each night, after Chelee' had gone to sleep, I would sit down at our kitchen table and think about what I had learned over the last 29 years. Everything I had experienced riding my motorcycle had been to develop an incredible sense of movement, but what had been the steps to help me understand it? Over the next months I planned and plotted. I would work late, sometimes all night, and take a break by walking to the corner store for a sandwich. Then I would write a bit more, cross out things.

One night, on the way back looking up into the clear night, the stars are twinkling and shining, but they seem so still and peaceful. I feel the universe is so powerful in a way I don't comprehend. I stop looking up and walk back to the apartment to work on the rider programme. I begin to think about what I glimpsed in my yard all those years ago; knowing that what I sensed then would become clearer one day. To help others I need to go back to the beginning.

Chelee' opened the mail one morning and could not believe what she found. There were tears in her eyes and you could see the relief in her face. A cheque had arrived from Jimmy, who had bought a piece of property from me almost a decade earlier. Now he had sold it and, without any obligations and out of the blue, he was sharing the profit he had made. That cheque enabled us to buy the Ford truck we needed and to have some vital spare cash for the first school.

Breeze, Louisiana, 2010

Here I am at 5am, learning the right way to fold linens from Mrs Ada at the Courtyard Marriott in my home town. And since I've been here I've grown so much wiser. What incredible moments I have had both spiritually and with others.

Mrs Ada and I finished our work and I went back to my room to get ready for my walk. I looked out of the sliding glass door to see what the weather was like. It looked clear but I could see the trees blowing in the wind and I could feel from touching the glass doors that it was cool. I put on my jacket, grabbed my iPod and headed out. As I started through the parking lot the most amazing, comforting feeling came over me. I couldn't see it but I knew it was there. I could feel it in the crisp, cool breeze.

I would never take it for granted again.

I had to go to England for the Birmingham Classic Motorcycle Show. I took an early flight from Shreveport to Houston. Then I would go to Newark and then on to Birmingham. Not long ago I'd have looked at that itinerary and said, 'There's no way I am flying to all those places.'

At Newark I got a Starbucks and sat down to people-watch. Airports are the intersections where our paths cross. But it's an intersection where there are no stop lights. People are just going through the intersections and not really looking in any direction for each other; all they are looking for are signs of where to go next.

Not paying attention to each other.

Just looking for a sign.

Before too long I was at the Birmingham Expo Hall. I signed autographs for a couple of hours. I enjoyed these interactions with fans. Even the younger ones are familiar with my racing and sometimes there would be three generations sharing a moment.

I went up on stage with a couple of other motorcyclists from the UK. One was Mick Grant, who just so happened to be one of the riders on the NSR500 Honda at the 1979 British Grand Prix at Silverstone. That was the broadcast that began my understanding that I was supposed to ride for Honda. There was a speedway rider too. We all took turns answering basic questions from Gemma the host. I got into the mode of Freddie the ex-racer, ex-riding instructor, ex-broadcaster. It was like pulling on a favourite pair of old jeans. I can put my mind in neutral and recall any race.

But this time my feeling was different. As we kept talking and sharing stories, for some reason I felt I should talk about a moment when my faith could have been tested. The only example in my thoughts was the 1984 South African Grand Prix at Kyalami.

In my head, I remembered it was the first Grand Prix of the season and it was a week after the Daytona 200, the most important race in the United States and where I had finished second to Kenny Roberts. We had battled for the 500cc world title the year before.

I had noticed in the last ten laps or so of that first practice session on Friday at Daytona that the rear of the bike was starting to feel different around the corners, especially on the exits. I finished second and I remembered telling the HRC and Michelin engineers that there was something wrong. One of the exhaust chambers from one of the four cylinders developed a crack. That affected the horsepower by about 30 per cent. It cost me the win but I think it helped me to finish.

A week later at Kyalami they used that wheel with a fresh tire. I went out and was going around 50mph, compared with the 180mph-plus at Daytona, when the rear tire just exploded. I went down and could immediately feel that both my feet hurt.

That story was going through my thoughts when Gemma thanked us all. I thought I should have brought up Kyalami 1984, but it was too late.

'Any questions for the guys?' said Gemma.

A gentleman from the second row stepped forwards and took the mic. He looked right at me and started: 'Freddie, your crash at the 1984 South Africa Grand Prix when the wheel exploded and you broke your feet ...'

All I could do was look at him and shake my head. He continued: 'Did that event make you question your faith in God?'

For a moment I could not take my eyes off him. I had the biggest smile on my face and he kept smiling back. The 1,500 people in the hall were so quiet you could hear a pin drop.

'Absolutely not, it didn't make me question my faith. In fact, it made it stronger because the wheel didn't come apart on me at 180mph but at 50mph.'

And I told them the whole story, how I was taking off my gear when Erv came over and told me they thought the carbon-fibre plates that connected the ream to the hub had come apart and basically exploded into particles. And that it was the wheel that was on the bike when I had been going 180mph the week before. And how Dainese wanted me to test a new back protector that day and how I kept putting it off until I came in that afternoon, put it on and went back out minutes before the wheel exploded.

I told the audience that I said to Erv: 'I know my feet are broken but I am here. If that wheel had come apart at Daytona I might not be.'

After Mick and I answered a few more questions, I made my way off the stage. I looked at the second row of seats but there was no sign of the gentleman.

The first thing I wrote about before going to the airport was how different this trip to the Birmingham show was from the last time, a decade earlier, when I was sitting in a car outside with a stack of *Rain Dance* prints, just a couple of weeks after my experience in my townhouse. At that time I felt alone and lost. I didn't really know what that meant.

Now I do.

Chapter 15: **DESERT SKY (1997–2007)**

LAS VEGAS was a neon metropolis in the desert. It was growing at a rapid rate, like petrified ripples in a brightly coloured pool. The outer limits were constantly spreading outwards and a city was literally rising from the dust. Some may have thought it an incongruous destination, but while I was never a gambler, Vegas had a true dynamism that I enjoyed and it was an exciting place to be during that time. In the late 1990s there were up to 5,000 people moving in every month and I imagined it was like the Gold Rush in California in the 1840s.

On that first day of school I had a deep sense of anticipation rather than nerves. It was not quite Kevin Costner in *Field of Dreams*, with its 'build it and he will come' message, but I was confident that this would turn out all right. There were four of us to start with – me, Nick, Nick's friend Andre, and Chelee' handling the catering and sign-ups. We had 11 bikes for students and used the infield road course inside the Super Speedway. There was no marketing budget and all we had was that press conference the previous September and a small ad in *Cycle World* magazine.

I understood what I wanted to teach but had no experience in communicating it. At first I rambled on for too long in the classroom, not understanding the attention span of the students, or their ability to absorb what I was saying. But we got through that school in March 1997 and we went from strength to strength. I started to realise that the great thrill of what we were doing was not showing how clever we were, but understanding what each rider was struggling with and adapting the message for them. I think that is the joy of teaching, not just regurgitating what you know and hoping it hits the target, but tailoring the delivery for the different rates of learning. One size did not fit all and I grew to understand that.

I trusted Nick's judgement. It worked and he became the lead instructor. Andre helped him with the bikes and assisted Nick and me on the track.

At the same time, Chelee' and I were trying to start a family and decided we needed some help with the business. I hired Gregg Kearns, who was the sales manager at the local Honda dealer, and he joined in October 1997 and was there until the end.

That first year we only had schools until the start of June because it was 110 degrees Fahrenheit (43 degrees Celsius) in the Vegas summer, but it was a success. It quickly grew to be more than just a motorcycle school, with American Honda looking at ways we could combine riding experiences with promoting the sport.

Later, in the spring of 1999, I would build a classroom in one of the buildings at the circuit and we began to get exposure beyond the normal motorcycling press. Major magazines such as *Forbes, GQ* and *Men's Journal* began to feature us. I was content for the first time in an age. Those days when I would look into the vast Nevada sky made me feel I had found our place. Chelee' and I were building a school from nothing but our own hard work and the support of others. I imagined it would last for ever.

I remembered how Mr Irimajiri, the first president of HRC, had told me that you should be able to stand in one place on the factory floor and see from the start to the end of the assembly line. That way you can catch a problem sooner. You see the entire picture. When he built his Honda plant in Marysville, Ohio, that simplicity was the key. Now, on that simple inside road course, I recognised the situations that would give those moments of learning the greatest chance – those moments of wonderment.

Nick and Gregg were exactly the ones to help me build the school – we did it together – and to learn the reasons we were supposed to do it. We were not the only ones doing schools and it wasn't that I was saying ours was the best. That wasn't the purpose. I knew I wanted to create a programme to share the sensation of riding a motorcycle with others and get the most from it, to ride safer and to not be afraid. From that, maybe more important and intimate lessons could be learned. What I realised was it was the trust to bring others on board to help and to grow as individuals. It was a privilege to share that with each person who came to the school.

Business was booming. The Motorcycle Industry Council set up an awareness campaign called Discover Today's Motorcycle, and one result of that was we started doing a few things with celebrities. One day in the fall of 1998 Gregg said he had received a call from a guy in Japan who said his name was Keanu Reeves.

'Do you think it's the actor?' he said.

'I'm sure it is.'

'He doesn't want to be treated special. Just wants to come to the school. The only thing he asked is does Freddie teach the classes?'

I'd read that he was working on a sci-fi movie, but we made contact and he came along to the school. He was extremely humble and kind, a good rider who worked very hard to learn.

It turned out the film he was working on was *The Matrix*, which came out in 1999 and changed his life.

Keanu was our first celebrity. Lyle Lovett, the singer, was another and I kept a bike at the school for him for many years. There were many others who loved to ride. Actors like Catherine Bell and Francesco Quinn, Anthony Quinn's son, came. It was a great time.

Away from the track and the school, life was not so smooth. Like many couples, Chelee' and I did not find it easy to start a family. We went to a fertility clinic and the stress and toll of that was doing neither of us any good and we separated for the first time. Finally, we decided to stop going to the clinic and after we had given up Chelee' became pregnant.

A month before our daughter, Jordyn, was born there was another problem. Jordyn's heartbeat was elevated and tests revealed the umbilical cord had got wrapped around her neck. Chelee' was put into neo-natal intensive care. Sitting in that hospital, listening to that soft heartbeat, it was out of our hands. They were thinking of a C-section. Luckily, Jordyn managed to untangle herself and so she was not born until she was due. I said to Chelee': 'I guess she's stubborn.'

She said: 'Like you.'

That was the first scary thing that happened to my little girl. The second would be one of the most traumatic days of my life, but when she did arrive on 16 November 1998 it was incredible. During that first hour with her she never let go of my little finger. There was a purity in that moment of connection. It was the most powerful touch I had felt in my life – and I had felt a few. She had me right then. She knew it was me, her dad. Before she was a month old she would sleep all through the night from 8pm to 8am. I wondered how anyone could hurt something so perfect and innocent.

We went back to Louisiana for Christmas in 1998 and to introduce Jordyn to our family and friends. I can picture Dad holding her in his arms, generations stretched by time and location but bonded by love and blood. It would be the last time Dad would get to see her. It made me think about Mom's dad too as he had passed when I was only a year old.

After getting home from a day at the track, I couldn't wait to go out on to our patio with Jordyn. She was just putting words together. She would hold on to my little finger and we would look up into the desert sky.

It was satisfying to create a business. The following year I was at a track near Atlanta doing a broadcast and I called home to Shreveport. I talked to Mom and then Dad came on. Nothing particular was said and I hung up and tried to get to sleep in my hotel room. Something was running around my brain that night, though. The next day I was due to fly back to Vegas on a direct flight, but there was a feeling that was bothering me. I didn't know why but I decided I should go back to Shreveport. I changed my ticket. I had not been back apart from the holidays in 1997 and 1998, but it felt like I needed to go.

Then I called Mom who was surprised.

'Is everything okay, Freddie?'

'Yes, Mom. I just want to stop by Shreveport on the way back to Vegas to see you guys.'

I went home and spent four days with Mom and Dad and we really talked. Then I sat down with Dad and we spoke about lots of things – about his life on the railroads, those endless trips to races, and the stories we could remember. Then we spoke about how I had said I would never respect him again. It had been left unsaid for 13 years, but I stressed that vow was no reflection on the sacrifices he had made for me and which I appreciated.

With tears welling up in his eyes he said: 'It's okay. I would do it again.'

You can't imagine how thankful I was for that. The last thing we did was hug each other and say: 'None of us are perfect.' It was the last time I saw him. A month later Mom called saying that Dad had passed away. We flew back for the funeral. Standing at the graveside, listening to the pastor talk about Linda, Danny and me, I realised there were things I did not know about my dad. I had never seen him step foot inside a church, but in those last few months he had opened up to the pastor. He had thought about whether there was anything more, as you might towards the end. We had never spoken about anything spiritual but I felt happy he had wanted to know and was just glad he had found someone to talk with. He had spoken about what music he wanted played at his service – 'Amazing Grace' – and I found myself gaining a fresh insight into my dad even though he was gone.

I got back to Vegas and waited for the end of the century. A lot of people were in a panic, and the new millennium would lead to no end of theories about how the world would plunge into disaster. All the computers were going to crash, and we backed up ours like everybody else, but we survived and faced 2000 with optimism and direction.

We were doing 18-plus race schools a year and, as the years rolled by, the numbers in each class rose from 11 to a maximum of 25. I also started doing consultancy work for the American Honda factory road-race team at the AMA Nationals. If a rider needed something, I would give my thoughts. I was happy to help. In addition to that, I took over the west coast distribution for Michelin race tires. Life was busy and had purpose, just working and taking care of the family.

The teaching side was developing too. Telemetry on bikes was a fast-growing field and, after being widely used in Grand Prix racing for some time, began to trickle down to the grass roots. We progressed to filming students, which was a huge improvement in teaching. If they could see what they were doing it made it easier for them to visualise what they needed to do. I also began riding with each student to show them two things – we were teaching them what I did on the bike and I wanted them to feel the transitions. It was about touch and anticipation. It was a shock to some to see how subtle and smooth my movements were.

In 2001, I began to work with Nicky Hayden who was riding for Honda in the AMA Championship. His crew chief, Merlyn Plumlee, and I noticed he struggled with the same issue each weekend. In first practice on Friday he would be really aggressive on the front brake entering corners. He would then want to make a change to the front suspension to compensate. The result of stiffening the front of the bike was it would not hold its line in corners.

When Nicky was more experienced I made a series of suspension changes one day at the school to show him what it felt like when the rider made the adjustments rather than expecting a fix from the bike. It was a case of becoming more aware. I really enjoyed that time working together with Nicky and Merlyn.

I was invited to Japan to join Mick Doohan, now a five-time world champion, to ride Honda's new RC211V, the brand-new four-stroke Grand Prix bike. The stage was Motegi where the last 500cc championship had been won by Valentino Rossi, before the advent of MotoGP, a rebranding of the top class to cater for bigger four-stroke machines.

While I was in Motegi, the president of HRC, Yasuo Ikenoya, asked me what I thought about Nicky being in MotoGP.

'I think he can do it,' I said. 'I think if you build him a bike he can win the World Championship.'

Nicky was the hardest-working rider I had worked with. He reminded me of myself riding in my yard, just wanting to be the best that he could be. He would come to the school as a normal student and just ride. If I told him to do 40 laps to work on something he would do 80. From the back of my workshop I could look out over the track and the Vegas strip was in the distance. I loved that setting and there would be Nicky doing lap after lap as the sun set. I thought that's what is going to win him the world title.

'Will you shake on that?' Ikenoya asked.

'Yes, sir.' I felt good about it.

During this period Nicky would win 11 AMA Superbike races in a row. One night, at the end of 2002, at about eleven o'clock, I got a call from Takayuki Arima, the vice-president of American Honda.

'Freddie-san, we have a problem. We need your help.'

'What's wrong?'

'We just got word that Nicky has signed a letter of intent to ride for the Yamaha Grand Prix team.'

'Really?'

'It's not official. We can't talk to Nicky directly and we have a right of first refusal. Will you help?'

I called up Nicky.

'I guess you heard,' he said.

'Sounds like you have a letter of intent. Look, I know Honda really want you to ride for them. I think it's where you should be, but it is your decision.'

There was a lot to consider and Nicky was under pressure from all sides. He just wanted to race so there was a lot to talk over with his agent. To cut a long story short he signed for Honda. Fast-forward to 2006 and Satoru Horike, the man who had designed and built my two-cylinder V-twin 250 bike in 1985, was the project leader for the Evolution version of the RC 211V Nicky raced. The Evolution was different because it had the engine lower and slightly forward compared with the RC211V that his teammate Dani Pedrosa raced. At the last race of the 2006 season, in Valencia, Nicky won a great duel with Rossi and he did, indeed, become the world champion.

A year later Nicky came back to the school because he was struggling with the new 800cc Grand Prix bike. He was the reigning world champion, but there he was, out there in the setting sun, the Vegas vista in the distance, riding through the field, still working. It was no different from the first time his dad, Earl, had walked up to me, at a track in Texas in 1991 and said he'd like me to meet his kids.

In January of 2001 Mom came out to visit for the last time. She had started to have some health issues with a hardening of her arteries. A couple of days before she was due to fly back to Shreveport, she said: 'If you want me to stay a little longer I will.'

I said: 'If you want to, Mom, but it's up to you.'

I remember the look on her face. Back then I shrugged it off, but it was a look that said she didn't want to go back yet. Dad was gone and she didn't have anything left to keep her busy. She didn't feel good and being out here, around her new granddaughter, had been a positive distraction. I didn't give that look the attention it deserved. If anyone should have sensed and felt its meaning it was me. She stayed just a few days more and went home.

Less than two months later Linda called me to say Mom had been flown to Houston Memorial Hospital. I caught a plane to Houston.

The problem was a dissected aorta but to get in there the surgeon would have to go through a web of other arteries. It was like open-heart surgery. When I arrived it was late evening and quiet. I had 30 minutes before Mom went down to surgery. She looked weak and pale and I knew that she was scared, even though her main concern was telling me that it was all going to be all right. I had faced so many things since I was a kid. Mom knew about some of them and didn't know about others. What I felt in those minutes with Mom was a complete and utter helplessness, but I knew she was strong. She was my mom and I had hope even though the doctor told me that the success rate for the operation was less than 20 per cent.

After operating most of the night, Mom came through.

'Her heart is strong,' the doctor said.

I knew that well enough. 'She's a country girl,' I said, but the doctor didn't, and couldn't, have any idea of the struggles she had faced, crouching in the dirt as her father fired a gun over her head, stuttering in unsympathetic stores, watching her husband and sons risk life and limb for decades. It was not about overcoming barriers for my mom; it was about dealing with them the best she could. That was all she knew.

Fortunately, my sister was able to get some time off and stayed with her in Houston and so I was able to go back to Vegas for the schools we had booked. If I have a regret – and I do – it is that Mom was in hospital for another two months and I was only able to make it back once.

During the first operation, the surgeon had nicked a small artery so it was not healing properly. It was the risk of that type of operation and they had to go back in. But eventually, after two long months, it was time for her to leave the hospital and start her rehab back in Shreveport. The doctors felt she would improve more in her own environment. I spoke to her the night before and she was more lucid than she had been in previous weeks. I did not tell her our big secret – that Chelee' was pregnant again – because I planned to do that when we flew back to see her in a few days.

The next day I had a school. I was in front of the class when Gregg opened the door and said my sister was on the line. I could tell from his face that something was wrong. I picked up the receiver and Linda was hysterical. She was in Nacogdoches Medical Center in Texas and Mom was in cardiac arrest. They had been trying to revive her for 20 minutes.

'I don't know what to do, Freddie!'

Linda did not have to ask, but I knew what she needed from me. She needed me to be the one to say stop and let her go. Mom had told me years before that if anything ever happened she did not want to be on a respirator. It was an awful thing to have to say, but I knew it was right.

'Linda, tell them to stop,' I said.

The last thing in the world that I wanted was for my mom to be gone, but the one thing I could never do was think about my own desires rather than her own wishes. You never know how you will react in those situations and you hope that you make the right calls. I believe I did.

'Linda, it's okay,' I said softly. 'I'm sorry I'm not there. You did the best you could.'

I hung up and went back and finished the class. I was in shock. Mom was gone. It had not sunk in and I went through the motions. I told Gregg I was going home to Shreveport. I drove back to the house and packed and we were on a plane that afternoon.

The last moments I had with Mom were at Wellman Funeral Home on Louisiana Avenue. It was near to closing time, viewing was over and they were locking up, but I did not want to leave the room. It was just her and me for the last time. The next day we had a little graveside service, just as we had done for Dad two years earlier, and I told the family about our news. We were going to have a boy. They were excited, the yin and yang of life's rich pageant.

A few months later I was getting up and watching the television when I saw a plane fly into a tower in New York City. The contrast between the beauty of that clear blue sky and the man-made violence made me shudder. It was that sinking feeling in your stomach when you know things will never be the same.

They shut down the airports when the full horror of 9/11 emerged. And it was then that I realised just how remote Las Vegas really is. On any given day in Vegas there are 100,000 people in hotel rooms. Only New York can rival it. And now these people could not leave. The airports were shut for two days and I drove past empty car dealerships, cleared by people desperately buying a way home. We had lots of clients from big business, the finance industry and Silicon Valley, and at that time everybody wanted to be at home with their families. There was widespread panic. Most people will never forget that picture of planes hitting towers. Trust and innocence were stolen in the horror of that day. It took me back to my childhood.

Connor arrived on 28 December 2001 and this time there were no traumas. We were happy and thankful to have a healthy baby boy.

It was not always easy caring for kids as shown by our 2002 trip to the Goodwood Revival in September. Chelee"s mom, Judy, came out to take care of Connor, while Chelee', Jordyn and I went to the UK.

We arrived on Wednesday and stayed at the Park Lane Hilton in London. My experience as a world traveller taught me that if you go to bed too early on the first day then the jet lag is worse. So I had the bright idea of keeping us all awake until around 8pm. If we got to then, then I knew Jordyn would sleep through the night before we headed on to Goodwood.

Across the road was the incredible Hyde Park and so I said

we should take a walk. Before long we found a playground and Jordyn started spinning, swinging and climbing. She said she wanted an ice cream, so I walked just out of the little play area to a wooden stall. I was just paying when I heard a piercing scream that I recognised as Chelee'.

'Freddie! Oh no! Where are you?'

I ran back and Chelee' was holding Jordyn and I could see that her arm was hurt. Panic flooded through me. I looked at her wrist. It was not just broken but completely displaced. Chelee' had gone completely white and was close to passing out. Jordyn had been bumped at the top of a high slide, which had no railing, and fallen.

We looked around for help but everyone just stared, not knowing what to do. We carefully started walking out the way we had come in. I was frantically asking for anyone to help. We had no phone. Hyde Park is a huge grass area in the middle of London and we were a long way into its labyrinth of paths. I looked at Jordyn's face and grimaced. Then, seemingly out of nowhere, a man walked up to us.

'Can I help you?'

'Yes, yes, we need an ambulance!'

'That will take too long. I'll take you. That's my cab over there.'

For some reason the taxi driver had driven quite a long way into Hyde Park. Maybe he wanted some solitude. Who knows? It was lucky for us he did, though. We got in and he said he knew exactly where to take us. Ten long minutes later he pulled into the back of a building that looked deserted.

'This is the children's surgery centre,' he said.

I thanked him and tried to pay him the fare.

'You don't owe me anything,' he said. 'Please just help your daughter.'

We walked in and there was no one there apart from a receptionist.

She said: 'Can I help you?'

'My daughter has broken her wrist.'

She looked at us and said: 'I understand but to come here you have to be referred by a GP.'

At that point a man walked in. 'It's okay,' he said calmly. 'We will need to open up a theatre to help her.'

I was grateful to the surgeon. There was talking but I was almost oblivious to the words. Still holding Jordyn in my arms, I just felt the most intense of emotions.

'They need to take her, Freddie,' Chelee' said.

I realised I could not let go and I have never cried so hard in my life. I had been broken myself lots of times but nothing compared with this. I was sobbing and squeezing, when Jordyn looked up at me and, with her good arm, put a little hand on my face.

'Daddy, it's going to be okay.'

With that touch, I knew she was right. Her touch gave me the strength I needed. I let go and they took her away. They said the operation would take 45 minutes. Two hours later the surgeon emerged. He explained that they would be monitoring her overnight. We were all physically and emotionally exhausted, jet-lagged and distressed. Chelee' and I slept fitfully, me agonising about keeping her up to beat jet lag. The surgeon and a nurse watched over Jordyn all night.

The next morning I said I was going to call the Goodwood people to cancel.

'No, Daddy,' said Jordyn. 'You need to go to the track.'

I was a basket case but her calming power was such a pure thing. I thanked the surgeon for his kindness.

'I want to tell you something,' he said. 'The greatest ride I ever saw was that one in the rain at Silverstone in 1985.'

So we headed south to the Goodwood estate and I was glad we made it to the revival because Barry Sheene was going to be there. I wanted to see Barry again. He had been an important figure from the beginning of my international career and a kind, occasional presence thereafter. The following year Barry would pass away from cancer, but I have never forgotten his generosity and spirit. It was nice to see him one last time. I got to ride the 1957 MV Agusta that John Surtees had won the world title on. It was a privilege. John did not let anybody ride his bikes and so I reassured him I would take it easy.

We got through the revival. Virgin Atlantic was the airline that sponsored Goodwood and so we had flown over in business class. Richard Branson was taken with Jordyn and her courage and he gave me his card. He said that we should go back in first class. You had to be 12 to do that, but if there were any problems he said I should pass on his number. At the airport, I duly handed over the card. There was a quick call and a 'Yes, sir' and we were bumped up to first.

When we got back to Vegas we saw our regular doctor who said the surgery had been so precise that Jordyn would be completely fine. I could not thank that London doctor enough. The break was so close to the growth plate that anything less could have caused her real problems in later life. We were so grateful for all the help and for the kindness of the London cab driver in Hyde Park.

One of the great fears of some professional racers is that their children will, at some point, want to go down the same route. When Connor was almost four we were riding home on a plane from Texas to Vegas when he told me that he wanted a mini-bike. I had been dreading this moment and began a series of diversionary tactics that I hoped would avoid the almost inevitable.

I knew all that could happen in this sport, all the bad things and the pain. I would never be a pushy parent and, if anything, wanted to push him away from that world. I had seen it time and again at the school. Parents would bring their kids and, within a few minutes, I could tell who really wanted to do this – often it was the parents vicariously living out some dream with no real thought for the child. I had a tremendous example in my own dad, who had never pushed but had always supported. Generally, it was the parent who didn't race but had always wanted to who was the pushy one.

When we got home from the airport I told Connor that he had never even ridden a bicycle without his training wheels. I thought that might slow this down for a few days, but he said: 'Okay, let's go outside and take them off.'

I said it was late and that we should leave it until after school the next day, thinking that he might forget by then, but the next day I pulled into the garage and there was Connor, standing with a wrench in his hand. He had not forgotten.

We had bought our own place and lived in a cul-de-sac with four houses on one side and four on the other, separated by a water fountain at the end. It was the home I'd always wanted. I took the wrench off Connor and removed the training wheels. I pointed him towards the fountain and began to push him. We took four steps and, when I felt his balance, I let go. He made it to about ten feet and then said: 'Okay, Dad, you can let go.'

'I already have, buddy.'

On hearing that, he turned to his right to look back at me. He gave me a huge smile and then a thumbs-up before crashing straight into a palm tree. I ran over. He had scratches on his hands and knees but he was fine.

'Great job, buddy, but just keep looking forward.'

'Don't worry about me.'

He was so excited and was soon riding around the fountain. I shivered. Connor's lips were turning blue in the cold but he did not want to stop.

'Come on, buddy. Let's go inside.'

He told his mom and Jordyn about his breakthrough. 'I did it, I did it.'

Then he came over to me. 'I want a mini-bike now.'

My next stalling technique was to say that he didn't have a helmet. I said he needed an Arai helmet because that was what Daddy used. I figured it would buy me a couple of months. Finally that helmet arrived from Japan, but still Connor was showing no signs of relenting. I gave up. American Honda sent him a little 50cc bike which was too big for him, and so for the first time in my life I actually bought a motorcycle. I went down to the store and signed the papers for a little Suzuki JR 50. I watched Connor ride and my first reaction was to slow him down. The last thing I am is a risk-taker. Connor was actually like that, too, far more cautious than his sister who would just get on anything and go. Jordyn would ride by feel.

I managed to divert him to four wheels before too long, mainly because he went to school with two brothers who both raced karts. I got a truck and started taking him to small meetings at the Vegas go-kart track next door to the Speedway. I quickly realised just how good my dad had been at supporting me. I had one kart to look after, which basically meant ensuring the chain was tight and the bolts were all tight, but we had a lot of issues. By contrast, Dad sometimes had five motorcycles to keep up, built from parts he had found in every place going, and I very rarely had any problems.

One night, late in his first full season in 2008, Connor had qualified on the outside of the front row for a race. It was a big deal for him because he was six and the other kids were older. That night I saw fragments of my childhood in him. When he got nervous he yawned, which is exactly what I used to do. He would take it a step further. On that pre-grid, in his little racing suit with his Arai helmet and little Alpinestars gloves and shoes, his head slumped down and he fell asleep. I remembered my stomach cramps when I was a kid after the races; this was his way to deal with nerves but less dramatic.

I woke him up and the race began. I watched and noticed that every time he went through the one right-hander, his seat seemed to slide to the left. He ended up third but he was steaming. As he pulled off the track he was shaking his head and talking away even though he still had his helmet on and the noise of the engine was drowning out anything that got out. I hunched down to his level and killed the engine.

'Good job. What's wrong?'

'The seat was loose,' he griped. 'Every time I went around that corner I had to put my foot against the side of the kart to hold it.'

I said: 'Yes, but that's great! You figured it out.'

He looked at me like I was mad, that there was nothing great about that. And then I did the worst thing I ever could have done. Looking at him standing there in his little driving suit, with his hands on his hips, I started to smile. I should have known better and remembered what I had felt like that night when Dad and Danny had laughed at me after my first race at Lake Lavon. I tried to make amends.

'You know what you should do – fire your mechanic.'

Connor considered that and frowned. 'I can't fire my mechanic,' he complained. 'How am I going to get to races if I do that? I have to keep you.'

I stifled a smile. 'Good point.'

We loaded up and he was asleep before I even drove out of the track, just like I often was when Dad drove us home from a night at the races. I looked in the mirror and smiled.

All I knew for sure was these days with my kids were magical. We would go out into the night and sit in the hot tub and look up into the big purple sky. Our favourite game on a crystal-clear night was to spot the satellites as they flew over. If you were patient enough and focused really hard then you could just about make them out. The kids would grow excited and I'd have to quieten them because the desert nights are so silent that any noise is exaggerated and drifts from street to street. I would catch a satellite with the kids and marvel at how fast 17,000mph really was.

Breeze, Louisiana, 2010

On my way home from the Birmingham show I sat down in seat 37B on the flight from Newark to Houston. The window seat next to me was empty but they had said it was a full flight. For some reason, I just felt uncomfortable and that feeling grew stronger. It was not like something bad is going to happen, so much as:

I need to move.

I looked up and two people were looking my way. One was a flight attendant and the other was a man in his mid-to-late twenties. The young man started to walk towards me. I took out my ear buds.

He said: 'Excuse me, sir, that is my seat next to you. I just got engaged and I wondered …'

I stopped him mid-sentence. 'I'd be happy to trade seats.'

He had a shocked look on his face. 'Really?'

'You bet.' His fiancée met me halfway down the aisle and after she thanked me numerous times, I said: 'No problem. I wish you both the best.'

When I got to my new seat, 32E, I realised the uncomfortable feeling had gone. I sat down and said hello to the young lady next to me and the man next to her. The lady said: 'I just want you to know that in 10 minutes they will close the doors and if no one is in the window seat over there I am going to jump up and grab it.' She smiled. 'Don't worry. I can really jump.'

The man in the opposite aisle seat started talking first. He was from Scotland and said he could tell from my accent that I was from the States and, taking a guess, originally the South. He expressed an opinion about how America was dealing with issues in the Middle East and the lady put her ear buds in. 'I do not talk about politics or religion with strangers.'

She leant back and closed her eyes. I smiled. Then she opened them and made contact with mine and asked if I would wake her when the attendant came by with drinks.

'Absolutely,' I said.

She put out her hand and said:

'My name is Grace.'

I shook her hand and said: 'I'm Freddie.'

I just felt that I should have moved seats to be next to Grace. After a couple of minutes she opened her eyes and Grace saw that a couple had taken the seats she was eyeing. 'Oh well,' she shrugged. 'It wasn't meant to be.'

After 30 minutes, the beverage cart came around and I woke her up. We all got drinks and the man from Scotland, named Morgan, began talking about how rich countries and their corporations give to charities.

He was vocal in his opinion and I agreed with some points but said ultimately it came down to why they were doing it. We looked at Grace and I felt that, of the three of us, she would have the most thoughtful perspective. I could just sense it. She looked at us and said with certainty: 'I don't talk politics or religion with strangers.'

Morgan looked at her and shrugged at me. We did not speak again for several hours until it was close to landing. I said what came to me at that moment.

'Grace, why don't you tell me how you give your time for others?'

She looked up with a slight smile. Then she sat up and said: 'How about I show you?'

I smiled back. 'That would be great.' And we weren't strangers any more.

Grace had worked for her own media company in Nicaragua. She specialised in video photography and had a degree from Duke University. As others from her country wanted to get out of Nicaragua, she felt compelled to go back and help her people.

She took pictures for companies to use in ads and that paid the bills, but she believed her mission was to take pictures of those that others forgot – to give them a voice through her photos.

She showed me a video about six young men who had been in gangs but were now breakdancers. They qualified for a competition in São Paulo and had hope that it would change their lives. Then the sponsor pulled out and their hopes were crushed. Grace portrayed it all with no blame. At the last minute, after seeing the video, somebody came through and the boys went on their trip after all.

Then she shared her most intimate project. There were photos of six different women who had been physically abused and brutally raped. The photos were only of their hands. She explained they weren't allowed to show their faces because their lives were still in danger, that they had been incredibly brave even to have their hands photographed.

Grace described how she would take each woman and sit them down, take their hands in hers and make them feel comfortable. It didn't matter how long it took. She wanted each woman to know that they were special and brave.

As Grace went through each shot I noticed she would touch the computer screen with the tips of two fingers and lightly rub the picture of each woman's hands. I could tell that, at that moment, she was back with that woman, telling her it would be okay and that she could trust her.

She had tears in her eyes when she finished showing me the pictures and I recognised one of Grace's biggest gifts is empathy. She said she had taken the photos on behalf of Amnesty International.

'I just felt I should show you and that you would want to see them.'

For some reason, I told her that one day I wanted to climb Mount Kilimanjaro. She said: 'That would be great. Just let me know.'

We traded contact information. As I was walking by the gate counter she turned around and stopped in front of me. She looked at me straight and with tears in her eyes gently put both hands on my face.

'Thank you,' she said.

I could feel the sincerity in her touch and feel it in her voice. And I said: 'It was my privilege, Grace.'

I walked to the gate to catch my flight to Shreveport.

Part 3
EXIT
(2008 to now)

Chapter 16: **LEAVING (2008–2010)**

IT WAS not only satellites that were moving quickly. I felt a sense that the business, which was at its peak after ten years of building it from the desert dust, was not going to last. It didn't make sense because it had never been better. Why did I have that sense now? Within a year the financial crisis was in full swing, but not now in 2007. My question was not *how* did I know? It was *what* did this nagging feeling mean?

I decided I wasn't going to get angry this time. I had been there before. It doesn't help. It's a hindrance in every way. This time I would use my lifetime of experiences and skills. I would pay attention as I did when I was a kid trusting what I sensed and felt. I would put all of that to good use. No matter how difficult it might be and how long it might take. I was in this until the end.

The contrast to the way I was feeling with the success we were having in 2007 was perplexing. We could not run schools in the summer in Las Vegas because it was so blisteringly hot, but Alan Wilson, the track manager at Brands Hatch who had given me my trophy there on that Good Friday in 1980, had approached me while I was working at an AMA race weekend for Speedvision. He said they were building a track near Salt Lake and maybe I'd like to run some schools there. And so in the summer of 2006, when it was finished, we did begin to run schools away from Vegas and the business grew. I couldn't imagine it being any better. I was working with great people and students who were driven to learn. It was not enough.

Chelee' and I had been drifting apart for some time too. We

loved our kids unconditionally, but I would come to realise that, as a couple, we had stopped communicating, or never really had. I had never told her about how I felt that day in the motorhome in 1985. I wasn't happy and neither was she. We had a lot of conflicts and I am sorry about that.

I sensed there was more I was supposed to know as the distance widened between us. I had turned 40 in 2001 and really hoped I had settled into the life I would see and experience until the end. But that wasn't the reality. Everything around me was now changing. When she asked for a divorce it was not out of the blue. It seemed inevitable.

We had taken two breaks in the past. It's easy to look from the outside and see what someone else should do, but it's hard to have that same clarity when it's you in that unsettled emotional bubble. We had built a good place to share with others at the school, but unfortunately we didn't have that same open and compassionate place for us to share together. We had tried to make our marriage work for our incredible, beautiful children, but we couldn't make it happen.

Chelee' moved to another house in another neighbourhood and we agreed a custody arrangement where we would have the kids for five days at a time. Our marriage was coming to an end but the joy I got from spending that period with the kids was something I will always cherish.

We went on a last pre-booked ski vacation to Colorado together as a family in January 2008. The following summer the kids and I spent almost every day together as Chelee' was working. It was a simple time, baking cupcakes and making pancakes. The kids nicknamed me Freddie Crocker, after Betty Crocker, a fictional character used in food advertising. I baked for Jordyn and her friends who wanted to make some extra money by having a cupcake sale. One time I baked almost 100 cupcakes. They didn't make a lot of money that day, though, because they ended up eating about 50 of them. Even now, with the perspective of time, I look back and wonder at how, after 16 years of marriage and two beautiful children, and 11 years of working every day to build the school and other businesses, it all changed in a matter of months. When the financial crisis hit and the global economy crashed, it was over, due mostly to circumstances beyond our control.

Most of our sign-ups were via the website and they were dramatically reduced almost overnight. Banks closed, billions were wiped off share prices and jobs and businesses were plunged into crisis. It is easy to look back at what you might have done differently, but this time I knew not to fight it.

The crash was so quick and so drastic that there was nothing else I felt I could do and so I closed the school. It was really tough, not least because of the damage to relationships. There was the staff to consider and people who had signed up for schools, but we were struggling like so many people at that time. I was glad that Nick and the guys would manage to get the Yamaha sponsorship and start a school at Miller Motorsports, but I had come to the conclusion that I needed to leave Las Vegas. It was remote and isolated, as the rush to leave in 2001 had shown, and there was nothing professionally there for me any more.

After 10 years, I helped my last person at Las Vegas Motor Speedway when I did my final consultancy work for Honda with Neil Hodgson, the British rider who won the World Superbike Championship in 2003. Neil followed me around the Vegas track because I wanted to show him how I had learned to use the front of the bike on corner entry – loading just enough to let the rear unload at just the right moment to drift out. It meant that by mid-corner I had already changed direction. It was like what I had seen when I was 11 watching Kenny Roberts. I may not have totally understood the technical reason then, but I could see it and then feel the result practicing in my yard and knew it worked.

On that final day on the outside road course with Neil it looked like I was right in front of him. Then I'm leaning and going on the brakes and, instead of the front pointing towards the edge of the track, it's pointed towards the exit. It's all about the rear tire rotating while applying lean angle and it's so subtle you can't see it. You have to feel it.

Now I know that it can happen to me and so it can happen to you. If I have a gift from riding a motorcycle, a skill as an athlete, it is recognition. To have that much feel while using the front brake lever means I never ride without knowing exactly what grip pressure I have. I know where my feel is. Work on that awareness and you will be able to recognise those moments that matter in any walk of life and react how you need to.

Back then it was different. Neil was receptive, but at the end of 2008 Honda decided to pull out of AMA racing. The broadcasting was also coming to a close. I went to Daytona in 2009 for my last broadcast. I would do a few more voiceovers in the spring but it was time to move on.

The school shut in October 2008. I used what funds I had to pay everyone what I could and I had to sell my bikes. I moved out of my house in November and then, on 24 January 2010, I told the kids that I would be leaving Las Vegas soon. It was how I was going to take care of them. They understood as well as they could, but were not sure what it would mean. I did the events I could to make money – I went to an event at the Japanese Grand Prix; a dealer in Switzerland had a grand opening of his premier Honda store – but there was a conflict between the very practical side of my nature and the uncertainty of what I was doing.

I realised that from that moment in November 1985, when I was the new double world champion, to that day in September 2007 when Chelee' asked for a divorce, I had let anger, pain and disappointment creep in. I had closed that door to the place deep in my most true self – the place that I used to depend on innately, to sense, feel and trust, for direction.

I should have known better. And I was sorry but I wasn't going to make the same mistake again.

I knew deep in my soul that for me to move forwards I would have to be willing to trust again, just as I had before as a kid. No doubts. This time I would trust those feelings, thoughts and situations.

I was staying with my friends Mike and Christine first, and then with my friend Les. A few weeks before I left Las Vegas for the final time, my sister called and said, 'Why don't you come back to Shreveport for a visit? Or stay a while if you want.' We had spoken a few times in the past year and she knew the divorce was finalised and the school and all the businesses associated with it were gone. Her brother, who had accomplished so much in his sport and built a life in Las Vegas from the ground up, was now 49 years old and staying with a friend. She had every right to be concerned, but she only knew what I didn't have any more.

I understood most everyone would only see what I had lost. After the call I felt I should go back to Louisiana. For how long, I was not sure.

I met the kids and Chelee' at the train park, a little play area near where they lived, on 21 April 2010. I was leaving the next day. Of course, it was emotional, but I felt this was for the benefit of everyone. I had to leave Las Vegas to be able to take care of them. What I said to the kids, and what they said to me, is between us, but I felt such a deep ache and pain in my heart to leave them, however, it was what I needed to do.

The next day I was on the 7.15am flight to Shreveport.

I had one event planned for the summer. So I went to 1000 Bikes at Mallory Park in July. Then I was back at my sister's, with a backpack and one suitcase and everything else I had left in storage units in Las Vegas. Memories of my youth and racing career were in storage here in Shreveport.

More than ever I needed my old friend Mr Williams. I had no real idea of what I would come to understand but I felt that Mr Williams somehow did. 'Freddie,' he said to me one day during that period when I was back in Shreveport and living with my sister, 'this is going to be even better than before.'

We had always been close, and he had come in and out of my life at pivotal times, but in those few months from 22 April we would become closer than ever.

Chelee' and the kids moved to Houston during that summer. That was closer geographically but I missed the kids terribly. This had to be worth it. I flew out to Vegas to check on the storage and when I got back I had made up my mind. It was 23 July 2010 and I felt I was getting close to whatever it was. I told Linda, I needed to leave. I checked into the Hilton Garden and stayed there until ...

When I woke up in my hotel room at the Hilton Garden this morning, 2 August 2010, I knew today was the day. I had left my sister's on 23 July. I had been there three months and she asked where I would go. I just told her it would be fine. All the striving and uncertainty had prepared me for whatever it was. I had no idea but I knew it would be out there.

I got out of bed and, as I have done the last three mornings, I walked over to the window and opened the shades and looked outside to see what the weather was like. I was waiting and today, 2 August, was the day.

My room here on the third floor faces east. I put my hand on the window and could feel the heat from the sun through the glass on my fingertips. As I took my hand off the window I thought it was time. So I called Mr Williams to see if he could come by to pick me up around 11. Where would I go next? I didn't know, but I trusted I would soon enough.

Mr Williams pulled up to the front at exactly 11. I put my bags in the back seat and got in.

'You got everything?' Mr Williams asked.

'Yes, sir.'

He started out of the parking lot and paused at the exit.

Mr Williams said: 'Which way?'

Chapter 17: **BREEZE (2010)**

IT HAD been an incredible few months. Part of that was just trusting my own intuition and the belief that comes from a life of learning, knowing when to trust that sense that comes when you are willing to recognise the situation.

That got me to this place a few months ago. And being here has given me those moments with others that I knew was possible. It would lead me to more understanding, like the time with Jenny.

On that Wednesday afternoon in the third week of September 2010, Mr Williams and I had left my eye doctor's office after my appointment. We were halfway back to the Shreveport Country Club when I finally told Mr Williams I thought there was something I was supposed to ask Jenny, Dr Bartkowski's assistant.

'Do you want me to turn around and go back?'

I hesitated for a moment and said: 'No, not today, maybe tomorrow.'

Mr Williams said: 'Okay.'

That night I couldn't shake that sense so the next morning I did go back to see Jenny.

I walked in and she asked if there was a problem with my new contact lenses. I said no as I glanced around the office. I noticed a beautiful vase with a dozen roses sitting on a table.

I asked, 'Who are those for?'

She said, 'Those are for me. It is my 26th birthday today, but that is not why they are so special. It is because twenty-five years ago today my mom and dad brought me home. They give me flowers every year as a reminder of the gift I am to them.'

I smiled. 'That is sweet. It means so much to you because of what it gives them.'

She put her hand on her heart. 'Yes. It is about them and not me.'

I said: 'I understand, Jenny. I felt I was supposed to come back today and ask you something. Now I know. It was to ask you about the flowers and see that in you.'

She smiled and leaned in. 'Not many recognise that in each other.'

'Maybe it is because they don't know how to recognise it, but I believe many want to, and this is priceless, Jenny.'

Now I understood why I was supposed to go back and what I was supposed to ask her. It was one of those trigger points.

On the day before Thanksgiving I got a message from Lisa, my friend, neighbour and PR rep who was instrumental in me getting some work in Europe back in 2009. She set up my Facebook account and keeps me up to date. She said a Facebook friend had messaged me. Her name was Kathryn Hampton. She was Ronnie's daughter, the little girl who had been listening at the bottom of the stairs when I went to pick up her sister Mary-Ann and take her to the sweetheart banquet in 1977. Before I went to Thanksgiving lunch with Martin and his family, I sent Kathryn a message to say I was in Shreveport and where I was staying. When I got back from Martin's in the afternoon, she had replied. She had got my message while sitting in a gas station in Dallas, around the corner from where she lived, on her way to Shreveport. She would come by to pick me up around 3pm.

While on Facebook, a sequence of photos cropped up on my page. They were of a motorcycle racer crashing. I could tell it was a low side crash in a left-hand corner and I could tell from the bike's position what had most likely caused it. I was also pretty sure from the landscape, the curbing and the asphalt texture which track it was, but that wasn't what intrigued me. I had the feeling I was supposed to help this person. It was 25 November 2010 and I hadn't thought about helping anyone since I closed the school in the fall of 2008.

I clicked on the name and sent the person a message.

'Hi, came across your photo and if you like I can give you my opinion of what happened and why.'

I walked out the side door and saw Kathryn, who was smiling. It had been almost ten years since I'd seen her when Chelee' organised a 40th birthday party for me in Vegas.

She was driving the perfect car for her – a Mini Cooper. There was a black terrier on the back seat.

'And who are you?'

He turned his head and raised his eyebrows.

Kathryn said, 'My name is Skittles. Skittles, this is my friend Freddie.'

'Really. I had a cat named Skittles. What are the chances?'

We went to see Kathryn's aunt Susie and had some of her pie. I was waiting for Kathryn to ask why I had been at the Courtyard Marriott for almost four months but she didn't.

Instead, she just said, 'I could tell you were all good when you got in the car.'

Kathryn took me back to the hotel after lunch. It was great to catch up. She said, 'I would like to go to Natchitoches tomorrow to see the Christmas lights. Would you like to come with me?'

'Sure,' I said. 'That would be great.'

When I got back to my room the motorcycle racer had answered. Her name was Kristin Casey and she couldn't sleep. It was about 4am in Australia and she was wondering about the crash. So she went online and saw my message.

We started communicating. It is a small example of what a great thing it is to pay attention. I was online doing something else when I first saw her pictures and I thought, 'You know what, I'm going to see if they want me to help.'

It helped her going through that weekend and she was able to improve on what she was doing wrong. When she got back from Australia, I went down to a track day at Jennings, Florida and I helped her there. We talked about many spiritual-related things and I found her so insightful.

The next day Kathryn and Skittles came by and we headed down Highway 49. Natchitoches is the oldest permanent settlement in Louisiana. Its main street takes you back in time to a simpler way of life. I hadn't been to see the lights in 25 years. The displays were everything I remembered. Then we drove on to New Orleans.

I just got the feeling to tell Kathryn about how I'd wake up each morning and write some or read from the Bible that Martin had brought to me. She asked what Book or scripture and I said, 'Just wherever it opens.'

And she said, 'Then just like we would do when we were teenagers.'

I remembered that so clearly. 'Right – just like that.'

We talked about how she usually planned everything meticulously, but had just felt that she should come over to Shreveport yesterday when she got my message. Then she knew why.

I said, 'I've learned that it's all about right here, right now. And that if you really pay attention to what you sense and feel with the right attitude then it will work out as it's supposed to. That doesn't mean it will be quick or easy. It will take patience and discipline and test your faith and will.'

Then Kathryn said, 'That's why I got so mad at you in 1985.'

'What do you mean?'

'We talked when we were teenagers and you would tell me that being in the moment is how you sensed and felt to ride. And you knew where that came from. But in 1985 you seemed to have changed and didn't talk about that any more. I could see that. You had forgotten. And it made me mad.'

I shook my head. 'You are right. How could I have changed so much to forget that? I'm sorry.'

'Don't be sorry. Just stay this way.'

And then, with a smile, she added: 'You don't want to get me mad again.' She was right about that.

We talked some more over the weekend before Kathryn had to

go back to Dallas and I had the most intense feeling that it was time to leave the Courtyard Marriott.

And then I thought, *with Kathryn?* I sat down and wrote:

If I am supposed to leave with Kathryn then she will bring it up.

I met her at the next-door restaurant at 8am on Monday. We talked about her interior design business and how hard it was to stay busy in these difficult times, but she had a few good and loyal clients.

Then she looked at me. 'What are you doing today? Or the rest of the week?'

'I don't know yet.'

'I feel really strongly that you should come back to Dallas with me. I have a spare room. You can stay for as long or as short a time as you want.'

I smiled. 'Maybe I should.'

I went back and started packing. I was leaving. I felt a tinge of sadness for leaving the people and experiences I had shared over the last four months.

I went to the laundry room and found Mrs Ada. I hugged her.

'What's wrong?' she said.

'Nothing, Mrs Ada. It's just I'm leaving.'

She was shocked. 'When and with who?'

'My friend Kathryn is coming by to pick me up and we're going to Dallas.'

Mrs Ada said, 'So when are you coming back?'

'I'm not. But I'll come and visit.'

Teresa walked into the laundry room and Mrs Ada told her, 'Freddie's leaving us.'

'When are you coming back?'

'I'm not, Teresa.'

She said: 'When did you decide that?'

'This morning at breakfast. Kathryn will be by in an hour. I will finish packing and come up in a bit.'

It was harder than I imagined it would be. After all that I had been through there, it was like leaving home, except it was more than that.

I felt privileged to have spent so much time with Teresa, Mrs Ada, Lorraine, Martin and the rest of the people in that time and place. I was a wiser and better person for it.

When I walked out, I said to Kathryn: 'You were confident I would come back with you?'

She said, 'I told you when I got your message I knew I was meant to come and pick you up. Then this morning I knew you were meant to come back to Dallas with me. It's time to leave.'

Chapter 18: **STRONGER (2010 on)**

SO KATHRYN, Skittles and me went to Dallas in her Mini Cooper, leaving Teresa, Mrs Ada, Martin and the rest of the people I had met in my four months at the Courtyard Marriott behind, gone but never forgotten.

I was seeing the events of a lifetime. What had changed after that moment at the Heathrow Sofitel when I had seen the photographs of Sarie? To put it simply, I could now recognise the deeper meaning of things. Before I just wondered.

I remembered when I had listened and, just as importantly, when I didn't. All the lessons gleaned from when I ignored my intuition were now weighing on me, like a burden that never leaves. It seemed like everything moved so fast but the reality is it had been a long time coming. I had been outside my comfort zone before. It had got me to Mr Honda's house. I had walked into the Courtyard Marriott not knowing why or what was different to the other times when I'd been there. While I was there I began to understand the reason. Now I needed to see what was outside my comfort zone again. But this time it was going to be away from the track, out in the world.

Kathryn was straight and spunky, a talented interior designer who had worked for major firms like Hanna-Barbera before her divorce. Her dream was to get back out west and use her creativity to the maximum. It was 29 November 2010 when we headed down the road to Dallas. We were helping each other go where we needed to go.

Through Kathryn I got to meet another important figure who would help me move this along. Her name was Georgia Patrick, a hard-as-nails, warm-hearted PR lady who worked in Washington DC. Kathryn had bought a table in support of a local charity being hosted at a horse-racing track in April 2010. We were all talking about purpose and how do we ever really know what that is. I began telling her about how I felt everything sort of falls into place. Georgia was not the sort to suffer fools, but she looked at me pointedly. When there was a quiet moment, she said: 'I'm supposed to help you tell your story. I just feel it.'

I could see the intrigue on her face. She was a very successful and practical businesswoman, but she called herself 'Sherpa', and now I had help on my side. She was the one who helped me begin to turn my notes into something tangible and write *Breeze*.

I had some events scheduled that May. One was in Italy with Zaeta, an Italian motorcycle company set up by Paolo Chiaia, who described himself as a romantic melancholic, and his friend Marco Belli. They were designing a street tracker for getting around urban communities. Their great friend was Graziano Rossi, dad of Valentino, and we did a cool demonstration event in Verona together, old-school flat-tracking, just sliding around in the dirt. Then it was on to Northern Ireland.

Leading up to that trip, I slowly started to open up to Kathryn, who had always been the only other kid I would talk to about anything approaching spiritual matters when we were young. I told her about my experience by Mom and Dad's graves, my stories, my dad wanting 'Amazing Grace' at his funeral, hearing 'The Lucky One' by Faith Hill and 'Strong' by LeAnn Rimes, feeling the words meant more than just pop rhymes, more than minor-chord sentimentality.

I felt 'Strong' was in some way connected to this somehow, maybe as part of the leaf fire part of my story. But I wondered how there would be a story of my life when I had resisted talking about it for so long. Talking to Sherpa and Kathryn was the first step to me telling my story, but I was only willing to share so much at that stage in May of 2011.

I did feel one day I would get to California. I felt that was the next step and then I would know where I would go from there.

I called Kathryn on Skype one night from the event in Northern Ireland and she said she had been driving back and forth from Shreveport, working on a project, when she had seen a big advertising billboard saying LeAnn Rimes was going to be in concert in Marshall, Texas on 3 June, just 35 minutes from Shreveport. She was letting me know that we were going. I said, 'Okay, great.'

Before I knew it, we were ten rows from the front on the right side of the aisle in a small venue of only around 300 fold-away seats. I had never imagined I would ever go to a LeAnn Rimes concert but here I was. She told the audience that this was her first concert after a break and she was not going to use a set list. After a couple of songs she was trying to fix her hair behind her ears and a lady from the second row said she had a hair band she could use.

LeAnn said: 'I was just thinking I could do with one. How lucky for me?'

Between each song she would walk to the back of the stage and I realised that was when she was letting the band know which song she wanted to sing next.

After the third song she said: 'Three months ago I put this next song in my set list. I've never sung it live in the US before, but it's a song that's close to my heart. It's called "Strong".'

Kathryn looked at me with a smile when she realised that LeAnn was going to sing 'Strong'. It was a nice confirmation of why she felt the urge to buy the tickets. She realised we were really supposed to be there. I knew that Kathryn was supposed to come and get me at the Courtyard Marriott and that we were supposed to come tonight. It had nothing to do with my old friend Kathryn and me. We were two people always striving to understand more, brought together on this journey. She helped to set the wheels in motion for what was to come next. I didn't know what that was yet, but so far, each step I had chosen correctly was a confirmation we were moving in the right direction. But it wasn't time to tell my story yet. The next thing was to get to California. Things seemed to be connecting, just kind of falling into place. Georgia had said they would. LeAnn had sung about her life being stolen, and fearing she would never get 'me' back.

When I looked at my notebooks from what I'd written in those first few weeks at the Courtyard Marriott it was about what I could do in my world of motorcycling. They were very practical projects. I had evolved from then and knew there was more to tell.

When I walked into the Courtyard Marriott that August day I did not know it was a project driven by the spiritual because I never assume. Believe me, I am also aware that the description of the spiritual scares and turns off many people; maybe it did me too. Because for many people, religion and spiritual things are things we should just acknowledge on a Sunday morning or a Wednesday evening and then put away. In today's world it's not easy to make the right choice. Sometimes there is scepticism and doubt and it is hard to trust after so much disappointment.

After the concert we walked out and noticed a motorhome to the right. It was obviously LeAnn's. Kathryn said, 'Do you want to go and say hello?'

I said, 'No. Maybe someday she will read about it.'

During the short drive to Shreveport after the concert, looking out at the clear moonlit sky, I couldn't get the song 'Strong' out of my thoughts. It was a perfect confirmation with its line about being strong even when it hurt.

Over the summer of 2011 I felt we were moving forwards. I was weighing up a few ideas. I began doing a few things with Michelin UK and wondered whether there was a way of telling the story through doing some riding with others through Europe, maybe with the help of Michelin and their travel website. I had met Charley Boorman at the London show in January. He had done a couple of great documentaries called *Long Way Down* and *Long Way Round* with Ewan McGregor. They had ridden around the world; maybe he and I could too.

Then Kathryn asked if I remembered a boy, a few years younger than us, who used to come over to her house on Pines Road when we were kids. His name was Randy Brewer and she said he was in Nashville now and had his own production company. She said maybe she should call him. She got his number and called. He said there was a guy he knew, Chris Hicky, who directed music videos and was a motorcycling fan. He would put us in touch. A month later Kathryn needed to go to Irvine, California, for a few days for a job, so she said I should join her and set up a meeting with Chris. When she had finished her work, we went up to Santa Monica, a place I'd never been to other than as a tourist visiting the pier with its carousel and roller-coaster.

That night at the hotel, on the eve of our meeting with Chris, Kathryn googled his name to see what else he had done.

I will never forget her asking: 'What song was it you listened to and wrote about in your notebook after visiting your parents' grave?'

'The Faith Hill one?'

'Yes.'

'"The Lucky One".'

'You won't believe it. Chris directed the video.'

I sat there in silence for a moment thinking, 'Strong' and now 'The Lucky One'.

Each of these apparent coincidences made me surer about what I had experienced. The next day we met Chris and told him about how I knew I was supposed to ride for Honda, and he said, 'You need to write your story.'

It felt right to him. When I got back to Dallas I knew it was time to start writing. Over a six-week period that spring I wrote *Breeze*, the story of my four months at the Courtyard Marriott and why it was so significant to me.

It felt good to get it out and the events began fitting together like pieces in a puzzle. On 1 June 2012 my friend Aldo Whittenberg got in touch with an idea of me doing more appearances and classic events in Europe in 2013. Then John Burns, an editor and writer from *Cycle World* magazine, sent an email saying that if I got to California sometime then we should get together and see what we could do to mark the magazine's forthcoming 50th anniversary. A week later Kathryn saw an advert for a job opening with a design firm in California and she felt it was time to go west for good. The door was opening. Things began to move fast.

In the last week of June, Honda Mobility invited me to the 50th anniversary of the Suzuka circuit in September. Other work came in too from events in Europe. They amounted to exactly what we needed to put Kathryn's stuff in storage and pay for the move to California.

The hard part was I would be so far away from the kids, but deep down I knew I had to see this through.

On 28 August 2011, I left for Japan and on 10 September I began my new life in California. A few weeks later I touched base with Chris Hicky. He asked me to send him *Breeze*. I felt he had a part to play in this; he had directed 'The Lucky One' and he had a role in knowing I should go to California. Yet something told me this was not the right time. Maybe he would help in the future, I wasn't sure. Recently, I found that he had made a number of small films with a spiritual theme. That was part of the story – how being open to seeing the connections between us gives direction to what's next.

That winter I prepared for my travels and work and writing more. *Breeze* was precious to me but it was not the full story. Finally, the time was right to tell it all.

Chapter 19: **SENSE (On the way to tell my story)**

IT IS early morning, 29 December 2016, in East Finchley, London and I am writing this by the light of my phone. I have just finished making corrections to some chapters for the book. As I tell my story I realise it is about recognising the simple spiritual beauty of moments shared, good and bad. It is about connecting with others. Only my hesitation to trust myself will limit my willingness to share this story.

My mind flicks back to the day I took a flight back from an event in Madrid in September 2012. I had left my phone in the plane coming from Los Angeles on Friday. So after the event on Monday I went to the airport a little earlier than normal to visit the Delta Airlines customer service desk to see if my phone had been recovered. It hadn't.

'Thank you for checking,' I said.

The agent smiled and studied me. She leaned in and said, 'We just received an update and the flight you're booked on is delayed but Iberia has a direct flight leaving in an hour. Go over to see Raul and say Rose sent you.'

I said: 'Thank you, Rose.'

I went over and they had one seat left. 15B.

I thanked Raul and headed to the gate.

Once on board I had a thought. Wouldn't it be great if I meet someone like Grace again? It had been three years since that moment. With just a few minutes until they closed the doors,

15A was still empty. Then I looked up and a person arrived and took the vacant seat.

After take-off we introduced ourselves and began to talk. The woman said she needed to make this flight but she didn't think she was going to because she had taken a 10-hour bus ride from the south of Spain and there had been delays. She told me her dad was a doctor and she was involved in a research project in genetics at UCLA.

I asked, 'What inspired you to choose genetics research?'

'I want to understand why this all happens,' she said.

I smiled. 'That's exactly what I'm trying to figure out too. Do you believe everything happens for a reason?' I asked.

She said: 'Absolutely.'

'I believe it too,' I said, 'but it is more complex than that and cleverly simpler also. It is what we are willing to see. What we are willing to believe. It's part intuitive and the other is driven by human nature so it is a constant choice in every moment of every day.'

Her name was Lorena and she told me about how she suffered with terrible asthma when she was a little girl. She could barely go out or do anything until she was ten when she told her doctor-dad that she was not going to take her medication any more. She said, 'I told him I just think it's going to be okay.' She had never had asthma since.

After she shared her story I knew to share mine with her.

'I had broken many bones in my life racing, especially in my feet. My shattered feet caused me intense pain and burnt almost constantly for decades. I had all kind of treatments, I had surgeries and took medicine for the pain. Too much.

'I didn't know what it felt like to have a day not worrying or focusing on the pain and how to alleviate it – not until that Wednesday in October in 2007, when I had a feeling that my feet were not going to hurt any more. And I just stopped taking my medicine.

'The pain went but I was so practical. How could this be? How could I explain the sudden change after all those years?'

She asked: 'Had you ever felt like that before that day in 2007?'

I said: 'No, but the next day I woke up and I felt no pain in my feet. I still sometimes wonder why it happened. I think it is partially mindset but also the fact I believed that it could happen. I had started to focus more on what's out there. I had had many glimpses in my life so I believe it's what I was willing to see and where I was willing to go that maybe had something to do with it.'

She said: 'Me too. Do you believe in miracles Mr Spencer?'

'Yes, I do,' I replied.

Then she said: 'It's why I am trying to connect the genome to what is the beginning, that moment when the spiritual becomes physical.'

I smiled. 'We are on the same quest. Now I know why we are on this flight.'

After we landed and we got to customs, I said: 'Thank you Lorena for sharing your story with me.'

She thanked me and my last visual image of Lorena is her smile and for that I'm thankful. Here was a really strong young scientist, riding a bus all night, to make a plane so she could contribute to the world. We were on the same flight but we are all on different paths. You don't need to be on a motorcycle or to be a scientist but you must be aware and willing to believe it is possible to have a moment like I had with Lorena. There are many elements that go into making a moment like this happen.

We can choose to use the gift of free will to embrace the good feelings and share them with others. Then, in turn, we receive a feeling of contentment and fullness that comes from helping with purity of heart and soul. Lorena enabled me to talk about what I had experienced, something that had nagged away at me as I was unable to rationalise it and voice it. Lorena had given me the chance to share my story with her as I had given Kim the chance to share her story with me.

Give in to fear and doubt and we not only let ourselves down but also those we are supposed to share the moments with – Teresa, Mrs

Ada, Kim, Lorena and Mr Honda. Complacency closes the window to that place in your being that provides spiritual nudges, the place that leads to leaps of faith. Take that leap and find the right path and you, too, can find the enlightenment that is your purpose.

I feel my relationship with Kenny Roberts changed in September 2012 when I attended the 50th anniversary of the Suzuka circuit. He was still unhappy about Sweden 1983, but he was there, along with many other champions of the bike and car worlds. They held an anniversary party and spoke to each of us in turn. I was the last. I understood why. I was the one who had given Mr Honda his dream. I asked the compere if he wanted me to tell that story. So I explained the drama, the emotion and how, eventually, in 1983 I had got to Mr Honda's house. 'He gave me my dream and I gave him his,' I said. You could have heard a pin drop at that point. And then the silence was broken by Kenny who shouted from the back as if on cue: 'You were lucky.'

I couldn't help but smile and I said: 'Well, sometimes it is better to be lucky than good.'

Everyone stood up and cheered. Kenny and I had brought the house down again.

The next day Kenny and I were interviewed on a stage in front of about 2,000 fans. I wanted him to understand how hard it had been. So I said: 'Every lap I ever did, every hour I rode since I was five years old, all the years of racing in National Championships, the struggles, the opportunities I got and the equipment I had to ride, all the mental, physical and emotional effort and any talent I may have – it took all of that to compete with this guy.'

Maybe I should have said it sooner.

Things have been better since then.

Entry, middle, exit – when I was a little boy I assumed everyone went on feelings that you either trusted or didn't. When I got older, I lost my way. Now I have gone back to trusting my intuition but this time I have the wisdom to know it wasn't ever about me. It was what I would learn along the way that would enable me to tell this story and help others. Would I do anything different? Of course, but I would go through all of this again to understand the gift that was given to me.

I know that my story may seem extreme to most, the highs and lows, the danger I put myself in even when I knew I shouldn't. I was always aware of the risk. I know the difficulties of everyday life, but I also recognise the purpose and the path. It has been vital to recognise the smallest of glimpses through my life, even when I didn't want to, and then use all that I had experienced and learned. It comes down to not dismissing the moment like I did when I visited my parents' graves in 2007 and was more focused on getting everybody in the car to go to lunch and getting an upgrade on the flight home. It has not been an easy ride.

The night Mom left the hospital my phone rang. It was Linda. She said Mom wanted to talk with me. Mom got on the phone. She sounded great as she talked about how she was going home the next morning and, as we were finishing, she said: 'Freddie, I didn't want to bother anybody.'

Those were the last words my mom spoke to me.

I said: 'I know, Mother. You always tried to do your best. I love you.'

She gave the phone back to Linda and I said, 'Is she okay?'

'Yes, she just wanted to talk to you. I will see you tomorrow.'

The power of those last words did not really resonate at the time, but I can now sense her incredible loneliness, that maybe she felt this was the end. It all matters. Every moment of every day, striving to understand more about out physical purpose, we have the independence to wonder. And each day is a gift that we should embrace.

In May 2013 I was sitting admiring the beautiful sunny day, watching the crowds of motorcycling enthusiasts walking along in Varano, Italy, gazing at the incredible machines displayed when suddenly I had a sense that something was going to change. It felt personal in some way but then it went away.

I was due to attend a new classic event in Normandy created and run by a team of four people. On Friday evening, Aldo, his colleague Karine and I arrived in a picturesque French town and Aldo called Nadia, our contact for the event. She was busy welcoming other guests who had already arrived and so her colleague Alexandra said she would come and meet us in the town square and take us to the restaurant where they had a welcoming dinner for all the invited champions. Alexandra and I had only met twice before, in March and April in Paris to discuss the event with Aldo and Nadia. At the end of our second meeting I just told her to always keep her spirit and passion. We did not exchange a word until May.

But that evening, in that beautiful town square, as it started to drizzle like it often does in Europe in May, I felt the beautiful intimacy of when it is right. As Alexandra walked across the parking lot to meet us there was a rare moment of recognition and I knew I was supposed to share more with her. I never expected it. I always assumed that this last part, after everything I had been through in this story, would be only me, but here I am in this village in Normandy, France and Alexandra is walking towards me.

As the weekend went on I realised that, although we were from different cultures and generations, we shared the same spiritual connection. Just as with Levy C, I knew not to let any prejudices and judgement interfere. I knew there was something I had to tell her and I felt our spirits understood each other. I saw the incredible spiritual being that she is. She had seen so much, gone through so much and could see everybody for who they were without judging them.

I felt comfortable enough to talk to her. For the first time in my life I talked about all that I had struggled with, the abuse I had suffered when I was a kid, the shyness, shame and introversion that followed, wondering what I was meant to do. Without question she was the one and I am grateful that I was paying attention when she walked into that town square.

I went back to LA a couple of days after the event and we talked on the phone every day for eight months. Then, in January 2014, I took a plane for Paris. We haven't been apart for more than six days since.

When I trusted that I should open up to Alexandra and share the struggles and experiences I had had as a kid, I realised that I could and *should* share this story wider. I hadn't done so before, as the last thing in the world I wanted was for people to feel sorry for me. I didn't need that – I had my motorcycle to help me and make me stronger, and the support of many exactly when I needed it. My family, my friends, my team, my teachers who believed in me, my hometown, the support of all the fans, the motorcycle community, and even strangers on a plane or train.

My concern was always for those who suffer similar experiences and lack the support and help I had in pursuing my goals.

In January 2016, Alexandra and I went to a 'Freddie Spencer talk show' in Ipswich in the UK. We took the train from Euston station in London. Mark Chapman, who I had met a few months before, came to see me at the event because we had agreed to visit his engineering company in Norwich the next day.

We drove with Mark's business partner because Mark had damaged his car in a car accident on the way and didn't want Alexandra and me to ride in it. So we got in the car with Andrew Foot and, after talking for a few minutes, he asked: 'Have you ever thought to publish your story?'

I looked at Alexandra in the rear-view mirror and said, 'Yes, I have.'

Andrew said he knew someone in publishing and would I mind if he got in touch with them.

I said: 'No problem.'

Nine days later I was on the train to the centre of London to meet Lorna from Penguin Random House.

I started to tell her my story.

'It's about more than my career and motorcycling,' I told her.

'That's why we're interested,' she replied.

I knew this was the place.

In the past few years since leaving Las Vegas I've lived in Shreveport, Dallas, Los Angeles, Paris, Marseille and London and I have met some incredible people. It is those people who make the story complete. They are the reasons why it matters.

Daniel from New York; Amrit who helped us and we helped him just when the three of us needed it; Gloria, who was not supposed to be in that cafe in Paris the night we met her; the Shrewsbury man in the hotel; the pastor in Northern Ireland who drove four hours from Dublin to come to tell me what he was supposed to; Sebastian on the train from Paris to Rouen; little Verane in the south of France; Aldo and the travels all around Europe in his van just like when I was a kid with Dad; Bernard Garcia, my ex-teammate with Yamaha in 1993 and the owner of the Freddie Spencer Riding School, 4G created in 2013, his boat, his parents and Clémence in Marseille; the incredible family with cystic fibrosis at the France–Switzerland border; Dave from Fort Lauderdale in the train from Venice to Paris; Henry and Jessy in Santa Monica; the missionary man from Pennsylvania in Montpellier; all the way to East Finchley and everyone I met at Amici Deli.

There are so many more and it is these never-ending connections and intersections that matter, a criss-crossing of paths to create a spider's web of humanity.

All the moments I had with songs in this journey over this last six years – 'Amazing Grace', 'Strong', 'The Lucky One' – and the connections to LeAnn Rimes and Chris Hicky were special, but it went deeper than that. The real lesson is that over the centuries we have created beautiful things that touch emotions and which people share, a piece of music, a book or a movie. We have been given ways to remember moments, individually and collectively. It was through all my riding experiences that I was able to hone my skills and as I got better and more precise it opened up another window to something else – to understand what I now see about the universe and about you and me. It shows us that we can evolve together in all we see, sense and feel to be that reflection and to strive to know a higher purpose.

The message of this book is one of hope that there is more. It's not about money, fame or success, all those things we are sold on a daily basis. It is about the hope that by paying attention to the moment you can feel the ones that matter and recognise the situations that will lead to enlightenment.

As a kid I trusted myself and had faith in the future. I grew into mid-life and tried to run from that understanding. Most people struggle with that battle, even if not on a conscious level, because there is a comfort in not knowing. I made many mistakes but each unsettled feeling told me it was never enough and I always knew I needed to know more even if I tried to convince myself otherwise.

In this world we sometimes prejudge people, choose sides, try to fit in, forget the stories that can only happen if we are true to ourselves. It is like the motorcycle racer who has to be 100 per cent in the moment, seeing, sensing and feeling, but at the same time needs to look ahead.

It is about seeing beyond the things that limit us.

This is my story.

It is the story of you and me.

Picture Credits

Section 1

Pages 1–7: All photos courtesy of Freddie Spencer.

Page 8: Top photo and third photo courtesy of Hero Drent. Second photo © Marc Sproule. Bottom photo courtesy of Freddie Spencer.

Section 2

Pages 1–5: All photos courtesy of Hero Drent.

Page 6: Bottom photo © Highsider.com. All other photos courtesy of Hero Drent.

Page 7: Top photo © DPPI inc. All other photos courtesy of Freddie Spencer.

Page 8: Top photo © Juan Goto/pointplus photo. Third photo © Pete Cagnacci/Throttle Roll. All other photos courtesy of Freddie Spencer.

Index